Inside the Hurricane

Calvin Patrick

Copyright (c) 2012 by Calvin Patrick

ISBN 978-1479353613

Some names and descriptions have been changed.

Acknowledgements

The Author gratefully acknowledges the dedication of his secretary, Ann Greer, who diligently transcribed notes, negotiations, meetings, and correspondence that are articulated in this book.

To my very special sister, Nadyne McGehee, for the many hours of editing. Without your encouragement the book would never have been finalized.

To my family, Carolyn, John and Joyce for their grace in handling huge stress issues when I was forced to transfer and move to another state. No one knew what the outcome would be.

Dedication

We dedicate "Inside the Hurricane" to the millions of workers who struggle each day just to feed cloth and shelter their families and who so often feel that they are not informed . Also to the Officers and stewards who serve. This book will help you understand the struggles on behalf of employees. It is often wished by those who lead, "If you could only be there with me." The Eye of the Hurricane will place you there and open the window of understanding the complexities in representing your interest. It will help you learn from the mistakes, the joy and the human interaction that is encountered with peers, leadership and the workforce we all serve. It is intense. You will learn as you enjoy.

Forward

Inside the Hurricane" places the reader at the Bargaining table, with the negotiators and carries him/her behind the scene listening to private conversations and strategy. The reader will share in the intense excitement of negotiations. These Negotiations involved five separate bargaining tables with five Companies and five separate contracts, which created extreme conflict and a very difficult climate for reaching agreement. It describes outside forces and the impact they have on negotiations. Struggles are revealed between competing leaders who have different constituencies, objectives and goals. How the member is manipulated or manipulates the process is illustrated in detail. The winners, rewards and failures, relationships, power struggles, death, and heartache is shared. In spite of all the obstacles, including a 30 day strike, a contract was negotiated and a relationship was built with the Company, It is based on minutes of negotiations, tape recordings, meetings, news articles and extemporaneous notes taken at the time.

The book is in three sections:

1. The first is a blow-by-blow description of negotiations including the 30-day strike. It shares the internal union conflicts the use of media and public politics and how all the issues are resolved with the gift of an unbelievable issue that settled the strike.

2. The story then transitions into a union political campaign. Running for Vice President of the Union. Retaliation, demotion and forced to transfer to another state in order to keep his job. The turmoil and isolation resulting in these

activities. , The aftermath in negotiations with then South Central Bell and later with BellSouth and The Communications Workers of America. (CWA)

3. A number of stand alone arbitration cases involving immorality and sex and how personal morality effects decisions that have unpredicted results.

"Inside the Hurricane" Excerpts

Editorial / Johnson City Press Chronicle.

"Members of the striking Communications Workers of America are not so caught up in their own situation that they cannot recognize real needs elsewhere.
(Supporting United Way) ----------------The Communications Workers, on strike though they may be, have set a good example for the entire community."

President Glen Watts: "When I received word of the settlement while in North Carolina, I wasn't in command of the ship. I know Calvin Patrick feels on the spot because of a failure to communicate.

Vice President Morton Bahr (Later President of CWA) of New York and New Jersey: "The United of New Jersey strike is a bad strike at a bad place and at a bad time."

National Director Rudy Mendoza "It's a good agreement and hard to turn down."

Vice President Ben Porch, over North Carolina:--" The problem is we understood there would be communications when we left Kansas City. This was the total discussion. This was our time to break through with a COLA. My personal feelings, this was a sellout."

Vice President Avelino B Montes over United of the North West USA: "This agreement is better than what we've got or can get in United of the Northwest."

Vice-President W.W. Brown over Tennessee: "I take full responsibility for the agreement being reached"

Chief Negotiator for North Carolina Patrick reached an agreement without approval and now when everyone is ready to settle, Patrick can't get an agreement.

Vice President W.C. Button over United of Indiana; "We cannot get this agreement in Indiana".

Man and Wife Janitors -- "At my lowest point, two members, a man and his wife, both janitors, came by my office. They were upbeat saying, "We've had to suffer all our lives. This is just a little more. If we are going to have anything in life we are going to have to sacrifice."

Calvin Patrick, "Just hold on, I am fixing to get the knockout punch if my information is correct."

Calvin Patrick: Rudy Mendoza's Efforts to lead the United Telecommunications Locals was vindicated in 1981 When The CWA Executive Board changed Union Policy* placing The Independent Telephone Director in the process of Bargaining. Had he had this authority in 1979 there would be no story to write.

Chapter 1: Keenland Racetrack	11
Chapter 2: Bargaining Strategy	16
Chapter 3: Re-election Enhanced	19
Chapter 4: Strategy But Not Policy	22
Chapter 5: The Company - New Players	28
Chapter 6: Opening Statement	32
Chapter 7: A Backward Glance	34
Chapter 8: 13 Lil'ole Girls	37
Chapter 9: Difference in Philosophy	40
Chapter 10: Decertification	43
Chapter 11: Things Must Be Done	45
Chapter 12: Hurricane off the Carolina Coast	47
Chapter 13: Clearing The Air	48
Chapter 14: You Can't Say Those Things	54
Chapter 15: It's Easy to Strike	56
Chapter 16: Exception to Wage Controls Approved.	64
Chapter 17: Strike Vote	69
Chapter: 18 15 Hours to Go!	74
Chapter 19: The Last Nickel Is In Bucket	81
Chapter 20: All Hell Breaks Loose	84
Chapter 21: Summit Meeting Called	88
Chapter 22: Sabotage The Agreement	93
Chapter 23: Back to Original Strategy	100
Chapter 24: Called to Washington	104
Chapter 25: Bad Faith Bargaining	108
Chapter 26: Strike Date Set	111
Chapter 27: CWA President Attends Union Meeting	114
Chapter 28: Media War Begins!	126
PHONE WORKERS, UNITED STILL IN STANDOFF	127
Chapter 29: Must Have a Media Black-Out	132
Chapter 30: May Not Go With COLA	138
Chapter 31: Strike Inevitable	143
Chapter 32: COLA Or Strike!	146
Chapter 33: CWA News "The Last Hours"	158
Chapter 34: The Strike Is On	163
Chapter 35: Meeting with Advance Team from White House	166
Chapter 36: Political Involvement Helps Cause	169
Chapter 37: Can't Allow the Company to Win Media War!	170
Chapter 38: "Settle Before United of Indiana Contract Terminates."	176
Chapter 39 : Ups and Downs of Continued Negotiations	192
Chapter 40: Building Up Strikers Spirits	208

Chapter 41: Company Criminally Immoral 217
Chapter 42: The Knock-Out Punch 221
   Election CWA Vice President District 10 227
      Three Years of Frustration and Uncertainty 242
      Watts Kept His Commitment. Almost!!! 246
   Campaign for Vice President 1983 250
      The nightmare was over!!!!.-----Not Quiet!!!! 259
      Roshto Files Objections to the Election 260
      The nightmare was finally over 263
Epilog 265
Arbitration of Cases and Grievance Handling for Employees 267
   Case #1 If the Member Could Only Be There!!!! 267
   Case #2 Arbitrate or not to Arbitrate 271
   Case #3 Scabs Have rights Too 275
   Case #4 The Hot Dog Case/Off Duty Sexual Activity 277
   Case #5 Morally Right/Legally Wrong-Fired 280
   Case #6 Pastor and Secretary Allegedly Involved in An Affair! 282
   Case #7 Information From Call Given to Police-Stops Crime 284
   Case #8 Employee Denies Sexual Encounter-Has Witnesses 285
   Case #9 Do Unions Support Bad Employees? 299
   Case #10 Company Sandbagged by Supervisor 303
   Case #11 Finally 305
Biography 306

Chapter 1: Keenland Racetrack

Time was running out and the stress was tremendous. The contract would terminate at midnight tomorrow. CWA Chairman of the Bargaining Committee, Calvin Patrick, was frustrated and short tempered with the bargaining committee over issues within the committee. The entire bargaining committee was very edgy.

It was the 28th day of May 1979 and negotiations had been ongoing for two months in Lexington, Kentucky between The Communications Workers of America (CWA) and General Telephone of Kentucky. Both the Company and Union were working very hard to resolve their differences after strikes of seven and five months each in the two previous contract negotiations. There were major issues that must be resolved if a third strike was to be prevented.

Local president, Carol Moss, in frustration said, "we are not bargaining today even if it means no contract by the deadline and we strike." Carol, very tough and at five feet four inches, weighing one-hundred-twenty pounds, had been local President for five years and did not take crap from anyone. Her disposition had come from her childhood with a cruel father who took great joy in putting his brogan shoes on her head holding her down as she squirmed to get out from under his brutal behavior.

Carol Moss: "I just can't take it anymore, I am going to call the Company and advise them we cannot meet until tomorrow at 1:00 p.m." Turning to the Union bargaining committee she said, "We are going to the races!"
Patrick said, "We can't treat the Company that way, they are waiting for us now."
Carol responded, "Calvin we've got to have a break. These 18 hour days are destroying our unity; we are biting each others heads off and it will do us good to take a break."

Bargaining Committeeman, Ned Wilson, said, "What if some of our
people see us at the track? How are we going to explain when the contract terminates in 36 hours and we don't have an agreement?" Carol responded, "We will face that issue if it arises, we are not going to bargain today. I believe a little break will benefit all of us." Wilson had reason for concern and worried about going out on strike again as they had done three years ago when it took five months to resolve the issues. He knew very well that the Union had not recovered from it.

They left the hotel at 9:10 a.m. with a soft breeze blowing. The sky was a deep blue and the temperature was 78 degrees. They drove west toward Keenland racetrack on highway 4, passing acres of beautiful bluegrass pastures with neat white wooden fences and large barns. Grooms were grooming horses next to the barns as mares grazed and their young colts galloped a quarter of a mile away from their mothers and then turned and raced back.

Arriving at the track at 10:00 a.m. Patrick exclaimed, "what a beautiful serene place" As they entered the grandstand it was filled almost to capacity. The bugler was dressed like an English hunter following the hounds as they chased the fox. He had a top hat, green coat with tails down below his thigh, and white pants and black knee high boots. He called the horses to the post with a long horn.
They sat halfway up in the stands. There was a hushed gentle noise rising. They looked toward the starting gate. To their surprise the race was on. There were no loud speakers. When the horses reached the three-quarter mile post, the crowd noise gently increased in the background as the fans cheered for their favorite horses. The noise reached a maximum crescendo as the horses crossed the finish line, then very gently subsided into a hush. The fans went to cash in their earnings.

The bargaining team, guided by Carol, headed to the paddock, which was filled with hearty pin oaks, sycamores, and maple trees. It was very comfortable under the trees. There were grooms, owners, trainers, jockeys and other fans getting one last look at those magnificent horses before they ran the next race. They watched as the horses paraded to the saddling ring and were saddled by their trainers. The jockeys filed into the paddock eyeing their horses and each other.

As the bargaining team stood an arms length from the horses they looked like real race fans selecting the next horse they would bet on. They then walked leisurely to the betting window, placed their bets then headed back to their seats. The jockeys took their mounts atop the thoroughbreds, and the outriders escorted them through the paddock onto the main track where the main event awaited them. There was no announcer saying "Their off". The race again started without a sound.

As Patrick sat on the end seat he felt a touch on his shoulder. He looked up and saw Christina Preston. She smiled and continued with three men to the seats near the track. Why was she in Lexington? He had to speak to her. After the 4th race Christina followed the men toward the paddock. Patrick caught up with them. Christina had stopped supposedly going to the girl's room. Patrick ask, "Where are you staying Christina?"
Christina "We are at the Hyatt Courtyard for two nights."
Patrick, "What a beautiful surprise. I sure would like to have coffee with you."
Christina "It will be difficult. We are at a personnel meeting and I just don't know."
Carol and the group had stopped about 30 feet in front of Patrick and were waiting. He told Christina, "I am going to try to see you." Christina touched his arm and headed to the Ladies room.

After the forth race Patrick had won two and lost two and was even on his two dollar bets. As they headed for the track kitchen located in the barn area, Patrick exclaimed, "That was a lot of fun and I am still even".

There were owners, trainers and jockeys eating a hearty country breakfast. The group ordered eggs, bacon and biscuits with gravy and a side order of country-style potatoes. There was a lot of banter over their ability to select the horses. All except Patrick had lost every race. After eating they paid the six dollars each for the breakfast and went back to the track for three more races before heading to the hotel.

As Carol drove Patrick back to the hotel he exclaimed, "I really appreciate your insistence on us coming here. This place is unreal: No mechanical sounds and everything is so peaceful and beautiful". To himself he was thinking, today will not soon be forgotten! As they drove in silence Carol ask, "Who was that good looking blond?" Patrick said, "What Blond?" Carol smiled and kept driving.

The following evening negotiations ended several hours before the contract deadline with the Company and Union agreeing to a substantial raise and a unprecedented cost-of-living allowance (COLA). After two strikes in the two previous contract negotiations of seven and five months each, the Company and Union were looking forward to 3 years of labor peace and an improved responsible relationship between the two parties.[1]

---

[1] *A month later CWA had its annual Kentucky State meeting. With 150 attending from 13 Locals, including the two Locals from General Telephone of Kentucky. The President of General Telephone of Kentucky and the Company Bargaining Committee also attended. It was a fun evening and all the Locals were overwhelmed at the banter between the Union and General*

Telephone of Kentucky representatives. Many responded that they wished they had this kind of relationship with their employer, South Central Bell. Calvin Patrick was given a large collectors print of a wildcat and thanked for the accomplishments achieved in Negotiations.

Patrick received a letter from Local President Carol Moss dated April 20, 1982, which said in part, ----------- We sure do miss having you as our State Director. You were and are a mean little shit, but at least you got the job done, and a hell of a job at that. I still love you just like I do my brothers - - - Well I know you just want the facts. - - We all love and miss you. Sure wish you were here for negotiations. Carol Moss, President Local 10372.

Chapter 2: Bargaining Strategy

Immediately after the Communications Workers of America (CWA) reached agreement with General Telephone of Kentucky, CWA National Director of Independent Telephone Companies, Rudy Mendoza, wrote to my boss, CWA Vice President, Willard Brown:

"---it appears at long last we are entering a new era with the General Telephone of Kentucky in our industrial relations. I think it should also be said that Calvin Patrick played a most significant part in reaching agreement with this Company. ---I just wanted you to know Cal not only did a job in achieving a tremendous package but has laid some real groundwork for building a relationship with this company---."

Mendoza, as the CWA National Director over all independent Telephone Company contracts for CWA , worked under the direction of the President of CWA, Glenn Watts[2] with so many independent local unions in companies such as General Telephone and Electronics, United Telecommunications of Kansas City, ALLTEL, and many other Corporations, Mendoza's job was very difficult, as each of these locals had their own separate contracts. Mendoza's job was like herding a bunch of cats, so to speak, as each local could decide its own fate without regard to other locals.

Mendoza had worked for General Telephone of California and had been active in the CWA starting out as a job steward working his way to the top of his local. He had

---

[2] *Glenn Watts: President of CWA, a 600 thousand-member Union mostly in the telecommunications industry, was the final decision maker over several hundred contracts in CWA, including A.T.& T. He was known as a fair and honest leader.*

run for the CWA National Directors job believing he could give leadership in bringing about change in the independent telephone conglomerates where CWA had hundreds of contracts all across the Nation.

Mendoza was well aware of the kind of pressure CWA had placed on the A.T.& T. Company over the years, to have one national "Master Contract" for all 23 companies. A.T.& T. had resisted and several strikes occurred over the years.

While these strikes had national repercussions, A.T.& T. had resisted a "Master Contract" through the years saying each Bell Company was responsible for all decisions made in that Company.

CWA had used a strategy of reaching an agreement in one A.T.& T Company and then all other A.T.& T companies had to meet that contract "pattern", giving the same raises and benefit packages as was negotiated with the "pattern" setting A.T.& T Company.

Finally In 1971 negotiations with A.T.& T. National bargaining was achieved with a "Master Contract" for all 23 A.T.& T Companies. One bargaining table was established for all Companies.

With this knowledge, all the Independent Telephone Company Locals where CWA had contracts were looking to CWA to achieve a single negotiation table for each of their Companies like CWA had in A.T.& T.

Mendoza felt he was the man who could accomplish this goal. His objective was to coordinate bargain within each of these Cooperation's and in time achieve national bargaining as CWA had accomplished in A.T.& T.

While this was a worthy goal, Mendoza's problem was that these Corporations were saying that each franchise made its own decisions and CWA must bargain with each franchise.

After the successful agreement in General Telephone

of Kentucky where I was able to negotiate an outstanding contract with a cost-of-living clause, (COLA), Mendoza began to think of a grand strategy for bargaining in United Telecommunications, headquartered in Kansas City, Kansas.

Chapter 3:   Re-election Enhanced

Mendoza knew that if he was successful and achieved his bargaining goals his chances of reelection would be enhanced in the upcoming National Union elections, which were a year away. He knew he had no other choice as the local Unions were becoming impatient with the National Union leadership. He was aware however that a similar strategy had failed in past negotiations.

On June 8, 1979 Patrick and United Intermountain Local 10871 President, Darrell Freeman, and Vice President Bob Brown traveled from Johnson City, TN to Kansas City to a United Telecommunications conference led by CWA National Director Mendoza. Also present was Glenn Watts, President of the CWA in Washington D.C. and several National Vice Presidents of CWA, each with jurisdictions over the several districts of CWA.   They were also on the CWA National Executive Board.   Also present were all of the local presidents and chief negotiators, for each of the United Telecommunication Companies, where negotiations were starting.

Mendoza chaired the meeting telling all present that the purpose of the meeting is to develop a coordinated bargaining strategy for the upcoming contracts in United Telecommunications. He explained the position we were now in. "Four of United's Companies had contracts that were beginning to terminate."

1. "In United Telecommunications of New Jersey there are two locals. One is a CWA Local and the other is a Local in the International Brotherhood of Electrical Workers (IBEW). The contract expired on June 1 and CWA went on strike, with an offer of only a 6.4% raise. This was not enough to catch up with inflation, running at a yearly rate of 10-12%

per year." The (IBEW) Local had accepted a final offer of 7%. This was their legal right and their choice. "This leaves our CWA Local on strike and in a difficult position."

2. "The contract in United Intermountain of Tennessee/Virginia will be expiring on August 23 and negotiations are about to commence with Calvin Patrick as Chairman of the Union's Committee." Mendoza outlined a strategy of not reaching an agreement and continue working after the contract expired.

3. "The contract in United of Indiana will expire on September 15. They are to negotiate but not reach an agreement and continue working after the contract terminates.

4. "CWA won an organizing campaign in United of Norfolk Virginia. During the campaign the Company had given the employees a raise and now were considering taking the raise back. There was no contract in Norfolk and a decision had to be made as to striking that Company.

5. "The United of Carolina contract will expire on October 1.

"And there are other contracts terminating down the road but for now the focus will be on the above five companies".

Mendoza explained the strategy was to strike all of the companies at the same time, around October 1. With five thousand employees on the street "it is felt the United Company will have no choice but to negotiate nationally from the Corporate Headquarters in Kansas City." Mendoza concluded.

The United Locals knew that CWA contracts in A.T.&T had cost-of-living allowances (COLA) since 1971, and they were pressuring for a Cost-of-living Allowance (COLA) in their contracts too.

On December 28, 1978 President Jimmy Carter had instituted Wage-Price guidelines due to high inflation. Employers could not give wage increases higher than 7% per year. However, within those guidelines, if a company and union made an agreement that had a COLA formula they would be allowed to agree to additional wages above the 7% to keep up with inflation and not violate his Wage-Price Controls.

Mendoza felt A Cost-of-living Allowance (COLA) could be achieved as a result of the coordinated efforts. He went on to say, "This is not a policymaking meeting. We are here only to discuss the issues in each unit and to see what each units problems are".

Chapter 4:   Strategy But Not Policy

Patrick liked Mendoza's strategy but wondered why we were here if we were not going to develop a plan of action where all would be required to stick together and all would strike together and come back together. In other words, all would have a contract or none would have a contract.

Patrick's District 10 Vice President, W. W. Brown, had chosen not to attend. He had been involved in a similar effort in 1974 when the Union in General Telephone of Kentucky, General Telephone of Indiana, and General Telephone of Ohio, had agreed to a coordinated bargaining strategy and all had agreed to strike together. The General Telephone of Kentucky contract expired first. No agreement was reached and Brown had carried them out on strike. General Telephone of Ohio and General Telephone of Indiana each reached agreements and did not strike, leaving General of Kentucky stranded, on strike by themselves, for seven months. With this knowledge, and knowing Brown did not have confidence in the current strategy, Patrick listened very carefully and took notes to be sure he made no mistakes.

President Watts announced CWA "will negotiate wage increases that protect the purchasing power of our members." He brought us up to date on President Jimmy Carter's wage price guidelines and the fact that we could only negotiate a maximum increase of 7 percent. He stated that CWA had stayed within the wage guidelines by negotiating a cost-of-living allowance (C0LA) in General Telephone of Kentucky where Patrick had been chief negotiator. The guidelines allowed the parties to assume a maximum inflation rise of 6 percent per year and on this basis we could negotiate within the guidelines but still be able to receive increases of 8 - 9 or 11 percent should inflation reach those levels.

Mendoza told the participants that United Telecommunications was insisting on no COLA and would not go above the 7 percent maximum established by the Presidential wage guidelines. He said the Union's job was to convince the Company to change their mind, and negotiate a COLA that would produce substantially more than the assumed 7 percent maximum. In doing so the Company would comply with the guidelines and at the same time be able to legally give additional wages.

National Director Mendoza was elected, in part, by the local presidents at this meeting and felt pressure to deliver a COLA formula and a common termination date for all contracts in the upcoming negotiations. The fact that United of New Jersey was on strike after rejecting the 7 percent wage package, and their sister, IBEW local, had accepted the 7% and did not strike, put CWA and Mendoza in a very bad position with the local presidents throughout the nation.

Mendoza stated the objective in pursuing this strategy "is to obtain the corporate involvement necessary for the achievement of the priority demands adopted by CWA. Those demands include:
"1. Substantial increases in wages, which will protect our members purchasing power.
2. Increased job security.
3. Improved insurance, including basic medical, major medical, life and sickness and accident insurance.
4. A dental plan.
5. Limitations on Managements rights to subcontract work.
6. Improve pensions."

Discussions flowed back and forth for two days with local presidents being very outspoken. In a memo to all concerned parties sent after the meeting Mendoza stated;

"There is a general consensus among the local leadership that the Union can use the wage price guidelines to its best advantage since the "system" has as yet refused to negotiate cost-of-living adjustments that result from inflation rates in excess of 6 percent in any one year period. Existing inflation would, therefore, produce substantial pay increases under wage price guideline settlements that include a COLA provision." Mendoza's memo used such terms as "I believe", "there is a consensus", "therefore possibly joining together." He failed to give specific directives.

During the meeting, however, the United of Tennessee Local President, Darrell Freeman, had expressed concern that his local's top priority was not a cost-of-living, but catching up with employees' wages in United of Carolina. Those members were making fifty cents to one dollar per hour more than the members of his local.

Each local president and his local at this meeting had their own contract. Those contracts were not dependent on the other contracts. Each of the locals had the right and obligation to send out any agreement made without regard to what happened in other locals and their contracts. The only way we could achieve Mendoza's objective was for Mendoza and the President of CWA to give Union Staff a directive not to reach an agreement until all other local contract settlements were achieved. This was not done and was the fear we had, based on the General of Kentucky strike of 7 months.

In a memo to Patrick's supervisor, T.J. Volk regarding the meeting, he pointed out that "from my vantage point if United Telecommunications find out what is being attempted, I am sure they may offer an adequate settlement (possibly without a COLA) in United of Tennessee. If this happens what choices do we have except to send the offer out for ratification? If we are in this position it may destroy the coordinated effort."

Patrick sent copies to his Vice President and the Executive Vice President in Washington who was technically involved with Mendoza at the Washington level of the Union.

No response or no instructions were given to Patrick as to how he was to proceed if the Union in United of Tennessee was placed in this position. Without direction, if the goals for the United Local were achieved, then the Local could exercise their right to send the agreement out for ratification. Patrick foresaw the problem since a COLA was not a priority for the United Local.

While at the Kansas City meeting, United Telecommunications Chairman of the Board, Paul Henson,[3] came by during a reception and circulated for an hour. Bob Brown, Vice President of United of Tennessee, told Mr. Henson that the corporation had better rethink its position because a 7 percent wage increase would not fly with his members.

Mendoza, upon returning to Washington, must have felt from what he had heard at the Kansas City meeting that there must be a problem in United of Tennessee.

On May 29th, to remedy this problem he arranged a meeting in Tennessee to talk to Patrick's bargaining committee and the Local Executive Board, to see if he could

---

[3] *Paul Henson, Chairman of United Telecommunications in Kansas City, began his career as a warehouseman and grew to become an internationally known leader in telecommunications. Henson was the architect behind the emergence of Sprint Corp. As a leader in the communications industry, he served as chairman of Sprint, formerly United Telecom, for 25 years, stepping down in 1990 to become chairman of Kansas City Southern Industries. He died in 1997.*

excite them over the idea of making a strike issue over the cost-of-living formula.

Local Vice President Ronnie Renfro's note to Patrick regarding that meeting, which Patrick was unable to attend, stated: "Mr. Mendoza talked about negotiating for a cost-of-living and making it a strike issue. He said New Jersey was on strike, pressing for a cost-of-living with their contract. Mendoza wanted New Jersey to strike until they got a COLA. If a COLA was not forthcoming, United of Tennessee would strike and before the end of the year we would have United of Carolina, Indiana, Norfolk, Ohio and New Jersey on the street. With this pressure Mendoza was sure the "system" would cave in and grant "COLA".

Renfro had told Mendoza that he did not feel that a COLA formula, by itself, was a strike issue for his people. He did not think his local would stay on the street for another local, not knowing whether another local would go on the street "to support us". Renfro asked Mendoza if he could guarantee, "If we strike, will the other locals strike when their contracts expired." Mendoza said, "no", he could not.

The Local Executive Board went on to tell Mendoza that they had conducted 10 meetings within the Locals jurisdiction to find the issues for negotiations. A COLA was not a high priority even though there were some members very strong for it.

On June 12th, not satisfied with the results of this meeting, Mendoza wrote Vice President Brown saying: "Local President, Darrell Freeman, and other officers expressed concern that the members might accept President Carter's Wage restraints, provided there is no retrogression by the Company. I am sure these officers' concern is sincere. However, I know Darrell Freeman can be counted on to generate interest among the membership and I think it is imperative that a meeting take place prior to the start of bargaining so that the leadership can motivate the members." Mendoza concluded, "I am concerned that unless we do something to impress the United System Corporation, we will continue to subject ourselves to great criticism."

On June 18th, Vice President W.W. Brown sent Mendoza a telegram responding to his request. "I believe Patrick has established himself as being thoroughly capable of handling relations with Company management including United of Tennessee/Virgina President W.W. Hill. If you can handle relations at the corporate level, I believe we will be able to handle relations at the Company level. I will advise Patrick of your concerns." (Brown forwarded a copy of Mendoza's letter to Patrick.)

On June 14th Mendoza had written to Patrick asking for him to request that Intermountain of Tennessee/Virginia supply the Union data to cost out the contract, which included data associated with the wage price controls under President Jimmy Carter.

On June 19th Patrick responded to Mendoza regarding his request for data stating, "I am very reluctant at this early date to approach the Company for the specific information requested by you as it infers to data needed to negotiate under the (COWPS) Council on Wage Price Stability, Carter's wage price controls. My instructions are to negotiate as if there were no wage price controls. If at some point we need that information, I will obtain it as requested. All other information is being requested.

Chapter 5: The Company - New Players

United Intermountain Telephone Company, (United of Tennessee/Virginia) located in upper East Tennessee, and 140 miles into Virginia, was organized by CWA in 1967 and Local 10871 held jurisdiction. The Local represented 1300 members who worked for United Intermountain.

United was formally a family owned Company and had been purchased by United Telecommunications . Historically the president of the Company would not meet with the Union at the highest level, even informally. This had created a barrier in solving problems and negotiating a contract between the Company and Union for several years.

The Company was divided into five districts and each had managed itself until around 1977. Patrick had characterized that type of management as a committee of 100 running in 100 different directions. The Company was criticized editorially and by letters to the editor in the 3 area daily newspapers. The Company's activities with the regulatory commissions and other politicians were just as bad. One of the committee of 100 felt that the more grievances the Company received the better the job the supervisors were doing, and he caused his share of grievances.

In 1978 United Intermountain had brought in W.W. "Dub" Hill as the new president. He was the final decision maker. He had been president for about two years and was still finding his way, especially in Labor Relations. Prior to his presidency no United Intermountain president ever met with CWA. CWA was now trying to develop a relationship with the Company, which must include the President.

Hill seemed to respect the Union and had met with us on several occasions. We had a degree of confidence in developing a positive relationship between the Union and

Company if we could overcome some "old time control" management problems.

The contract was to terminate on August 23, 1979 and our first negotiation session was set for June 22, 1979. Local 10871 had conducted elections for the bargaining committee from among its almost 1300 members, and had chosen:

Bob Brown Vice President of Local 10871 from Kingsport, Tennessee, who was always cheerful with a fresh joke and was an inspiration to the bargaining committee.

Judy Graham, from Greenville, Tennessee, was an Area Representative in CWA Local 10871. She was dedicated to her task and loyal to CWA Local 10871.

Darrell Freeman, Local President and a committee member by virtue of his office, was very dedicated to his local and was involved and very influential in Tennessee State Politics.

Sandy Barry, Local 10871 Secretary/Treasurer, was the Union note taker. Sandy was very capable and had designed the note taking process to where one could instantly find every time an issue was discussed and the date of the discussion.

The Company committee was chaired by one of Kingsport, Tennessee's outstanding labor lawyers, Ed Norris, who had been the Companies chief negotiator since 1967, the year CWA won the National Labor Relations Board conducted election to be the bargaining agent in United Intermountain Telephone Company.

Norris was involved in the strike and decertification of the Union at the Kingsport Press, which involved one of the nation's longest strikes lasting from March 11, 1963, continuing into the spring of 1967. Norris was proud of his role in the Kingsport Press Strike and shared that with CWA East Tennessee Director Calvin Patrick at their first meeting.

Jack Gaddis was the new Human Resources Director coming to the Company within the last 60 days. Gaddis would be the top Company spokesman. He worked under the direction of the President of United Telephone Company of Tennessee/Virginia, and reported directly to United President W.W. Hill.

Dan Luethke was the Companies note taker and had been working in the labor relations department for 9 years. Luethke was a very honest and upright person that the Union held in high esteem.

Bob Nicar was over the Operator Services Department. Bob had a reputation of doing the right thing.

Bill McDonald had been recently promoted to General Plant Manager. While the Union did not know him, he came over as a very sincere and honest person but was untested in our relationship.

This was a new team of managers, but they had been unwilling to exercise their authority over some of the established officers and upper management who had been creating problems for the Company, the employees, and the Union.

As we were entering negotiations for the 1300 employee bargaining unit, Patrick wanted President Hill and the Company Bargaining Committee to understand our mutual problems. The Company Bargaining Committee and President Hill needed to know two officials of the Company were misleading them. The Company Bargaining Committee must know that these two men were continuing to cause a cancerous condition that could keep us from reaching an agreement.

While these two officials were competent in terms of dealing with equipment and telephone service, they did not express any ability of how to motivate or deal with employees. They had been known to discipline an employee for doing a "good deed" which received favorable newspaper coverage for the Company, but this "good deed" had caused the employee to be 15 minutes late for work.

They were also noted for watching employees going on coffee break. Supervisors under their direction trembled at their names. These two officials were known in the Union as "the Cancer" and "the assistant to the Cancer". They had totally destroyed the relationship within their jurisdiction with the employees and the Union.

Patrick's plan was to use the bargaining table as a forum to lay out some misunderstandings between the Company and Union, caused in part by the "Cancer". These problems had been building prior to Patrick coming on the scene in 1974, and had involved his two Union predecessors. Patrick's hope in all of this was to expose the "Cancer" and to clear the air and start a "responsible relationship" between the parties.

Bargaining was to commence on June 22 and Patrick had notified the Company that he wanted to tape his opening remarks, and for the Company to share them with President Hill.

After an hour of discussion, anger, and accusations, by the Company Bargaining Committee, accusing the Union of committing an unfair labor practice by wanting to tape the meeting, an agreement was reached and Patrick's opening remarks were taped.

Chapter 6: Opening Statement

Patrick started the conversation: "I have just completed negotiations in General Telephone of Kentucky. In that Company we have built a responsible relationship based on mutual trust and respect. This came after two strikes: The first in 1974 for 7 months, and a five-month strike, which started in late 1975.

"We accomplished our objective because there was trust between the president of that Company and myself.[4] There was trust between the Labor Relations manager and myself. We did not agree on everything, but when we didn't agree it was because of sound business principles from their viewpoint or a viewpoint of the Union that was different. Differences were not based on personalities.

"With President Hill we are moving in that direction. If you managers here at this table will become "the leaders" of this Company I believe we can be successful. That is what I have been trying to do in this Company, but two high-level Company officials continue to be defensive. They don't trust

---

[4] *A. On December 19, 1979 the President of General Telephone of Kentucky, Payton Adams penned a personal letter to Patrick, "As we close out 1979 I want to personally thank you for assisting in making our Company have a successful year. "In the years of dealing with Union personnel, I put you at the top of people I know that are outstanding Union leaders. "I shall always be totally grateful for the assistance you gave me in improving the relationship of our craft and management employees in our Company". B. January 21, 1980 On Patrick's Promotion and transfer to Birmingham: From the Chief Negotiator for General Telephone of Kentucky: "It's a pleasure to send you most sincere congratulations. With my very best regards Calvin. You have my Professional trust and respect as well as my personal friendship. Dick (Salvi)*

Calvin Patrick. They don't trust the local Union leadership. Because of the problems these two officials have caused, the local leadership and the members do not trust the Company. This cancerous condition may well cause a strike unless it is removed.

"We must get to know top Company management. You can't deal successfully in labor relations unless you know the Company leadership and there is mutual trust. That doesn't mean we'll get an agreement at this bargaining table. If we have mutual trust but do strike, we'll know that what we are saying to each other can be believed. The strike will be over an honest difference of opinion, and sometimes we have strikes to settle those differences. The "Cancer" is keeping this trust from becoming a reality.

"The assistant to the Cancer" has been telling President Hill that Calvin Patrick wants to generate grievances. That is the most asinine statement I have ever heard. I don't want grievances. The Local President and Executive Board don't want grievances. I'll admit that down in the ranks we've got some bad apples, but you hired them. They are your employees and we can't do anything about that. Most of our members, your employees, are honest people who want to do a days work. They want to be paid for it and have good benefits. They want to feel good when they go home at night.

"The "Cancer" and the " Assistant to the Cancer" are creating this chasm and causing our problems. Until that cancerous condition is removed from this Company or until you managers at this table become "the leaders", and really take control and make tough decisions the "Cancer" doesn't like, we're never going to have a responsible relationship that can work."

Chapter 7: A Backward Glance

Patrick's taped opening statement continued. "The other morning I went back in my mind through the history between CWA and this Company. Problems from the beginning have been caused by the same people. In 1972 before I came to this Company, the Union told the Company, you've, (the Cancer), made a bad decision. The employees are going to walk out. They walked out. Then the "Cancer's" decision was reversed. While the Union staff was getting the employees back to work, Mr. Norris you got an injunction after agreeing not to. The Union had tried to communicate, to trust, and to believe the Company.

"In August 1973 negotiations, I was not here but Mr. Nicar you were, and at the midnight hour the Company came with your final offer. You had made some changes in the definition of "callout". The Union Bargaining Committee asked, is there any change in the intent of "callout"? The answer was "No". The contract was signed and low and behold there is a different interpretation. The employees blamed both the Company and Union for this change. We had trusted."

"I took over the responsibility of this Company in November of 1974. In 1975 we had a wage re-opener. Mr. Norris, you and I had a conversation in your office. The first thing you told me was that you had been responsible for busting the Union at the Kingsport Press. I guess you were trying to impress or frighten me. Our relationship started off very negative[5] Later in the negotiations for the 13 Lil ole

---

[5] *Kingsport Press Strike Collection, 1961-1982 is in the Special Collections Library at East Tennessee State University. Dale K. Larkin, who was born on February 16, 1955 in Kingsport, Tennessee, compiled them. He attended the public schools of*

girls in the Data Processing department you accused me of lying. You have never told me what I did wrong. That has bothered me."

"During our first conversation I laid out to you how I would like to conduct the mechanics of negotiations. I then had to reverse my position. Later I told you I had been instructed to change. At that time I couldn't say anything. I didn't mean to mislead you, if in fact I did. But it was only about the mechanics and the timing. I was reprimanded by my boss over that issue and had to file a grievance: A misunderstanding between my boss and myself. The result of the grievance was a standoff. I wasn't guilty, my boss wasn't wrong."

"The only other time that I know I may have mislead you was when you approached me in 1976 and told me that I had made an agreement to move negotiations from the Ramada Inn in Kingsport to the Holiday Inn in Bristol. I honestly don't recall our conversation in that context. I may have made that agreement, but you brought it up at the bargaining table and you were negotiating about it across the table. I wish you had asked me to recess negotiations, and then in private ask. Calvin, don't you remember? Those are the only two times I could have mislead you. It wasn't intentional in either case. I feel this has caused a problem

Liberty Hill Elementary and Church Hill High School in Church Hill, Tennessee. In 1972 Larkin began working for United Inter-Mountain Telephone (UIMT) and joined the Communications Workers of America (CWA), Local 10871. Through his affiliation in CWA Local 10871, Larkin served as president of the Sullivan-Hawkins/and Hancock Counties Central Labor Council from 1982-84. Larkin served on the staff of The Communicator, CWA Local 10871's newsletter, from 1982-83. He received his Bachelor of Science degree in communications and political science in 1987 from East Tennessee State University. Larkin still works at United Inter-Mountain Telephone and participates in the activities of CWA Local 10871.

between us that should be removed. If there is a problem we need to talk about it."

"In the 1976 Negotiations the Company wanted to reopen the no-strike clause after the Supreme Court ruled on the "sympathy" strike. We had already agreed on the "no strike" clause, but reluctantly reopened and renegotiated it. Because of that renegotiated strike clause, we asked a question and understood from the Company bargaining committee that if we were to organize an unorganized group of employees in this Company, they would be placed in the contract with the 1300 organized employees. Because of this oral understanding the "sympathy" strike issue was not important and we agreed to the change."

Chapter 8: 13 Lil'ole Girls

"In February 1977 we won an election involving 13 women (13 Lil'ole girls) in the data processing department. This made top management angry because the women worked, took breaks and lunch in the same area as corporate management. The Monday following this election, a meeting was held and the general manager over that department was fired. Mr. Wilson, Vice President of Labor Relations, was striped of his authority over these employees, removing him from the negotiations that were to take place. Shortly afterward he went into depression and committed suicide on April 8th."

"When we were ready to negotiate, Ed you called me to set up negotiations. We agreed to a date and I said it should not take too long to negotiate since we would be placing these employees in the same contract as the 1300. You responded you were not going to do this. I ask you were you sure? We had a verbal agreement (that Vice President Wilson was aware of) from 1976 negotiations to do so. You repeated we had no deal."

"Later Ed, I ask you, have you talked to everybody about this? You said, "I have". But the night you and I were at the funeral home after the death of Vice President Wilson you admitted you did not talk to him. I knew he was a sick man because of the things that had been done to him, because of the Monday Morning massacre when his authority was striped away."

"The "Cancer" forced you to change your position. You could have told me off the record, "Calvin I did make a commitment to you but the Company has changed their position". I understand that you are the Company's mouthpiece and have to negotiate what they tell you. But you did not talk to me. I had trusted you as the Company spokesman. You had given me a commitment."

"During the negotiations for these 13 Lil'ole girls, you stated that you were not on retainer, each job was separate. So now I can't trust you as a Company mouthpiece that can be depended upon. I hope you understand this is nothing personal, but the "Cancer" keeps changing his mind and you have to mouth it across the table. The Union trusts and the Company rebuffs us. "Later in 1977 you modified your position and said that as far as the 13 Lil'ole girls were concerned, I had said the Union wanted to place them in the large contract, and Ed, your statement was "we'll get a contract". Now from a naive person trying to accept a person's honesty, if I tell you I want to place them in the same contract with the other employees and you tell me "we'll get a contract", what am I supposed to believe? I believed as I have interpreted. You meant that we would place the 13 Lil'ole girls in the same contract with the 1300 CWA members. We did not do either for 22 months. So which is the reasonable position? "On June 13, 1977 I went to the "Cancers" office and had what I felt was an excellent conversation. In my notes of that meeting I stated; "I went away with a good feeling". I had trusted, trying to establish a relationship. A few days later in a telephone conversation with the "Cancer" he said; we (the Union) had the Company in the corner because of these 13 Lil'ole girls having higher benefits than the existing contract. If they kept these benefits it would be a red flag for the existing bargaining unit at the next round of negotiations. I had responded that the Union had been aware of the higher benefits of the nonunion employees for years and it had not created a problem in the past. The "Cancer" said he was sorry he had to put me in this position but that was the way it was. "After it became apparent that we could not reach an agreement for the 13 Lil'ole girls, we advised you we had gone as far as we could and we would just quit negotiating until the Big contract we are now about to negotiate. We would get justice when we negotiated for the 1300. I had a meeting with the13 Lil'ole girls in April of 1978 and told them what their options were. I told them if they wanted to decertify the Union (by voting it out) "I'll help you". I told them that the Vice President of CWA had wanted me to strike the Company and the Union would take care of them. I had rejected that solution, as no viable option, because the "Cancer" in my view would hire new employees to replace them. I told the 13-Lil'ole girls we would get justice when the big contract came up for negotiations in 1979. I asked them to make a decision together, to decertify or stay with us. We would support any decision they made. "They chose to stay with the Union. Someone had committed a grave injustice to them in the past. It was not money. It was a cancerous, inhuman condition worse than seeing the tragedy on television yesterday when that newsman was shot.[6] would just as soon have had someone shoot me. To realize, I have to deal with people who have such low mental feelings for human beings as that. "So negotiations ceased. The 13 Lil'ole girls decided to wait another year and 4 months, if necessary, to get their contract. I continued trying to find a way to get through to top management and build a relationship."

---

[6] *MANAGUA, Nicaragua, June 20, 1979ÒABC Television correspondent Bill Stewart, 37, was shot and killed today by a Nicaraguan National Guard soldier while attempting to film war destruction in a Managua neighborhood. Stewart's Nicaraguan interpreter also was killed in the incident, filmed by eyewitnesses who described it as a deliberate shooting carried out after Stewart had been ordered to kneel. [Dramatic films of the shooting, made by survivors among the ABC crew, were shown on U.S. television evening news programs.] The Washington Post June 21, 1979, Thursday,   Final   Edition By Karen DeYoung, Washington Post Foreign Service*

Chapter 9: Difference in Philosophy

"On September 28, 1978 I talked in private with a Company official who I had confidence in and asked him for his opinion as to what I could do to improve relations between the Company and CWA at both the local and at my level." He responded, "It was not a personality clash but a difference in philosophy." He said there was a power struggle inside the Company. He hoped President Hill would soon take over in fact, rather than just in name, then things would change. I had been asking for a high level meeting for 18 months and continued to press. In November the Cooperate officers agreed to sit down and talk. This was the first time in the history of this Company that the President was willing to participate in any kind of dialogue with the Union. The date was to be December 4, 1978. "I worked for a week preparing data for the conference, knowing since I had requested the meeting I would be expected to take the lead. The meeting was attended by most of the Cooperate Officers of the Company including the "Cancer". I laid out six problem areas that the Company and Union needed to work on.

1. Problems the Company was having with the Public Service Commission.
2. The Personnel Department was unable to resolve issues due to outside interference.
3. A lack of trust on the part of management and not living up to commitments made with the Union.
4. The Company's negative attitude with the Union.
5. The inability of both parties to resolve problems at lower levels.
6. A take-it-personal attitude rather than "lets resolve the problem".

In my opening remarks I had stated there was a Cancer eating away, destroying the Company in the eyes of the public, with the employees, the union and the Public Service Commission. Being a very provocative statement, President Hill seized on this, wanting to know what the cancer was. I advised it must wait until last. He agreed. We spent 3 hours during the morning session. The Company bought lunch. The afternoon session went very smooth. We discussed other Companies where CWA held contracts and I had the responsibility of administrating those contracts. We discussed the number of grievances and arbitrations in those contracts and depicted graphically how far out of line grievances and arbitrations were in United of Tennessee/Virginia. There was an exchange of ideas and discussion on the problems. Both President Hill and the "Cancer" indicated they had no disagreement with the statistics as had been laid out. However, there was no commitment on the part of the Company to help resolve our collective problems.

When we touched on the problems in negotiating a contract for the 13 Lil'ole girls in the data processing department you could feel the tension building. I was rather forceful in describing the commitments that had been made and the fact that some employees had not had a raise in over 3 years. The Company did not want to discuss this issue. The "Cancer" started rebutting every remark being made. After about 15 minutes on this subject it was obvious the meeting must adjourn in order to maintain any foundation that might have been laid regarding the other matters of discussion. I was told later that the "Cancer" had said, "I told you that is the kind of person Patrick is." Whatever that meant. Both Local President, Darrell Freeman, and I came away with the feeling that the "Cancer" was, in fact, running the Company and that President Hill is about as effective, in the labor relations policies of the Company, as a eunuch in a brothel. President Hill had sat at the far end of the table where the least powerful person would normally sit at a meeting such as this. The "Cancer" had sat directly across from me.

I continued my remarks to the Company bargaining committee, "Dan, (labor relations manager Dan Luethke) at a grievance meeting two days later, you told me, "I could kick your ass for what you did to ruin our meeting after 6 hours of really laying out the problems in this Company". You told me that I had the Company's attention until I brought up the data processing problems of the 13-Lil'ole girls. Then in 15 minutes, 6 hours of work went down the drain. Dan, knowing that you are a very good Christian and these were strong words for you and because of my great respect for you, I took what you said very seriously. I was afraid that what you were saying might be true. I remember that after a long pause I was finally able to respond. "Dan, you may be right but those 13 Lil'ole girls have suffered unmercifully because they chose CWA as their bargaining representative. They are a part of this Company to. It had to be said. We will just have to wait and see."

Chapter 10:   Decertification

"In December the "Cancer" got involved in a decertification election of the 13 Lil'ole girls. One of them, without consulting with anyone in the Union, decided to ask the National Labor Relations Board to hold an election to allow a vote, to get rid of the Union by decertifying it in an election. The "Cancer" got President Hill involved and they wined and dined those 13 Lil'ole girls trying to get them to vote against the Union. Several had been without raises for 3 years. How long---how long---must they suffer for their beliefs. But they voted for the union, to continue trusting the Union. How could a Company have this kind of attitude toward 13 Lil'ole girls and deny them a raise? Every other non-union employee had received at least two annual raises. Why would the "Cancer" deny these employees a raise even when the Union insisted that it be placed into effect, even without a contract? What type of mentality would deny employees their bread and butter for three years? How can they be concerned for people?

"I turned to Company counsel Ed Norris. Ed, you don't believe that way. You would not do that. But the "Cancer" believes that way. What is humanitarian about that type of thinking? Ed, you have received three to four times as much for your legal fees defending the unfair labor practice charges against the Company trying to keep us from getting a contract than we were asking for those 13 Lil'ole girls. After the "Cancer's" unsuccessful try to get the 13
Lil'ole girls to vote against CWA, I sat up a meeting with President Hill for January 11, 1979. I felt maybe after the decertification attempt, he was beginning to see the problems as they really were. Much to my pleasant surprise he advised that he had asked all department heads to tell him in writing, by February 1, what could be done to

improve labor relations and reduce the number of grievances. He was asking the personnel department for a separate recommendation as to what it would take, recognizing the economics realities, to upgrade the personnel department to where they could handle personnel problems. He acknowledged that some management responded to the Union from an emotional viewpoint rather than a pragmatic business viewpoint and that there were changes for the better taking effect in this area. Regarding the election in the data department, he said the Company was going to have an internal meeting on January 12 and start in a new direction. They would be ready to meet with CWA on January 16 to negotiate.

Glory to God, the long nightmare was starting to come to an end. President Hill had given me hope. What did Calvin Patrick and Local President Freeman do? We compromised and reached an agreement for the 13 Lil'ole girls on January 29, 1979. Mr. Hill had been President over two years. He had finally shown us that he wanted a new relationship by some of the things he was doing and we compromised to reach an agreement. The agreement was one we could be very proud of. But it did not take into account for the three years that some of the Lil'ole girls had been without a raise.

Chapter 11:   Things Must Be Done

"Jack, (Gaddis) within 3 months you took over as the new Human Resources Director after the incumbent was demoted. Bill, (McDonald) you took over as the new General Plant Manager. I believed we were on the threshold of mutual trust but the "Cancer" is still in power. He is still causing us serious problems. So there are some things that must be done in these negotiations to show the members and us that you, the leaders, at this bargaining table, are in charge and not the "Cancer".

1. The Company has denied me a pass to Company property for 5 years. Contractually and legally I am entitled to a pass. That is number one in restoring trust.

2. Ed, you told me across this table in 1976 about a strike that was caused by a personnel manager and union representative not getting along and it ultimately caused a strike. We have tough negotiations ahead of us and because of all the new officers on the Company bargaining committee we need to prevent that kind of a problem. You and I must have a heart to heart discussion.

3. The officers of this Local have serious reservations about trust because of the past problems I have elaborated on. They need some assurance the Company is serious about a new direction. So there is something tangible the Company can do between now and the next time we meet to show these officers you mean business. Look at those grievances that are now 2,3,4 and 5 years old that we have been unable to settle. Make some tough decisions that the "Cancer" will not like and settle two or three cases. This will be some tangible evidence that will at least indicate to these officers you are serious about becoming leaders and want to go in a responsible direction.

4. If we are to remove the "Cancer" from this Company you,

the new team, have got to become leaders, you've got to make the tough decisions. I ask you to work with me and the Local in establishing a firm foundation for the future."

Chapter 12: Hurricane off the Carolina Coast

I concluded my remarks by telling a story in allegory form. "There is a hurricane off the Carolina coast. It is headed this way and may effect negotiations. We can head it off-- maybe change its course, provided the Company comes with a cost-of-living allowance (COLA). If you fail, the Hurricane will sweep across this Company and take negotiations out of your hands. You men at this table, if you will become leaders, can prevent that from happening. You say Kansas City is not controlling negotiations. Then stop this hurricane before you get swept away."

We presented our proposals for the Company to study and agreed on our next meeting date, July 2, 1979.

I was not through with the "Cancer". I had met United Telecommunications Chairman of the Board, Paul Hensen, at the reception in Kansas City. I wrote him a 3-page letter and requested an investigation of the "Cancer". Subsequently a detailed analysis of the problems with the "Cancer" was sent to Chairman Hensen.[7]

---

[7] *This information was learned 3 years later in a conversation with a Company official.*

Chapter 13: Clearing The Air

On July 3, 1979 United of Tennessee's Chief Negotiator Attorney Ed Norris requested a luncheon meeting with me to clear the air regarding our personal relationship. In two and one-half hours we discussed our relationship from the beginning, the misunderstandings and commitments made and the perception of those commitments being broken.

Norris stated that I had insisted in 1976 on moving negotiations from his office suite conference room to a motel. Historically negotiations had been conducted in his facilities. The move had inconvenienced him because of his many clients. I explained, the local officers had insisted that a neutral location be used. They felt the Unions private conversations could be overheard or even monitored. I had agreed that neutral ground was the best place to conduct negotiations and because of their perceptions I felt it in the best interest of reaching an agreement.

Norris was likewise miffed because after moving to a neutral location at the Ramada Inn in Kingsport he had later wanted to move to the Holiday Inn in Bristol, Tennessee, which was nearer to United's headquarters. I had addressed this issue at our first meeting on June 22 and had nothing further to add.

Norris was upset because in 1976 negotiations he had brought an off-the-record offer of 8 percent in wages plus 1 percent in pension improvements saying this was the Company's final offer. The Union rejected that offer. Norris had gone back to the Company and after much discussion with them, finally got them to commit to a 10 percent wage package including a 1 percent improvement in the pension plan. He had understood the Union would accept this as a final offer. However, I had rejected that offer. He again had to go to the Company for additional money. This had caused him much embarrassment. I could not recall such an understanding and advised there must have been some misunderstanding on his part.

Norris admitted lying to me regarding conversations with Vice President Wilson about the commitment made to place the 13 Lil'ole girls in the bargaining unit with the 1300 employees under contract with CWA. He said this was the only time he had ever lied in his life. The reason for his lying was that he was afraid I would go to Wilson, who had gone into depression shortly after the election in the 13 employee bargaining unit. Further, he was upset because of my insistence on placing these 13 employees in the 1300 employee bargaining unit.

Norris admitted he had probably contributed to the Company's attitude toward the Union. For that he was sorry. We agreed to put the past behind us and work more as professionals in our relationship.

Regarding negotiations, Norris stated the Company wanted to take the high road and it would be left up to the Union. The Company had orders not to negotiate a COLA and they were committed to stay within the Presidential wage guidelines. There would be no dental plan. All other items were flexible.

I advised Norris the Union was willing to stay within the Presidential wage guidelines, provided the Company granted the COLA. If he felt the Company was taking the High road by denying COLA he was sadly mistaken. I advised him I must know by August 10th whether the Company was willing to change its position on a COLA. If a COLA were not forthcoming by then we would lose control of negotiations and would be in the middle of the hurricane.

Our conversation terminated with Norris stating that he felt better about our personal relationship, but much worse about negotiations.

Norris asked me to speak to the Kingsport Rotary Club after negotiations. He said this would be a first time a labor leader had ever spoken to this club. I agreed to speak provided we reached an agreement.

On July 13 bargaining resumed as both the Company and Union started explaining our proposals. On July 24, United's bargaining committee chair, Jack Gaddis and Labor Relations Coordinator, Dan Luethke, asked for a meeting with Local President Darrell Freeman and me. Gaddis stated that in response to my request on June 22 the Company was granting me a Company pass. Today they were responding further with tangible evidence that the Company wanted a better relationship.

They would agree to settle a case that was going to arbitration by granting holiday pay that had been denied. They would also reinstate an employee who had been discharged and they were setting in motion guidelines to prevent the selection of "wrong" employees for promotions, which was causing many grievances.

The meeting concluded with Gaddis stating the Company had listened very closely to me on June 22. They too were concerned about labor relations and felt we had turned the corner.

On July 24th I received a letter from President Hill stating that the Company had filed a petition, testimony and exhibits with the Tennessee Public Service Commission on July 10 1978 and a year later they had not been granted a hearing. He stated, "I am writing this letter to compare for you our operations in Tennessee with other independent Telephone Companies." He further stated that even if the Commission had granted the Company petition they would still be $20 per telephone below the average of other Companies. His final paragraph concluded. "We continue to need a hearing and adequate revenue. Our inadequate level of revenue affects every employee and every customer in our service area. Our ability to pay and our ability to perform are limited by the Commission and its refusal to allow the Company the revenue needed for a normal operation."

It was clear part of the intent of Hills letter was to place the Union on notice that the Company did not have money for a COLA, as we were insisting on. He made no suggestion that we attempt to help the Company with the PSC.

On July 25th Local President Darrel Freeman and I met with President Hill and the Vice President of Operations, Charles Browning. Before Browning came into the meeting President Freeman had a private discussion with President Hill regarding some Company officials and problems with the PSC.

We presented a copy of President Carter's remarks during a question and answer session at the CWA convention as well as a copy of CWA's economic statement, emphasizing that if the Company was going to attempt to negotiate by the guideline as set out by President Carter, that they further were mandated to give a COLA as stated during Carter's Question and Answer session at the convention.

Mr. Hill responded that the Company had two problems. One was the earnings of the Company and the fact that they could not get the Tennessee Public Service Commission to grant the Company a hearing on the filing that was now over a year old. The Commission had denied the petition and now it was in the Courts. We advised the Company that while they may have a legitimate position from their point of view, we cannot accept that position and will not be intimidated by it. President Carter had set out a way for both parties to be successful in negotiations and we would be waiting for the Company to modify their position.

We ended the meeting by offering to attempt to get

the PSC not to appeal the courts decision, and grant a hearing for the rate increase, otherwise a PSC appeal would delay the Company getting an increase for another year. President Hill was receptive to our trying to help.

Negotiations were conducted on August 1st and 2nd with the Company supplying requested data in order to cost out the contract. No substantial progress was made except the Company continued to emphasize their interest in improving the relationship with the Union.

The Union bargaining committee had asked the Company to come forward and agree on three proposals before a Union meeting on August 7th.

> 1. Grant a cope check-off. (A one time each year deduction from employee's check if the employee agrees)
>
> 2. Grant a check-off for the Locals hardship fund. (If employee agrees)
>
> 3. Pay the bargaining committee members' wages during negotiations.

The first two proposals would only cost the Company the money to set up the computer for the deductions. The third would cost the Company $4,000. While the cost would be minimal to the Company, it was a large figure for the Local with its limited income.

The Company had proved to the bargaining committee that they wanted a new relationship. The Union bargaining committee wanted to take these agreements to the members at the August 7th meeting and prove to them there had finally been a change in leadership and the "Cancer" was at least sidetracked.

At the bargaining session on August 7th the Company rejected the three proposals saying they had demonstrated to the bargaining committee their desire to change attitudes. They were right. But would the membership believe it.

Chapter 14: You Can't Say Those Things

At the August 7th membership meeting I felt compelled to give the membership the message that the Company wanted a new relationship, even though the three proposals had been rejected. The Bargaining Committee had come a long way toward trusting the Company, but were opposed to my trying to lay the groundwork for a better future relationship between the membership and Company. They rightfully felt that we might lose the memberships trust and confidence.

The employees did not feel positive about the Company, but because of my appreciation for what had transpired since January of 1979, I decided to go forward with attempting to bridge the gap between the Company and employees, even though I knew I must say some negative things about the Company in order to maintain credibility with the bargaining committee and membership.

Seven hundred members attended the meeting. There was an uneasiness in the air as several members told me prior to the meeting that they would have a contract by midnight August 23rd, or strike, with or without the "damn Union". The meeting went smoothly as Local President Freeman conducted normal business for 45 minutes. Freeman then turned to bargaining and spoke firmly about supporting the bargaining committee. He urged those who were threatening to strike to wait on the committee to make a recommendation.

In introducing me, Freeman stated there would be some things I would say that they might not agree with. He was sure, however, they wanted it told, "Like it is". "Calvin Patrick, your National Union Representative and Chair of the Bargaining Committee."

I received a cordial applause.

"I come tonight very upset at individuals telling me they are going to strike if we don't have a contract on August 23rd, regardless of what the Union says. It is a big responsibility to put 1300 members on the street knowing that 3000 dependents are looking to them for a livelihood. If anyone ever wanted to strike this Company, it's Calvin Patrick. Some of you know just a small amount of agony that we have been through for 22 months trying to negotiate a contract for 13 Lil'ole girls who work for this Company in the Data Processing Department. Many of them did without a raise for 3 years because of an attitude in this Company. You can't realize the heartbreak for me, for President Freeman, and the bargaining committee for those employees; the lost sleep, lost vacation time, and time away from our families. You can never understand the loneliness when I asked my CWA Vice President for advise, and the only help he could give me is to say, 'You have my support, strike the Company, we can keep picket lines up for two years if necessary---.' The frustration of making the decision not to strike because I knew the Company wanted to replace the 13-Lil'ole girls and get rid of the Union. The isolation of not getting any feedback from my Vice President on this issue for 16 months because there was nothing he could do. Yes, I want to strike, but what kind of person am I if I caused others to suffer because of my anger and hurt."

Chapter 15:   It's Easy to Strike

"It's easy to strike--but it's hard to get back---. We are going to have our disagreements. We all won't be happy with the results of negotiations. We may not want to strike. The Company may force us to strike. We may lose control of bargaining if the Company doesn't come through with a cost-of-living formula. United of New Jersey has been out since June 1st, that is 67 days. They still do not have an adequate wage offer."

"The Cooperate Headquarters in Kansas City is trying to take away the raise they gave to the employees in United in Norfork, during the organizing campaign. You, the average members, are simply not in a position to know what is going on in other parts of the country. So to say you are going to strike regardless is irresponsible. You must trust your committee to do what, in their view, is best and then we will bring the contract to you and let you vote to ratify the contract or reject it and strike.

The Company has proved to the bargaining committee that they want a more responsible relationship. On June 22, we asked for some tangible evidence and they came through for us. You know we have a new Company President, a new General Plant Manager, a new General Manager in the Data Processing Department, a new Human Resources Director and we have some new supervisors. You haven't seen the results as we at the bargaining table have. I asked the Company to give you some tangible evidence of wanting change. It would have cost a little over $4,000 . They thought we were just bargaining. They really did not understand how important those 3 proposals are to you. They don't understand the problems you have had with the "Cancer". They do not understand your feelings. We got our answer today, 'No! No! No!' Do you know what the

Company is interested in?

-"Supervisors going to used car sales." The crowd responded with laughter and much agreement.

-"Top Management going around with binoculars trying to find employees on long breaks." Echoes of, "Right, Right" sounded throughout the audience.

-"The Company won't listen to employees who tell them that customers don't want employees servicing equipment at certain times thus causing two or more trips to the customers primacies. Right?" Again, laughter and clapping filled the air.

-"Supervisors taking care of personal business on Company time." This brought on an overwhelming round of applause.

-"Supervisors taking over an hour for breaks." A member truly fed up with this injustice yelled, 'You mean two hours.'

-"Top level officers of this Company making public statements that get into the press and cause problems." A round of applause filled the room.

-"Managers that make excuses to customers that trouble can't be cleared because employees are working for the Union."

-"Employees can't find supervisors when they need help." Applause confirmed this serious problem.

-"Supervisors directing employees to change customers service, but it is never changed on the records, therefore revenue is lost." More applause.

-"Employees don't have the equipment to perform their work.

-"Last but not least, an officer of this Company gets drunk and tinkles in the fish fountain of a very luxurious hotel where he has been sent to influence the Public Service Commission." At this true account, the members burst into laughter and a period of prolonged applause.

"The Message I am trying to give you as employees

and Union members is this, The Company has problems with its employees, the public, and the Public Service Commission. I do not believe in deriding the Company when I say these things. It's important to you that this Company is successful, therefore we can not be irresponsible like some of the management we have spoken about."

"When you abuse your breaks you are wrong. Today I received a report that in one location the employees had to cough and clear their throats when they pass a certain office because employees are hiding and up to no good. This is wrong." (Chuckling). "When 5 or 6 employees go to the same restaurant for coffee in Company vehicles you are helping create a negative image which hurts the Company. We've got to give a days work for a days pay, but we want, and demand, a fair days pay."

We may be on the street. We can't make a judgment 16 days before the contract terminates.

We can have successful negotiations, even with wage price controls, but the Company hasn't shown any leadership so far. I am depressed; I don't know where they are going.

I hope you will trust the committee. We may have to go beyond the 23rd of August. We don't know. That is a collective decision made by many within the Union. This is a very large Corporation. What is happening in other parts of the Country is playing a part in what may happen here.

If someone jumps the gun and gets us on strike then we may all be in trouble and could lose control of negotiations. Events then would overtake us. Based on past history, we aren't going to get a lot more on the street than we can before a strike begins. If the Company is doing their job they will offer the very last nickel before a strike. Why? If the Company gives more after the strike starts, then the next time we negotiate we won't believe them. That is the pressure that keeps the Company honest.

We will be talking to others within the Union who know what is going on in the rest of the country. We ask you to trust the bargaining committee to do the right thing. We will then bring a recommendation to you to ratify or to vote to strike.

I hope the Company comes through with a COLA. We've told them how. I don't believe they are listening. I know they are preparing for a strike".

After my remarks there was 30 minutes of hard questions about negotiations. I then closed the meeting with this summary.

"The Company tells us they are in desperate need of the rate increase that is currently before the Public Service Commission. They have been advised, rate increase or no rate increase, we will not be denied justice because of the failures of those who have preceded the present management team. If we are not successful at the bargaining table and strike, I want to be in a position to continue to respect and trust President Hill. I trust you will continue to respect your supervisors even though they will be required to cross our picket lines. We don't want any violence on the picket lines.

What happens on August 23 is left up to the Company!!! They have been placed on notice. We will have justice!!!" The Bargaining Committee received a standing ovation.

On August 8 the Union met with the Public Service Commission. Present were all three Commissioners, Johnny Thompson, Legislative Chairman of Local 10871, Darrell Freeman, President of Local 10871 and Calvin Patrick, East Tennessee/Kentucky State Director. Our purpose was to see if the Commission would grant a hearing for United Telephone, without automatically appealing the court's decision which was expected shortly."

A synopsis of the meeting:

1. The Commission felt the Company did not have the expertise to perform the job both with the public, and with the Commission.

2. They felt that Cooperate Headquarters in Kansas City was calling the shots and not allowing United to develop personal relationships with the Commission.

3. The Commission had wanted the Company to remove 8 town upgrades from their filing. They said that these town upgrades would have been routinely upgraded, but the Company refused to separate them from the filing.

4. The Commission wanted a personal relationship with the Company and for the Company to come to the commission staff and get their input. It would be helpful to have the Commissions thinking prior to making a filing.

5. The Companies attitude must change. They must show the Commission where improvements are being made. The Company must be willing to have enough confidence in the Commission to acknowledge the bad side of internal audits and tell the Commission what is being done to correct problems identified by these audits. It was very clear that unless the Company changed from an adversarial relationship to one of respect and cooperation the Commission would continue to deny every filing and keep the filings tied up in Court for as long as possible.

One Commissioner agreed that he would grant the hearing once the court made their decision. The Union felt that a second commissioner was coming around. The third commissioner was hard against United primarily because of their continuing to criticize him, but there were rays of hope if the Company would make positive changes in their relationships with the Commission.

Bargaining continued on August 9 and 10, with the Union completing explanations of our proposals. The Company wanted to agree on the contract language where there were no new proposals and no dispute. We ask for a delay.

On August 10, I received a call from National Director Mendoza advising that the New Jersey IBEW Local had voted and settled their contract with the 7 percent wage increase. He stated "we are adamant, CWA will never get an agreement in New Jersey with only 7 percent on the table. We will continue to strike." Mendoza set August 20, as the date for his research assistant to come to Tennessee and cost out an agreement, using a COLA formula and President Jimmy Carter's wage guide lines.

On August 13, the Company continued to press for agreement on language where there was no dispute in order to be able to report progress in negotiations. We responded that we had asked for tangible evidence to take to the employees. The Company had failed to give this tangible evidence and had proposals that were retrogressive, therefore we would not agree on the non-controversial language. At the end of this meeting the Company advised they would be meeting on August 14, with an expert on President Carter's wage price controls and should know at our next meeting how far the Company could go on wages. We responded that we were not negotiating under the wage price controls unless the Company accepted our offer to negotiate using a COLA Formula.

On August 13th Darrell Freeman and I met with President Hill to share our conclusions about our meeting with the PSC on August 8th.

President Hill was very defensive at the beginning of the meeting. After advising him we were only there to share information we had received from the Commission, and were simply trying to be helpful and to deliver a message, he listened very carefully, taking notes. My conclusion was that President Hill was objective enough to take corrective actions, one of which would be the removal of one vice president in charge of public relations and a member of the Company Board of Directors. He was the Company person who worked with the PSC.

On August 14, I met again with President Hill and discussed bargaining, pointing out I was looking for more than just an agreement. I wanted to establish trust between management and craft. I ask him to remove the retrogression from the bargaining table and grant:
1. The Hardship fund check off, where the Company would make deductions from employee's checks once a year.
2. Pay for the bargaining committee during negotiations, and
3. Grant the CWA cope check-off where the Company would make periodical deductions from employees' checks who had requested the deductions.

These were very small money items that would be very meaningful to the local leadership and would help in developing trust. The officers and stewards were in need of these items to help the Local Union. Mr. Hill was noncommittal.

I advised Mr. Hill that I had requested an answer about a COLA formula by August 10, but August 10 had come and gone and we had not received an answer. I advised him I would be having a press conference on August 17 if no COLA was forth coming. I would be telling the public that the Union was willing to stay within President Carter's wage guidelines provided the Company came with a COLA formula. President Hill responded that we had the Company in a difficult position on COLA "with President Carter supporting your position".

President Carter had spoken to the CWA convention in June of 1979 and had responded to a question from a delegate who was concerned that employees who were caught negotiating under the wage guidelines could not catch up with inflation. President Carter had suggested that if companies and unions used COLA formulas, with certain assumptions regarding inflation, then the buying power of the employees could be maintained. This was the approach we were now using in United Telecommunications.

President Hill thanked me for sharing CWA's position and suggested that we keep in touch.

Chapter 16: Exception to Wage Controls Approved.

After negotiations on August 15, the Company advised the Union committee that they had met with their expert on wage controls and had received approval from Kansas City to an "Exception to the wage controls." However, the Council on Wage and Price Stability (COWPS) would have to approve the exception. The Company would try to get approval on the basis that the employees had fallen behind other companies who had cost-of-living formulas in their contracts.

I restated CWA's position. "We will get a contract using the wage controls provided you come with a COLA formula. That is the only way we can reach an agreement".

On August 16, we advised the Company that we were looking with favor on their proposal on Operator Services Computerized scheduling. Since it was a radical departure from the present scheduling and was controversial it would have to be for a one-year trial period. I announced that I was conducting a news conference tomorrow. I explained that previously my agreement to a news blackout was based on the Company making movement on a COLA formula. "We have not received any indication that a COLA formula is forth coming".

Company spokesman Norris was very upset about getting involved with the press. He accused them of "yellow dog" journalism.

The Kingsport Times headlines read:

"Phone Workers Set To Strike Next Week"

-**August 17,1979** Johnson City--"Some 1300 United

Intermountain Telephone Co. workers stand ready to strike next week if difficulties continue in present contract negotiations. Calvin Patrick, CWA Director, said the main snag in negotiations has been the Company's failure to present an acceptable Cost-of-living Formula." He continued, "The Company is telling the CWA bargaining committee that these are most difficult times because of the presidential wage and price guidelines.

"CWA has responded to this statement by placing the Company on notice that the Union will do everything within reason to prevent a strike." Patrick said. "We have given the Company an outline on how an agreement can be reached within the guidelines; however, as of today we have received no definitive response from United".

Patrick said, "The Union is willing to stay within the President's guidelines. He added that President Carter told CWA representatives at their annual convention last month that cost-of-living increases are an acceptable part of his guidelines. The purpose of the press conference was to simply let the public know the Union is willing to stay within the guidelines, but must have a COLA formula to be successful.

Mr. Hill, president of United Intermountain Telephone Company, responded, "Previously the Communications Workers of America and United Intermountain Telephone Co. have observed a mutual blackout in releases and statements to the media during negotiations. Since Mr. Patrick, the chief negotiator for CWA, had issued a statement today, we can say that the current negotiations are indeed most complicated and difficult by reason of the President's guidelines and the slowness of the negotiations is regrettable. Nevertheless, the Company will continue to bargain with the CWA in good faith. We are optimistic that a fair and equitable agreement for all parties concerned, our customers, the public and employees of the telephone Company, can be reached before the expiration of the current contract."

During negotiations on Friday, August 17, I again emphasized that we must have a COLA formula in order to reach an agreement. The Company was again reminded of the hurricane off the Carolina coast. We later learned that Jack Gaddis had taken this as bargaining rhetoric but others who had negotiated with me knew I meant what I was saying.

Negotiations continued Saturday and Sunday with no response on a COLA formula. By Monday, August 20, I was becoming impatient. Time was becoming a factor. While I was not looking for the Company's bottom line on economics, I needed to know if they were going to accept the principle of COLA. The Union's position was acceptable with the public as indicated by the response of the press conference on August 17. It was our intention to use the press, if necessary, to keep up the pressure.

At 11:30 a.m. I advised the Company my economist was coming in today to cost out a wage and benefit package using the presidential wage guidelines and a COLA formula. Time was running out and I needed an idea of where we were going economically.

Company spokesman Norris responded that we had started out negotiations with an understanding to agree on language first and he felt we would be better served to continue working in that direction. I responded, "while that may have been the understanding, the Union placed the Company on notice June 22, regarding a COLA. When we receive the Company's commitment, to negotiate using a COLA formula, then we will continue our agreement to negotiate language before wages." Norris responded that the Company had been seeking diligently on ways to give the employees a fair and equitable settlement above the 7 percent wage guidelines, but without a COLA formula. "A COLA is not feasible in this Company". He advised "the Company is working on the economics at this minute. When we get authorization, it will be communicated to you. We agree we are running out of time".

I responded that the Union must have an understanding on a COLA formula as I have those to whom I must communicate with.

Jack Gaddis had joined the Company team at 12 noon and at 12:30 p.m. requested a recess until 5 p.m. for the Company to review their position. Negotiations recessed on a very somber and downbeat note.

At 5:30 p.m. after reconvening, Company spokesman Norris stated that the time was short. Then in a most unprecedented move, as bad as our relationship had been, he proceeded to reject every Union proposal on the table.

At 7:00 p.m. negotiations recessed with the Union committee dumbfounded as to what was happening. We felt the Company must have received some bad news at lunch. Our hunch was that United in Kansas City was denying a COLA and leaving it up in the air as to what direction United of Tennessee was to go.

The Company's caucus room faced the hotel swimming pool. To show the Company that their strategy, whatever it was, had not upset the Union committee, within three minutes after reaching our hotel rooms, we were in the swimming pool. Within five minutes Local Vice President Bob Brown, 6 foot tall and much of a man, was prissing like a waitress bringing drinks held elegantly on a tray.

We were laughing and splashing water but out of the corner of our eye we could see the "Cancer" look from behind the curtain of the Company caucus room. Inside we were very confused.

At 1 a.m. on August 21, I could not go to sleep. I called Gaddis at his home, waking him up. I informed him the Company had made a serious mistake in reacting as they did at the bargaining table. I told him I would be in his office in Bristol at 9 a.m.

We met at 9:00 a.m. and had a friendly conversation. I reemphasized the Unions position. Nothing was said as to why the Company had reacted as they had. I went in to see President Hill and emphasized time was running out and there must be movement.

The Federal Mediation and Conciliation Service (FMCS) met with us in the afternoon session. The Company reversed themselves and started making concessions on Union proposals. As the session ended the Company advised they would be coming with a wage offer but no COLA.

On August 22 The Kingsport News reported that the PSC "Postpones making a move on Rate Hike of 3.4 million as requested by United Inter-mountain Telephone Co. The delay was approved to give the PSC staff and members time to study last weeks State Court of Appeals decision finding the PSC unjustified in denying United a hearing on its July 1978 Request."

On August 22, the Union pointed out the areas in language where we may be willing to move provided we were able to reach an agreement on economics. We further advised, "We would be having a meeting tonight to take a strike vote. We have no choice since the Company has chosen not to come with a Cost-of-living Formula."

Chapter 17:   Strike Vote

Local President Darrell Freeman opened the meeting. "We have trouble in negotiations, and tonight we come to you asking you to give us a vote to strike. We want you to give us a strike vote to show the Company we are serious about a cost-of-living clause in our contract. A strike vote will authorize the President of CWA, Glenn Watts, to set a strike date should we not reach an agreement.

Should you vote to strike and we strike, there will be over 70 picket line locations. If one hot head jumps the gun and causes a strike without it being authorized by President Watts, it could very well mess up negotiations."

Bargaining Committee member, Judy Graham, spoke to the members: "Over the last few weeks we have worked for you and tonight we feel we need a strike vote from you to show the Company that you are still behind us."

Committee member, Bob Brown stated, "You have the assurance that we, the bargaining committee are together. All we want is a fair share and we ask you to vote to strike." (Applause)

My supervisor, T.J. Volk, had come to Kingsport to assist in negotiations and spoke to the membership. "We are trying to reach a peaceful settlement, but this is the hard headiest bunch of management I've seen in my life." (Loud applause, clapping and yelling) Volk continued, "You need to seriously think about how you vote tonight. If you follow the rules and leadership there will be a defense fund to help you. If you do not follow the rules you may be on your own. If you vote to strike the Executive Board of CWA will be polled to approve a strike, subject to President Watts setting a strike date."

Volk continued, "There are two reasons for a strike vote. First, we want to build pressure on the Company, and second, we want to make contact on high corporate management and get them to do the right thing. That is all we want. If we don't have a contract by midnight tomorrow you don't necessarily strike. You wait until President Watts calls the strike. I want to point out to you, the Union calls and starts the strike but the Company is usually the one who will say when it is going to end. They have control over whether they do something better in improving the contract or whether you get anything at all. We don't know how long a strike will last. Again the Company decides when it's going to end. I'm not trying to dampen your spirits; just let you know the facts. We are looking at a very serious situation. The Company will know your feelings by the outcome of the vote tonight."

I was then introduced.

"This is a Union meeting!!! What a turn out!!! Things would be so much better if you participated all the time and not just once every 3 years, when we have contract negotiations. God, we need you!!! (Applause). We do!!! It gets lonely for a Local President and the officers and stewards doing the job you need done. Giving the time it takes away from their families. You have a good group representing you. A group you can be proud of. They stand up for you.

"We told you at our last meeting that we had gone to Kansas City on June 9, and met with the CWA leadership of all the United Telecommunications Companies in the United States. Your Union was concerned because of the injustices in the United System toward their employees. We were concerned about the backwardness and hard headedness, and sometimes down right stupidity of the management of this Company. (Applause).

"I said that to say this. They are concerned about what is happening tonight. We sat around the bargaining table today discussing the situations coming up. New Jersey has been on strike since June 1. They still have less than 7 percent on the table. Our contract terminates at midnight tomorrow. United of Ohio and Indiana are terminating around September 15, United of Carolina terminates October 1. . United in Norfork is in trouble. We put United of Tennessee/Virginia on notice June 22 that they must come with a COLA formula. (In the background--"they better do it too") (Applause).

"We've been talking, and frankly, up until yesterday we felt we were against a stone wall. But yesterday we had some breakthroughs and things have been moving.

"I want to say something positive about this Company. It is your Company. Even though we are in conflict I think we can be successful. The future will be brighter for us in terms of handling grievances. Hopefully, if we can get some support from the Public Service Commission, we will get economic justice in the future. It has taken President Hill over two years to assume the Presidency of this Company. He has taken over and I've come to admire him. We have a new General Plant Manager, Bill McDonald, and all of you know General Traffic Manager, Bob Nicar, who is part of the old team, but very honest. We have Dan Luethke; all of us admire him as honest and fair.

What I'm saying is we have a good group across the bargaining table. They have listened to us. They want to help us in the future. They have become real leaders, going out on a limb in some cases to help us establish a new relationship for the future. The problem in negotiations is not at this bargaining table. The problem tonight, my friends, is at United Headquarters in Kansas City. Let me tell you about United Telecommunications of Kansas City.

Profits per employee:
$2,900 in General Telephone
$5,400 in American Telephone and Telegraph

$6,900 in United Telecommunications

The money is there, but it is locked up in Kansas City. All they are worrying about is the Profit and Loss statement, the stockholders, not the employees. The money is there!!! (From the audience "lets get it, then") "We're trying!" (Laughter and applause)

"These figures came from Forbes Magazine. Profit growth jumped from 31st to 25th place among the top 500 corporations, a 19.4 percent increase between 1977 and 1978: Since 1974 an increase in profits of 150 percent. How much of a raise have you gotten since 1974? Tonight we don't have a COLA formula on the table to tell you about. President Watts pledged to President Jimmy Carter in October of 1978 that this Union would support wage price controls. Mr. Paul Henson, Chairman of the Board of United Telecommunications, sent a letter to President Carter pledging that United would support wage price controls. At that time inflation was running 7 percent. Things are a lot worse now, aren't they?

"President Carter came to our National Convention in June and a member got up on the floor and told the President that his Company was negotiating when wage price controls went into effect. The Local felt a responsibility to do their part in holding down inflation. That Company said they wanted to stay within the wage guidelines, and the Union agreed to a contract with a 7 percent wage increase. The member's question to President Carter was: "What do we do now? What kind of justice have we got, when inflation is now running 12-13 percent and we settled for 7 percent?"

"President Carter responded that there was a way to have wage justice: through a cost-of-living formula, A COLA.

"In United of Tennessee we are willing to stay within the wage guidelines and do what is reasonable, even placing a cap of 9 percent on a COLA formula. But we want the principle of a COLA in these negotiations. We can get a contract within the wage-price guidelines if the Company will come with a COLA formula.

"Let me tell you of another Company that did what we are asking for here in United. In General of Kentucky I settled a contract on June 6. In that Corporation the Chairman of the Board also pledged to President Carter to stay within the wage- price guidelines. But General of Kentucky realized that inflation had escalated and they came with a COLA formula that we could and did accept. That is the same formula we are trying to use here.

"Frankly, I think United of Tennessee wants to help us, The Company chief spokesman told me on June 7, that he didn't see how we could reach an agreement without a COLA. But we haven't had any help from Kansas City, and tonight we are asking you to send Kansas City a message! Do you want to send them a message?" (Applause)

The members voted overwhelmingly to strike.

Chapter: 18 15 Hours to Go!

We met with the Company at 9:00 a.m., August 23. Only 15 hours to go before the contract expires. I advised the Company we had kind words to say about the Company bargaining committee at the Union meeting last night, and that the membership had voted overwhelming to strike.

The Company laid out a wage offer for a three-year contract: Six percent at the go-down: 6 percent at the first anniversary and 5 percent at the second anniversary.

Without discussion we rejected the offer as ridiculous.

The Company accepted the Unions counter proposal on "call- outs". An agreement was reached on "day at a time" vacation for a one-year trial period. The Company challenged that the Union had not responded to many Company proposals. We advised that unless a COLA formula was forthcoming we wouldn't have an agreement; therefore it didn't make any difference.

At 10:40 a.m. negotiations broke off subject to call by either party. Norris asked for a private meeting with me. He stated there was no way the Company could get permission to offer a COLA formula.

He unofficially said he would offer a wage package under certain conditions. He then spelled out what they would like to offer:

1. 9.5 percent at the go-down
2. 7.0 percent at the first anniversary
3. 6.0 percent at the second anniversary
4. Should wage price controls be lifted there would be wage re-openers at the first and second anniversary.
5. They were willing to improve the insurance from 75 percent payment by the Company to 85 percent and the Company would pay 90 percent beginning at the first anniversary of the contract.

Norris said he could not place this offer across the bargaining table unless they had assurances that the Union Bargaining Committee would recommend it to the members for ratification.

I advised Norris that we were on a collision course if a COLA formula was not forthcoming. I then asked for a meeting between my research economist and a Company representative to understand how a final package would be priced out with both parties using the same criteria. That meeting concluded at 3 p.m.

Communications had not been secure at the motel. The Company, as well as employees, could monitor the circuits. When it was necessary for me to communicate with my Vice President I had been traveling 40 miles one way to get out of United territory and find a secure line. I needed to up-date Vice President Brown so I drove the 40 miles and informed him of the Company's' latest position. I asked for final instructions as to whether we should hold out for a COLA. After this conversation, he and I were convinced a COLA was not going to be forthcoming.

With only six hours to go before contract termination, Vice President Brown instructed me to continue to test the Company to the end and we would talk again before making a final decision.

At 9:30 p.m. negotiations reconvened with the Federal Mediation Service sitting in on the discussions. The midnight termination date was bearing down. I advised the Company that the Union bargaining committee could reach an agreement provided the Company improved the following:

1. A COLA formula with a 9 percent cap for each of the 3 years.

2. 100 percent hospitalization paid by the Company by the first anniversary.

3. Improve the life insurance.
4. Improve telephone concessions from 40 to 50 percent.
5. Agree to the check-off for the Locals hardship fund.
6. Agree to the check-off for CWA Cope deduction.
7. Improve Board and lodging and travel expense.
8. Improve the seniority for recall after a layoff from 12 to 24 months.
9. Grant long-term disability insurance that non-represented employees have.
10. Agree to the Unions proposal eliminating entrance level jobs until all existing employees had an opportunity to bid on the jobs.

Without comment the Company asked for a recess.

At 11:25 p.m. The Federal Mediation Service came to the Unions caucus room and gave us the Company's response:

No, to 100 percent pay for hospitalization

No, to a COLA formula

No, to the long-term disability insurance

The Federal Mediation Service left and we discussed among ourselves where we were. It was now midnight. We had instructed the officers, stewards, and members to continue working until we gave the word to strike.

At 12:55 a.m. August 24, the Company and Union committees met with the Federal Mediation Service. The Company advised the informal offer discussed with me earlier was now the Company's final offer.

9.5 percent at the go-down.

7.0 percent at the first anniversary.

6.0 percent at the second anniversary.

The Company would agree to a wage re-opener at the first and second anniversary should wage and price controls be lifted: This offer complied with the Presidents wage and price controls. However, the Company would offer an alternate proposal with exceptions to the wage guidelines provided the Council on Wage and Price Stability would approve them. That offer was:

9.5 percent at the go-down.

8.0 percent at the first anniversary;

8.0 percent at the second anniversary.

This offer would be placed into effect upon approval by the Council on Wage and Price Stability (COWPS). COWPS would have up to a year to approve the wages.

The Company conceded to 4 Union proposals.

1. Improve telephone concessions from 40 to 50 percent.
2. Improve Board and lodging and travel to $20.00 per day.
3. Improve seniority on recall, when on layoff, from 12 to 24 months.
4. All Jobs would be biddable except telephone operator and house service persons. (This would remove 5 jobs that previously were hired from the street without considering promotions from the employees on the payroll).
5. This offer was subject to the Union agreeing on all outstanding Company proposals.

The Company then chided me that it is now my turn to become a leader. "We have come with more that the Unions COLA formula would have produced. There is no reason for the Union not to reach an agreement." Gaddis smiled and said, "Calvin, we've both been leaders, lets shake hands on it."

At 3:30 a.m. I advised the Company we would take their offer under advisement and study it. We then recessed until 9:00 a.m.

The members were advised through our officers and stewards to continue working as we studied the Company's, complex proposal. We had a lot of talking to do and must check out the proposal with COWPS through our Washington office.

The News media told the story of negotiations.

Kingsport Times August 24th
"Deadline Passes; United and CWA Still Dickering"

At 8:00 a.m. I attempted to get CWA Research Economist, John Howard, from Mendoza's office to check with COWPS and see if we could obtain an exception to the Presidents wage-price controls. Howard went to his hotel room.

When Howard returned and reported his findings it was rather difficult to understand what he had found out. He was very reluctant to say anything that made sense. (Later I learned Howard was acting under direct orders from Mendoza not to cooperate with the bargaining committee.)

After much hell raising on my part, he finally said there were two possibilities on an exception to the wage price controls:

1. An acute labor shortage concept. If the Company felt it would be difficult to attract employees at the wages provided under the guidelines then COWPS would "make an exception" and approve higher wages.

2. The hardship and gross inequity argument. If the Company could prove that other workers in similar industry in the same community are receiving substantially higher wages "we could get an exception".

The bargaining committee knew that number two would work because wages in this Company were $1.00 per hour lower than 3 companies that joined United. Howard figured that total compensation over 3 years was 28 percent and would not be unreasonably high in light of argument number two.

At 10:43 a.m. I contacted Norris and asked where we were legally. He responded; we have been without a contract since midnight. [8] Norris and I agreed to break off talks subject to call.

As I was preparing to travel the 40 miles to discuss our next move with Vice President Brown a call came in confirming my suspicion that the telephone calls from the motel were being monitored. A voice said. "Just listen, I overheard a conversation from Jack Gaddis to a man in Kansas City. They said the Union had gotten the last nickel and not to give on insurance or anything. "The bucket is empty", he concluded. I asked how did I know he was telling the truth? He responded that he knew everything going on in negotiations. He then repeated enough for me to be convinced he was telling the truth.

I traveled the 40 miles and called Vice President Brown, giving him a status report on what had transpired since our last conversation. Brown instructed me to reach an agreement, but to continue testing the Company until I felt sure we have gotten everything possible.

It was not a question as to whether the employees would ratify an agreement, but the employees in Vice President Browns opinion, should have an opportunity to vote before a strike. I suggested that we check with Mendoza's office in Washington since they wanted us to go for a COLA formula. Brown told me as far as he was concerned we had an agreement when we were sure we had gotten all we could get.

---

[8] *On June 11, 1979 President Hill had written CWA President Watts and advised: "you are hereby notified that at 12:00 midnight on August 23, 1979, any agreement, written, oral or implied now in effect between the Union and Company will terminate." This was the Company's right to terminate the agreement but usually we extended contracts on a day-to-day basis in situations such as this.*

Chapter 19: The Last Nickel Is In Bucket

As I traveled back to Kingsport, I went over the events leading to this point in time. In my mind I knew with a 28 percent package, we had more on the table than we could have gotten with our proposed COLA formula, which had a 9 percent cap. We had exceeded the wage-price guidelines and there was no doubt the Company would get approval from COWPS if the Union worked in Washington to help them. The Company had given more than we were asking just to keep from giving in on the principle of a COLA formula. I knew that the employees who were pushing for a COLA probably did not understand what we were attempting to do with the COLA principle. They would not understand we had exceeded what we had stated publicly we would do. I had also emphasized this position at our last meeting. This issue would have to be resolved by the vote of the Local.

I knew the Union bargaining committee would feel comfortable in recommending the contract to the membership if we could improve on the Company offer on hospital insurance. That is the way we would test the Company. Improve the hospitalization offer. Upon reaching the motel and talking to the Union committee I found that indeed the hospitalization was still an issue.

With agreement from the Union bargaining committee, I called the Company spokesmen, Ed Norris and Jack Gaddis, and asked them to meet Local President Freeman and me in the breezeway of the motel. We asked them to remove any reference to getting a clearance from the COWPS and then if we were able to reach an agreement to just place the wages into effect. I informed them the hospitalization was still an issue and the Company must improve the insurance from 80 percent being paid by the

Company at the go-down to 85 percent paid by the Company. This would be a cheap price to get ratification and keep from being involved with the hurricane that I had talked about.

Norris and Gaddis responded that the Company had given more than they could afford and had every nickel on the table. I attempted several times to get them to reconsider, to call Kansas City and check it out. They kept repeating "no way, that's all there is".

I tried another offer of change. Under the present proposal the Company would be paying 85 percent of the premium beginning with the second anniversary. However, should inflation continue at more than 5 percent per year the employees would have an additional increase in premium. Therefore, the Company should pick up any additional cost of the premium above what the employee would pay if inflation remained at zero.

Gaddis again said, "we have the last nickel in the bucket. I've got my orders and will not ask Kansas City for another penny."

After discussing these events with the bargaining committee we agreed we had all we could get and the employees should have the right to vote on this package.

At 2:15 p.m. I advised the Company we had an agreement in principle on economics provided we could work out the language. Our position was that we take the 3-year package without the wage re-opener provided the COWPS would agree to the exceptions to the wage guidelines. But in the event wage price controls were lifted we would revert to the re-opener package. [9] The Company responded that we had an agreement on economics.

---

[9] *The Company later advised they had made a mistake in allowing the Union the option of the three year package with the option of a wage re-opener should wage-price guidelines be lifted.*

The committees were called together at 3:15 p.m. It would take several hours to complete agreement on contract language.

At 4:00 p.m. CWA President Watts called my supervisor, T.J. Volk, in the Union's caucus room and stated he had heard we had reached agreement. Watts was advised we had an agreement on economics, but it would be several hours before the language would be agreed to. President Watts said he was in Carolina with the Local Presidents of United of Carolina and was getting pressure because they had wanted COLA. Watts was advised that we had some tough language proposals on the table and by holding out for them we would not reach an agreement. Before hanging up President Watts asked Volk not to say anything about his call and if he (Watts) did not call back to go ahead and reach agreement.

At 7:50 p.m. the last language item was agreed to. President Watts had not called back. We shook hands across the table with Jack Gaddis. We had an agreement.

Chapter 20: All Hell Breaks Loose

At 2:00 a.m. Sunday morning, August 25, I received a telephone call from National Director Mendoza questioning why I had reached an agreement. He thought I knew where "we were all going together in these negotiations".

I asked him did he think it was a good settlement. Mendoza responded it was not a matter of being a good settlement. "We had agreed in Kansas City to work together and work for a COLA formula. I asked him why he had not been here to help in negotiations.

I was in a position to get an agreement and put the agreement out for a ratification vote. Vice President Brown instructed me to reach an agreement. I then found out from the Company, of all places, that "you were in California." I asked, who is criticizing my reaching an agreement? He responded, "no one, but I have been in touch with John Howard there at the motel". [10]

I told Mendoza that I had been at the motel for weeks and he could have contacted me, especially since I was responsible for negotiations. Now, "after an agreement is reached you suddenly have a need to communicate with me in the middle of the night."

Mendoza responded, "I've got the impression you would have reached an agreement no matter what anyone says. I'm not being critical because it looks like 28 percent over 3 years, but we were trying to get the Corporate structure's attention this year. Now we've got an agreement that doesn't have a COLA formula. I conveyed to you that Kansas City was looking at a different approach and this

---

[10] *Hotel records indicated Howard had called Mendoza 11 times. There was no way to know how many times Mendoza had called Howard at the motel.*

evening, when I talked to Vice President Brown, I ask; does this contract contain re-openers in the event there are relaxations on wage-price controls. He indicated yes, that was in the agreement. This is a departure from the past but I am not sure that President Watts wanted an agreement without a COLA formula. He and I are going to catch hell from the Carolina local presidents".

I responded, "What has the President or the Unions' Executive Board said? Have they ever issued instructions on how we were to negotiate?"

Mendoza: "Yea, I think the Executive has been told by the President that wage guidelines will not give our members economic relief."

Rudy, what kind of instructions have you received from President Watts?"

"My instructions are--what do you mean instructions?"

"I don't know. I don't have any instructions except to do what my Vice President directs me to do. All my directives come from my Vice President. I work for him. I'm out here in the field by myself except for my contact with him".

Mendoza responded: "I appreciate the fact that you are at the bargaining table--on the firing line--I'm not taking anything from you."

I responded, "What you are saying is that we should communicate more closely."

Mendoza: "That's part of it."

Patrick: "What else has the President said?"

Mendoza: "Precisely what I've said."

Patrick: "And what is that?"

Mendoza: "It's time we stopped taking a selfish view, just looking at one bargaining unit, relieving the corporate structure of pressure."

I asked: "What is President Watts saying since an

agreement has been reached?"

Mendoza: "He is in Carolina at the State meeting catching flack from the Local Presidents."

Patrick: "Rudy, I only have one boss, my Vice President. He is responsible for negotiations and he instructed me to reach an agreement based upon all the facts, which were discussed in detail. The decision was to allow the members to decide whether this contract was good enough to be ratified. If it is not ratified then the Company comes with additional concessions or we strike."

Mendoza: "The President's position is that we should have touched bases."

"You've said 2 or 3 times that you have called it to the Executive Boards attention and to the Presidents attention.

Mendoza: "Yes, and I think it was generally agreed---.

Patrick: But you never got instructions?

Mendoza: "Calvin, you are negative with me."

Patrick: "Rudy, at the Kansas City meeting you opened the meeting by saying "this is not a policy making meeting". Tonight you keep making "qualified" statements like "it was generally understood" I can't operate that way. I need directives; then I can operate. "The members in United of Arkansas, Missouri and Kansas felt they settled for less than they should have. United of New Jersey traffic operators settled for low wages. United of New Jersey Plant employees have been on strike for 2 months and 24 days. Where were you when these things happened? Two years ago in United of Carolina they went out prematurely and stayed for 30 days and one of the Carolina Local Presidents told Local President, Darrell Freeman, in my presence, that his group would accept 3 percent this time if that's all that was offered. With these known negatives and the fact that Local President Freeman told the meeting in Kansas City that a COLA was not a priority, you should be able to comprehend the problem.

"I suggest you get in touch with President Watts and let us get together and make a decision on coordinated bargaining with definite instructions. Otherwise I must go through my Vice President and use my skills and do the best job I can." [11]

---

[11] *On January 7, 1981, (over a year after the United negotiations were completed) a motion was passed by the CWA Executive Board on Structure, the responsibilities of Independent Telephone Director's Office, and the roll during bargaining situations and developing a clearer delegation of responsibility from that office to the CWA President's Office. This 6-point document made clear how agreements would be reached and that before the President of CWA approves any contract with independent telephone Companies, the Independent Telephone Director will review the settlement in an effort to achieve the goals established by the Bargaining Councils. (This document gave the National Director and the affected bargaining chair the clear guidelines needed in the 1979 negotiations. It also placed the National Director in the line of communication with the bargaining chair with specific directions as to the responsibilities and directives of each.)*

Chapter 21: Summit Meeting Called

"United Pack is settled", Read the Saturday Headlines.

The Company and Union had issued a joint press release.
"---Patrick and United President W.W. Hill jointly announced the settlement last night, saying the new contract calls for substantial increases in wages, hospitalization and other employee benefits." The two men agreed the settlement was "fair and equitable" and in the best interest "of all parties concerned".

As a result of my challenge to Mendoza about getting the President of CWA to make a decision on coordinated bargaining strategy with definite instructions, Monday August 27, found me in Washington setting in the CWA Executive Boardroom. All chief negotiators and their Vice Presidents from throughout the United States were there. President Watts opened the meeting by stating; "For a long time Local Officers have wanted coordinated bargaining. This objective caused the Kansas City meeting on June 9. There we had long discussions of possible things to do to get the Corporation to respond favorably to our needs. We had an objective to build pressure points with expectations of keeping the New Jersey Plant employees on strike, have United of Tennessee/Virginia strike and then on September 30, United of Carolina would strike if we did not get a COLA Formula.

"Compared to other agreements being reached, this is a good settlement. But when I received word of the settlement while in North Carolina, I wasn't in command of the ship. I explained to the Local Presidents in Carolina that I did not take lightly our reaching an agreement. In order to hold to our original plan I must make a decision. I'm under the impression the members in United of Tennessee/Virginia will accept the contract. Obviously if a decision is made not to allow the members to vote and ratify or turn the contract down, the Company would look on us in an unfavorable light.

Watts continued; "I know Calvin Patrick feels on the spot because of a failure to communicate. We need to determine how we communicate and operate internally. My own conclusion is that we must live with this agreement and learn from it."

President Watts then asked for comments from the group.

Vice President Morton Bahr[12] of New York and New Jersey: "The United of New Jersey strike is a bad strike at a bad place and at a bad time. The Company has 6.4 percent on the table with no increase on top pay. Once IBEW settled we knew we were trapped no matter what anyone else did."

Vice President Ben Porch, over Carolina: "This is a damn good settlement. The problem is we understood there would be communications when we left Kansas City. This was the total discussion. This was our time to break through with a COLA. My personal feelings this was a sellout."

Porch was asked about the membership in United of Carolina. He responded there were 2300 members out of 3200 eligible employees. (72% organized)

John Holder worked for Ben Porch and was chief negotiator for United in Norfork: Holder stated, "If this settlement could be reached in Norfork it would be a good settlement."

Vice President W.C. Button over United of Indiana; "We can not get this agreement in Indiana but if it would help New Jersey we would strike."

---

[12] *Bahr was later elected President of CWA in 1985 and served as CWA President for 20 years*

Grover Cantrell Chief negotiator for United of Indiana: "We can't get this kind of settlement in Indiana."

Vice President Martin Hughes over United of Ohio; "I have an excellent relationship with United of Ohio and do not anticipate any problems."

Vice President Jack Lovett over Arkansas, Kansas and Missouri: Money is not the problem but we are willing to do what is necessary."

Vice President Avelino B Montes over United of the North West USA: "This agreement is better than what we've got or can get in United of the Northwest."

Vice-President W.W. Brown over Tennessee: "I take the full responsibility for the agreement being reached. I was in daily contact and involved in every discussion. Calvin Patrick was following my instructions. There are persons in this room who had knowledge of negotiations and could have stopped us if they so desired. They chose however not to stop us. [13]

I was the last to speak and gave my reasons for reaching an agreement. "At Kansas City the meeting started out with a statement "this is not a policy making meeting." At that meeting everyone expressed their opinion for 2 days. Some wanted to go for a COLA, others had other priorities. But no one ever said we would go for a COLA and that every bargaining unit would be required to stick together. In fact, after that meeting Mendoza went to Tennessee to meet with the Tennessee bargaining committee and was asked by the bargaining committee could he guarantee that all bargaining units would be required to stick together. His response was "no".

"Another problem the Tennessee Local knew about,

---

[13] *Vice President Brown was referencing the call that President Watts had made to T. J. Volk in Tennessee after an agreement was reached on money but before the language was agreed to.*

this same strategy was attempted several years ago by Mendoza in General Telephone Of Indiana, Ohio and Kentucky. All three units were to stick together and strike. Kentucky was the first contract to terminate. They went out on strike but Ohio and Indiana settled. Kentucky was left on strike for 7 months by themselves. The Local in Tennessee did not put a lot of faith in what they were being told as a result of the General of Kentucky strike. In addition, they felt that there was no way, even with a strike, to get a COLA. For these reasons and after getting instructions from Vice President Brown, we reached an agreement."

One Vice President spoke up questioning the truth to what I was saying about the strike in General of Kentucky. President Watts quickly confirmed that indeed this had happened in General of Kentucky.

Mendoza added his comments: "It's a good agreement and hard to turn down. I was apprized to what was going on in negotiations in Tennessee, but my conversations with management indicated we could come up with a package that would please the full committee and be historical."

I thought to myself, Mendoza continues to hedge. He either had an understanding with the corporation or he didn't. He should stop saying Management "indicated". They didn't indicate anything at the bargaining table. Where is he coming from?

Watts: "We need to begin to act like a system. I did not communicate clear and explicit. We will be recommending ratification. Ballots will go into the mail on August 30, and will be counted on September 10. We are playing poker; each unit is to proceed in negotiations. I expect to be involved with the corporate level of United in Kansas City to see what we can pull off in the New Jersey and Norfork negotiations."

Very tired and emotionally exhausted, I flew back to Tennessee and prepared a bargaining report and ballots to be sent to the members.

I kept my commitment to Ed Norris and spoke to the Kingsport Rotary Club. Norris gave me a very warm introduction to the 120 business leaders of the community including a newspaper editor and the president of the largest manufacturing plant in Tennessee. I spoke on Unions and productivity. I also commented on the new management team in United Intermountain and my feelings that the public would be rewarded with better service and a happier work force. My remarks were accurately reported in the Rotary newsletter the following week. The time and effort had been well received.

Chapter 22: Sabotage The Agreement

From the moment the agreement was reached until the ballots were counted on September 10, a campaign was led by 40 to 50 United employees to defeat ratification. Their goal was to get the contract turned down by the membership and go back and bargain for COLA and failing to gain it, to strike. They did not understand the National Unions objective of not necessarily more money but the recognition of a COLA formula. In fact, had the Company come with the same money as was in the contract but had used the wage guidelines and a COLA formula, everyone in Washington would be praising what an outstanding job we had done. Another group, the telephone operators, were upset over the agreement on computerized scheduling of work, even though it was for a one year trial period and could be cancelled. They too worked to defeat ratification.

On August 30 at my request I received a telegram from Vice President Brown in order for there to be no misunderstanding about what direction we were going.

The telegram stated: "This is to confirm our conversations of Wednesday and Thursday August 29 and 30. After very careful study of the tentative agreement with United Intermountain of Tennessee in Washington on August 27, President Watts, Rudy Mendoza and I feel that this is the best agreement we can reach under the present economic conditions and guidelines we are working under. While we are not satisfied, we feel the membership should have an opportunity to vote on the contract and therefore ratification ballots should be sent out as per your instructions. We urge ratification." Signed W.W. Brown Vice President.

Ballots went out on schedule. A meeting was scheduled for September 4 to give an explanation of the agreement to the membership.

Hand written notices were placed on bulletin boards:

"If you want to know about Calvin Patrick signing an agreement without the CWA National offices' knowledge, call Mr. Mendoza at his Washington office 202-555-4517"

"DON'T MARK BALLOT UNTIL AFTER MEETING ON September 4."

Telephone calls went to Mendoza in Washington. Mendoza answered members' questions just as he had at the June meeting. Never specific but leaving the clear impression that Calvin Patrick had gone against instructions and the membership by reaching an agreement.

An employee who talked to Mendoza typed the following statement:
"September 4, 1979 2:15 p.m.

"I dialed 202-555-4517 and told Mr. Mendoza there was a bulletin board notice that asked that the members call him and ask why Calvin Patrick signed an agreement with the Company without the National's approval. Mr. Mendoza stated that he was not aware that there was a notice on the bulletin board, nor had he authorized such a posting. He said that he was available to answer any questions if members did not get satisfactory answers from the Local. However, he said he believed that Darrell Freeman and Calvin Patrick would be happy to answer questions. Both were good to talk to. He said he had received a lot of phone calls from members apparently because they had not received satisfactory answers elsewhere---and maybe because of this posting. He said that as it stands now, the contract has been released and that it was now up to the members. If the majority wanted to ratify the contract, then that will settle it. If they don't, then it is up to them to vote against the contract. "Then we will have to get together with the Company and discuss our differences." Mr. Mendoza also stated he understood a vote was taken before the agreement was reached to get a COLA or there would be no contract. He said he thought as a result of that vote COLA was an ultimatum, but Calvin Patrick made an agreement with the Company without COLA. He said he thought this was a big issue in the local. He stated the members could be assured that in the future, the National will work much more closely with the Local in those last hours to see that no misunderstandings such as this occur.

"Mr. Mendoza seemed quite upset that the Company had put the pay increase into effect "because there is no agreement until the contract is ratified by the members and the Company knows there is no agreement until that time." He said, "This is a matter I will look into."

"I thanked Mr. Mendoza for his time, and he in turn said he was glad to be able to help, and from here on out it was up to us."

Rump meetings were held in several locations. In each, emphasis was on turning down the contract and then getting a COLA or strike.

At the meeting to explain the contract on September 4, Local President Freeman gave a report. "Many members and stewards have attempted to keep the bargaining report and ratification ballot from reaching the members. "--The office secretary has been receiving vulgar and threatening telephone calls. --Notices have been handed out that Darrell Freeman and Calvin Patrick had sold out. --The Bargaining Committees' families including children have been receiving telephone threats, that if we didn't strike, things would happen to the families. --There are rumors that the Bargaining Committee will resign if the contract is not ratified. That's not true. --There was a rumor that Calvin

Patrick wasn't even at the Bargaining table for the last two days. That rumor is not true."

Freeman said these divisive remarks and behavior was dividing us and only the Company could gain from it. "--A rumor was out that the National Union was making the Bargaining Committee recommend ratification. He explained that the National Union could not tell the Bargaining Committee to recommend or not to recommend. "It's our sole decision and we recommend the contract. We are not satisfied, we argued and argued all the proposals. We've listened to you over the last 6 to 8 months going to every district, holding meetings asking you what you wanted and what you would strike for. We even sent out questionnaires about your desires. Based upon those meetings we feel we are in the ballpark of what you wanted. You can accept or vote the contract down. If you vote it down, your committee will be recommending to CWA President Watts that we strike."

During a question and answer period it became obvious that the operator service members were upset over the computerized scheduling. Per Diem for those required to travel was not enough. Another faction asked "Why are we here? We voted to strike unless we got a COLA formula. Lets vote this down and strike".

COLA was an emotional issue. The members concept of COLA was that under the Presidential guidelines, they would receive a 7 percent raise plus whatever COLA would produce because of inflation. As an example, if inflation were 10 percent then the COLA formula would add an additional 10 percent to the 7 percent raise for a total of a 17 percent increase in wages.

The Union on the other hand was trying to get the Company to accept the principle of a COLA formula with a cap of 9 percent. With a cap of 9 percent the maximum that could be received in a 3-year contract was 27 percent. Our hope was to be able to negotiate to remove the cap at the next round of negotiations.

Our position had been explained to the members at meetings. It had been explained on television and the printed press. But those who wanted COLA were not looking at COLA as Washington or the Bargaining Committee was looking at it. Consequently had the agreement been reached with the capped COLA we had been attempting to negotiate, these members would have been more upset.

Once again we explained the fact that under the Presidential wage guidelines a 3-year contract, without a COLA formula, could only have an 8 percent wage increase at the go-down: 7 percent at the first anniversary and 6 percent at the second anniversary for a total of 21 percent in three years. We again explained how we had shown the Company how we could use the COLA formula and legally stay within the wage guidelines but the contract would produce 27 percent over three years.

We explained that knowing this the Company had chosen to grant a 9.3 percent wage increase at the go-down, 8 percent at the first anniversary, and 8.35 percent at the second anniversary. This would guarantee a total of 25.65 percent increase in wages plus 2.35 percent in fringe benefits for a total of 27 percent. Had the Company agreed to the Unions capped COLA formula the Guarantee would produce the same 27 percent in both wages and fringe benefits. The Union was determined to get the principle of a COLA in this contract.

An angry member shouted, " You asked for a strike vote, we gave it to you. We should have been on the street on August 23" (applause).

Another member; you (Patrick) told us that the Company must give a COLA or else." (Applause and whistles)

I responded: we stated to you, the public, and told the Company we had a plan that would stay within the Presidential guidelines, and still give equity to our members.

The member responded; "You are a liar, you said we would have a COLA." (Applause)

A telephone operator who had threatened to get out of the Union unless we got a COLA, shouted; "The members were ready to strike at midnight August 23, but the bargaining committee has sold us out." She said she knew the Company could not operate if we had a strike with 90 percent of the employees on the street. She continued; "When we didn't strike on August 23, the momentum was lost and now some members don't want to strike."

I made the decision to quit trying to explain the contract as they were in no mood to understand what was happening.

I responded that we had done the best job we could do. "It doesn't do any good to hit the Company on the head with a hammer because we would still have to ask them to sit and negotiate. I don't believe they would feel kindly toward us with knots on their heads. In negotiations you do the best you can, then the membership must make the decision as to whether the settlement is fair or not. There is no way the bargaining committee can sell you out when you vote on the contract."

"Regarding whether the Company can operate if we have a strike lets get the record straight. I hear this argument all the time but in an automated industry like ours, they will operate and do a pretty good job if 100 percent of the Bargaining unit goes on strike."

Another member who had been listening but saying nothing spoke up. "We are this Union, lets vote this contract down and get the Bargaining Committee back to the table. (Applause)

I responded that the ballots would be counted next

Monday. "I will be with Vice President Brown in Birmingham. He has made the decision that if the contract is voted down by one or a thousand votes we will be recommending to the President of CWA that we strike. But listen carefully, we only recommend, the President calls the strike, but only after approval of the CWA Executive Board."

It was obvious that 25 percent of those attending the meeting were very angry at what had transpired in negotiations and Mendoza's responses to telephone calls had made it impossible for the contract to be ratified.

On Monday September 10, at 5:25 p.m. while in Birmingham, Local President Freeman advised me the contract had been rejected: 615 voting no contract. 393 voted for ratification.

Chapter 23: Back to Original Strategy

At 6:30 p.m. I advised Jack Gaddis of United that the agreement had been rejected by a 2 to 1 majority. Gaddis responded that he was extremely sorry because he and President Hill had been raked over the coals especially about offering the alternative package with the two wage re-openers. Gaddis felt that this was a real plus for the Union. He didn't see any changes the Company could make but would be talking to his superiors and would get back to me.

I called Vice President Brown and we drafted the following message for the members.

"The membership has rejected the tentative agreement between CWA and United of Tennessee by a vote of 393 voting for ratification of the agreement and 615 voting not to ratify. Your bargaining committee has requested President Watts set a strike date. Vice President Brown has advised the Local to set up the strike machinery. The Local meeting scheduled for Tuesday September 11, has been postponed until further notice. Lets keep unity, together we can win, divided we fail."

I advised Vice President Brown that in talking to President Watts it would be my recommendation to strike September 30, and have United of Carolina go with us unless we can reach an agreement before that time in all units.

At 6:18 p. m. Jack Gaddis and Dan Luethke called me in Birmingham. They had talked with President Hill and Hill said the Company was willing to meet and negotiate and would be willing to rearrange the package, but that the Union had the Company's final offer.

On the lighter side Dan Luethke said that my speech at the Rotary Club had been taped and had been played to President Hill and that Hill thought I had made a lot of good points. They appreciated the kind words I had said about the Company.

At 6:30 p.m. I called Vice President Brown again and advised him of the Company's Position. Brown said he was going to call Mendoza and advise him of the vote and he would also contact President Watts tomorrow morning.

At 7:30 p.m. Local President Freeman called and said he had learned that the Public Service Commission was going to audit the Company. Freeman had asked the PSC to put off the audit until the labor dispute was settled.

TUESDAY MORNING SEPTEMBER 11

Vice President Brown advised that President Watts was very surprised the contract had been rejected. Watts then announced he was calling a meeting in Washington at 2:00 p.m. Thursday September 13. He wanted all staff, which who were involved in negotiations with United Telecommunications present.

I called Jack Gaddis and requested a meeting. Gaddis told me he was hearing the members had lost faith in me, because I had reached an agreement without a COLA. Gaddis didn't see the need for a meeting because the Union had the Company's final offer. I advised him that the Union has the responsibility to formally bring to the Company's attention why the membership had rejected the contract. We agreed to meet at 2:00 p.m. Friday September 14.

Tuesday night United President Hill went on television stating that United had their final offer on the table and the Union had agreed that it was a fair and equitable agreement. Nothing had changed since that statement was made.

WEDNESDAY September 12

I called Gaddis and advised him that we were going to Washington to discuss where we were in negotiations. He wanted to know what to expect. I said to expect the worst and then you want be disappointed.

Local President Freeman was getting a lot of reports that the members were getting restless and wanted to strike immediately. He expressed concern that they would strike regardless of what we may recommend. They did not want to wait for President Watts to set a strike date. I told Freeman that we must be factual with the members and wait for the appropriate advise from Washington. Freeman half heartily chuckled, "its easier said than done."

I called President Hill and discussed the situation and that we should keep the channels of communication open. I expressed my concern about his television statement saying the Union had agreed the contract was fair and equitable. While that may have been our view at the time, the members had spoken loud and clear by rejecting the contract. By repeating that statement now he was driving a wedge between the members and the bargaining committee. There was more at stake than trying to justify our respective positions, because at some point we would have a contract that the members must ratify. Hill responded that we must keep our communications channels open and he had "rather talk than walk."

Rumors were running wild. No COLA no contract. The 3-year agreement was too long, and employees were now finally realizing that their vote rejecting the agreement was also a vote to strike. Employees were again calling Mendoza. He was giving his reason as to why the contract was rejected. Mendoza was complaining to employees about the Company placing the negotiated 9.3 percent wage increase into effect before an agreement was reached. He would tell them that he would settle this issue later.[14] At

8:25 p.m. Jack Gaddis called. He was very upset. He told me that we were working without an agreement. The Company was suspending the check off for Union dues, and they were considering locking out the employees if the contract was not settled within a month. Gaddis said he knew what CWA was up to, coupling our contract to the bargaining in other United companies around the Nation. He said the Company was expecting a coordinated strike November 1, but they would not be intimidated. Gaddis said, "The Union has the Company's final offer. There will be no more insurance, no dental plan and no COLA."

I responded to Gaddis. "Jack you were put on notice on June 22, that a hurricane was off the coast of North Carolina. I gave you a way to keep the hurricane from overtaking all of us. But you wouldn't listen. I heard that you even said Calvin Patrick is bluffing. Now you and I have lost control of bargaining. It's not very smart to stop dues, and not to continue the contract on a day-to-day basis. You really know how to upset the members and make them mad as hell at you."

Gaddis had no response.

---

[14] *What ever that meant -- We never heard about it again, In fact we were glad that the Company put the wages into effect.*

Chapter 24: Called to Washington

Thursday September 13

Local President Darrell Freeman traveled to Washington with me. We had requested that President Watts meet with Freeman to discuss coming to Tennessee to meet with the members and prevent a premature walkout.

At 5:15 p.m., 3 hours late, the meeting started. Mendoza was presiding in Watts' absence. He explained that Watts had been and still was tied up in court and could not be present. He stated, "we are now in a position to attempt to do what we set out to do in Kansas City in June." He said that President Watts was thinking of increasing the defense fund in the New Jersey strike and for the bargaining committees to work toward tying United in Tennessee with Carolina and strike together. Mendoza continued: "Watts is inclined to place a strong emphasis on COLA, a dental plan, improving hospitalization and the check-off for the CWA savings and retirement trust fund."

Mendoza then asks each member of the group for their view of where we were.

Vice President Brown stated that in Tennessee we were with him 100 percent. He stated that if President Watts would travel to Tennessee and meet with the members he believed they would follow the leadership and not strike until the word came from Washington.

Vice President Ben Porch, over United of Carolina asked why Tennessee had rejected the contract.

Vice President Brown responded, "There are several factors.
1. There had never been a strike in Tennessee so they just wanted to strike not realizing the seriousness of it.
2. Several issues affect different groups, which collectively is a majority.
3. One group is insistent on improving the hospitalization.

4. The operators do not understand the agreement as it relates to computerizing the work schedule. "We have explained that the scheduling agreement can be terminated by either party but the telephone operators will not accept the new scheduling."
5. Some are adamant on a dental plan.
6. The most vocal group of about 25 percent of the members are insistent on a COLA and are willing to strike to obtain it."

Brown stated that Mendoza now has contacts at high levels of United Telecommunications that he did not have a few weeks ago. Brown continued, "That can be of help to us. The President of the Union getting involved at the corporate level can't do anything but help us resolve the dispute."

Vice President Morton Bahr of New York, responsible for the strike in United of New Jersey, gave an update of the New Jersey situation, "The employees have been out for 104 days. The New Jersey Company doesn't know how to bargain. They have written a letter that CWA is not striking for New Jersey but that this is a part of a master plan involving the entire country to obtain a COLA. He stated "We have $29.00 per week on the table but want a 9.35 percent raise which equates to $31.50 per week. That would settle the New Jersey strike without a COLA."

Vice President Porch stated the only issue in United of Carolina was COLA. Assistant to President Watts, John Carol, was the most knowledgeable person in the union about bargaining. He had remained silent through out the meeting. I addressed both Carol and Mendoza, "What does Watts want us to do?"

Mendoza responded, "We want in all contracts:
1. A COLA
2. A Dental Plan
3. Hospitalization- United to pay all premiums.
Executive Vice President George Miller, who also had been silent,

interrupted, "but what does President Watts want us to do?" Mendoza responded:
1. An uncapped COLA
2. A dental plan
3. Improvements in the premium payments on hospitalization
4. United is to grant the CWA check-off for the CWA Savings plan.
5. Each bargaining unit can add its local demands.
Miller: "with the knowledge of what President Watts wants, we all can keep on the same track."

Mendoza announced that President Watts would be polling the CWA Executive board for authority to set a strike date for September 30.

Freeman had been able to talk to Watts during a recess in the trial, that Watts was attending. As a result of that meeting Watts advised he would come speak to the members in Tennessee.

Freeman and I spent the night at the Capitol Hilton; both were very restless.

Friday, September 14. As Freeman and I flew back to Tennessee I suggested that we prepare a press release and that he speak to the Press that would be waiting. He deferred to me. As we flew along the Smoky Mountains spilling coffee as the DC 4 rose and fell in the air currents, we prepared the press release and discussed our strategy for the bargaining session scheduled for 2:30 p.m.

We arrived at 11:50 a.m. The press was waiting at the plane steps.

The press release read:

"CWA President Glenn Watts today set a strike date of 12 midnight September 30, for United of Tennessee unless an agreement is reached prior to that hour.

"Local President Darrell Freeman met with President Watts today and President Watts has agreed to attend a special called membership meeting Sunday at 1:30 p.m. at the Ramada Inn in Kingsport. President Watts will explain to the membership the reason for the delayed strike date. Freeman has urged the members to continue sticking together and we will be successful."

"The outstanding issues keeping the parties from reaching an agreement include a COLA formula, a dental plan, 100 % pay for the hospitalization plan, check off for the CWA savings plan and contracting out of work.

"We will continue negotiating in hopes of reaching an agreement prior to September 30. We want a contract, not a strike."

As Freeman and I headed for the Ramada Inn and the Company bargaining committee, we wondered what their reaction would be.

Chapter 25: Bad Faith Bargaining

Upon arriving at the Ramada Inn we met and had lunch with Bob Brown and Judy Graham, the other two members of our committee, to update them on what had happened in Washington.

The bargaining session got under way at 2:30 p.m. with all members of both the Company and Union committees present.

I opened the meeting by stating that we had come a long way during these negotiations. "Personal relationships which are important to the handling of labor relations problems have improved. The Union believes the Company has been honest and has tried to do what you felt was in the best interest of the members and keeping the Company solvent.

"On June 22, we stated that a hurricane was baring down on us and the only way to stop it was to agree to a COLA formula. You told us there was no way you would ever agree to a COLA formula. You then came with a greater percentage increase than would have been necessary should you have agreed to a COLA formula. You have convinced the Union bargaining committee that you are serious, and in good faith we accepted your final offer. That agreement was sent to the membership for ratification or to vote down. The members knew that to vote the contract down would mean a strike yet they rejected it and by doing so they have given us a new mandate. I have been called a traitor and that I sold out by agreeing to your final offer. I have had to go to Washington twice to explain my position. I am now following orders from Washington rather than from my Vice President. We are now in the middle of the hurricane that I have attempted to worn you about. Our destiny is being guided by President Watts who has given us until September 30, to reach an agreement.

"We have plenty of time before that date but I must emphasize, as I have since June 22, to reach an agreement it must include:

1. An uncapped cost-of-living. (COLA) the capped offer we were willing to agree to earlier had been withdrawn.

2. Hospitalization paid in full by the Company.

3. A fully paid dental plan.

4. The CWA savings plan Check-off deduction.

5. Six day work opportunity before hiring outside contractors.

6. The Locals hardship fund check-off.

7. The CWA cope deduction check-off.

The Union reserves the right to amend or modify our proposals. The money that is on the table is locked in and must be improved through the COLA formula.

I concluded by advising the Company the Union was willing to look at any responsible Company proposals. "We don't want a strike. We want a contract," I concluded.

Company attorney Ed Norris responded. Do you have any other proposals?

Patrick: I have listed the major obstacles, understanding that the proposals already agreed to will be satisfactory and placed into the agreement.

Norris: We need a short recess.

After 20 minutes we reconvened.

Norris: "We have considered your proposals and counter proposals. They are rejected and are ridiculous. We have given you our final offer and the membership rejected it two to one. We have an impasse and no contract. As of now there will be no check-off for Union dues. There is no grievance procedure. The Company will not finance a strike against itself.

"While you have been sitting here making these proposals the CWA headquarters in Washington was making a statement that a strike has been called for September 30. The Union has bargained in bad faith," Norris concluded.

At 3:29 p.m. the Company bargaining committee walked out.

The Union committee sat in silence for several minutes. Why had the Company reacted so irrationally? It was our conclusion they had blamed the reason for walking out on Washington because outsiders were now calling the shots for the Union. They had used this as a pretext to walk out without directly attacking our bargaining committee since we had come so far in our relationships.

Chapter 26: Strike Date Set

The headlines in the September 15 evening newspaper told the story:

TELEPHONE TALKS END ABRUPTLY:

"Renewed efforts to reach a contract between United and the Communications Workers of America ended abruptly yesterday with each side accusing the other of negotiating in bad faith.

"United negotiators, led by Kingsport labor attorney Edwin Norris, are sticking with a 25.65% increase already rejected by the CWA members.

"But CWA, led by Calvin Patrick, its East Tennessee Director is asking for an uncapped cost-of-living increase-- whatever the inflation rate would produce. No further meetings are scheduled but Patrick wants to meet again. I told them we do not want a strike, we want a contract, Patrick said. We stand ready and willing to negotiate and we are asking them publicly to bargain".

"United President W.W. Hill would not comment on Patrick's request.

"An announcement of the strike date, while negotiations were in progress, "coupled with the CWA's unreasonable demands today (Friday), led us to conclude CWA does not want to reach an agreement before September 30," Gaddis said. For these reasons the Company team promptly concluded negotiations Gaddis said."

"After 33 minutes in our session the Company walked out, refusing to bargain," Patrick said. "I did not want to comment on this because I thought it was very unprofessional".

"A special Union meeting has been called by President Freeman for Sunday. CWA President Watts will be present to explain why a strike will not be allowed until the end of the month."

SEPTEMBER 15

United President, W.W. Hill again went to the press and evening television. He was amazed that CWA had reverted to its June 22 proposals. The Company's final offer had exceeded the wage price guidelines and was fair and equitable. He stated that CWA did not want an agreement and that supervisors and non-striking employees will continue service if a strike occurs. He closed his statement by saying the Company would be willing to listen to any new offers from the Union.

It was 11:15 p.m. when the news went off. I called attorney Ed Norris, waking him up, and advised him I had seen President Hill on television and as a result I wanted a meeting at 9 a.m. Sunday. He said he had commitments for Sunday and could not meet. I asked for a meeting for Monday, September 17 at 9 a.m. He said he would get back with me.

Because of the Company's knee-jerk walkout, going on television, and in general trying to divide the membership, I decided I must be more aggressive. I went on the local information recorder and reported to the membership:

"On Friday your Bargaining Committee requested a meeting with the Company. After only 33 minutes of the Union explaining our position the Company walked out. It is obvious from their behavior they were emotionally upset. Their conduct was very unprofessional. Since the Company has chosen to go public with this issue, I categorically deny any bad faith bargaining and am surprised at such an accusation since the Company has an experienced attorney as spokesman.

"The Unions proposals price out lower than the rejected agreement, using a COLA formula and the wage price guideline rules. However, it would give added protection in case of high inflation rates of 11 to 14 percent, should they occur. That's the purpose of the COLA formula.

"Mr. Hill's charge that I had stated the rejected contract was fair and equitable is not a quote by me. It was taken out of context from the newspaper the Company is continually criticizing. I am surprised that Mr. Hill would use it as a reliable source. At the bargaining table we have advised the Company we want a contract, not a strike.

"The Company is using the press release about the strike deadline to break off negotiations. They are trying to frighten you, divide you, and use you, just as they did before you had a Union.

"Let's stick together and we will win."

Chapter 27: CWA President Attends Union Meeting

SUNDAY, SEPTEMBER 16

After meeting President Watts at the airport, in route to the meeting, I filled him in on what had transpired with the press and the lack of progress in negotiations. When we arrived the press was waiting for President Watts.

Question: "Are the employees going to strike?"

Watts: "It is interesting that you would ask that question. It's my understanding that after the members rejected the contract we went back to the negotiation table with the Company and they walked out. They have suspended the grievance procedure and stopped the dues check-off and are saying that Washington is in charge. Quite frankly I'm here to urge the members not to strike until the deadline of September 30, in order to give us a chance to negotiate an agreement that the members will find acceptable and will ratify. I'm surprised at the Company's action as it can only irritate their own employees. They may well cause some walkouts before September 30."

Question: "Do you feel there is enough time to reach an agreement before September 30?"

Watts: "Of course, if the Company will meet the needs of the employees. Yes, there is plenty of time. On the other hand it has been demonstrated by the management, since the members rejected the first agreement, the Company is not willing to enter into an agreement the members will find acceptable.

Question: "How would a walkout affect the public?"

Watts: There would be no immediate affect except in installation and maintenance of the equipment, new installations, etc. In time the switching equipment would need repairing and the employees would not be there to do it, so deterioration will set in.

"We are not thinking in those terms however. The employees who work for this Company live in this community and have families and friends in the community. They do not desire to cause disruptions to the community. On the other hand they do call upon the Company to treat them fairly."

Question: "There is going to be a Public Service Commission hearing giving the Company six months to clear up the problems or give the franchise to another Company. How will the strike affect that?"

Watts: "Obviously, with a strike underway there will be no opportunity for the employees to improve conditions here."

We entered the Ramada Convention Center, looking at 1000 members who were getting restless.

Local President Darrell Freeman opened the meeting. "President Watts has responded to my request last Thursday to come and reassure you he has full knowledge of our problems and is showing by being here that every Local and every problem is important to him, no matter how large or small the Local.

"Your bargaining committee did what we thought the membership wanted based upon the pre-bargaining meetings we conducted before negotiations began. We now have a directive, a new ball game, by your rejecting the agreement. We must stay together and forget our differences of the past. We are one Local. We can't be divided. You must give your bargaining committee your full support and let President Watts guide us.

Freeman then introduced me. - - - -Nothing but silence.

I introduced the head table, - - -silence. Bargaining committee members: Judy Graham, representing traffic operators; Bob Brown, representing plant and engineering; Local Vice President and strike director, Ronnie Renfro; Secretary-Treasurer, Sandy Barry; Virginia Vice President Dick Adams, Tennessee Vice President; Marshall Thomas, Dave Kent, CWA NEWS Staff; CWA National Director, Rudy Mendoza; CWA Executive Vice President, George Miller. -- - - - Still silence.

I began: "As of last Friday the Company walked out of negotiations after only 33 minutes of bargaining. They have canceled our grievance and arbitration procedures and our dues check-off. They have refused to extend the contract on a day-to-day basis so we are working without a contract and the protection it would provide.

"They have accused the National Union of taking over negotiations. That, of course, has been true since the beginning and they well know it. The Company knows that the President of CWA is the only person with the authority to settle a contract and that is vested to the staff by the President working through the Vice President of each district of CWA.

"I want to give you a brief history of where we have come from. Several months ago your President, Darrell Freeman, and other local representatives conducted 10 meetings throughout the Locals jurisdiction. There was disappointment because very few attended those meetings. Your leadership was trying to find your priorities for negotiations. We have negotiated based upon our feedback from you at those meetings.

"Two weeks ago we asked you to give us a vote of confidence by voting to strike, which you did overwhelmingly. This vote gave us a tool to produce an additional 4.5 percent that the Company had no intention of giving you.

"Your bargaining committee is never stronger than the membership. By your overwhelming rejection of the contract you have now given us a new tool to take back to the bargaining table. We will be successful in improving this agreement as a result of your strong support. You've told us Hospitalization is important. Is it important? (Loud applause)

You've said a COLA is important. Is a COLA important? (Applause.) You've said the CWA savings fund is important. Is it important? (Light applause.)

"We are receiving calls in the office that members did not understand they were voting to strike. The Company has picked up on this and has asked us to put out another ballot. Others are worried about the defense fund. The defense fund will be available.

"If we are to be successful we must not say things about each other or worry about the defense fund. We need to bargain together. How do we do this? You are the negotiators. We, your committee, mouth what you tell us at the bargaining table. You need to be telling your supervisor and higher management what they are doing wrong. What you need.

"I suspect that within the next two weeks you will get a letter from the Company saying your hospitalization will be terminated if you go on strike. That's an alarming thought as it is intended to be, to demoralize you. Whoever signs that letter should receive hundreds of calls letting the Company know that the insurance is no good and that they had better make it right. (Loud prolonged applause.)

"If you are strong your committee will be strong. We ask you to go out there and do a job. Be positive, work hard, and together we hopefully will reach an agreement. We don't want a strike, but strike we will, if necessary." I concluded.

I then introduced President Watts. "President Watts comes to us today as one of the founders of CWA. He understands your struggle in obtaining and then building your Local Union. He cancelled an appointment in Chicago to be with us today. He is leaving immediately after this meeting for California. President Watts is a compassionate labor leader. I'm confident if we follow his leadership the final decision we will make will be the best for all concerned. It's an honor to have with us today your President and mine, CWA President Glenn Watts." (Polite applause)

President Glenn Watts: "I told the press I have come to keep you from striking prior to September 30. United of Tennessee is part of the United Telecommunications system and is controlled from Kansas City, even though they try to get you to believe they make all the decisions here. We haven't been able to get Kansas City's attention in the past. Therefore they have had the advantage and we've had to deal on a local bargaining unit basis. But your action here has reversed that and now Kansas City is listening to us. When the staff and your committee brought a package that was above average, you rejected it. That's democracy.

"You've now got the system's attention but don't get it in your minds we've got them where it hurts. We haven't, but we are in a new posture."

Watts continued: "Why am I asking you to wait until September 30? Nothing is going to happen until then and North Carolina will be ready to go out with you and support you. You don't want to waste two weeks do you? (Laughter). I have no doubt from what I heard when Calvin ask you were those things important. I was listening carefully. You deserve more but we can't get everything you want. However, we can get more than you have got. The pressure is on the Company.

"When your sacrifice is over you will be proud of the day you strike, and will hold your head high. I hope you will never say that Glenn Watts said you would get everything you wanted. We don't have a magic wand, but if we stick together you are bound to come out of a strike better than when you went in. At this moment I believe there will be a strike because the Company said they would not give in on a COLA formula. They are philosophically against that concept, but in my opinion there is a possibility of getting it. I did not say there was a certainty but a possibility. I hope you will remember once a strike starts the leadership has a new situation to deal with."

"The leaders of this Union will not lead you down the primrose path of destruction. The total resources of the Union will be behind you. We've got 18 million dollars in the defense fund and we can support you for an extended time.

"Remember this, a strike in our industry is not going out and tearing down the Company brick by brick. You can't stop this Company from operating. You can cause inconvenience to the public, get them mad and down on you, but that's not good. The Company will keep going. We must keep the public with us; we must let them know we are not crooks or goons. We are citizens of this community.

"Dave Kent from our Public Relations Department will be working on P.R. You must speak to the press and the public telling them why you rejected the contract".

The meeting was then thrown open to questions.

Question: President Watts, who is authorized to sign an agreement?

Watts: Technically, I am. I will be in on any discussions that are made.

Question: Will we keep our insurance?

Watts: We will see to it that you do not lose your insurance by delaying payments. We will try to get the Company to pay for it or we will be making arrangements using defense fund monies so that no one is left without Blue Cross-Blue Shield coverage while we are on strike. (Loud prolonged applause)

I cringed and hoped the employees understood what

President Watts said. I had been defense fund director and knew the rules. Watts had made a technically correct statement for those of us who knew how the defense fund worked, but his statement, as perceived, would cause me trouble if we got into a strike.

Question: Why is a cost-of-living formula so important?

Watts: Inflation is running at 13 to 14 percent and you should be able to restore your purchasing power. The Company takes care of itself through the Public Service Commission. High-income people want wages indexed to take care of inflation. You deserve the same. If there is no inflation we are entitled to a 6 or 7 percent wage increase due to the productivity in our industry. We are entitled to a cost-of-living on top of the productivity increase to protect our earned wages, because we are always 6 months behind inflation. (Light applause)

Question: If there is an agreement in United of Indiana how will it affect us?

Watts: No one is going to settle before anyone else because I've got to approve the settlement. (Very loud and prolonged applause)

Question: Will we strike on September 30?

Watts: Unless you hear from the Union that a strike is not going to take place, we will strike. If an agreement is reached that we are satisfied with, which will justify not calling a strike, we will get that word to you as quickly as possible and let you vote on it so that if by any stretch of the imagination you should reject it, a strike could be called immediately. I don't believe we are going to bring you anything back that you are going to reject. (Light applause).

I looked at Freeman and shook my head. *I felt there would be no COLA and I would be blamed for it. But he was right; it would not be rejected.*

Question: A statement has been made that wages,

insurance, and benefits are better in surrounding companies. Is this true?

Watts: I understand that you are absolutely correct.

Question: Can we get wages and benefits that we negotiate approved by the Wage and Price Board?

Watts: I'm sure that whatever we negotiate we will get approved, because of the low wages in this Company. I'll simply say, anything we can get in negotiations we will get approved. If we can't get it approved, so what, there is no one who will take it from us. (Very light applause).

Question: Will we settle the contract without a COLA?

I murmured to myself, oh! Do be careful with this answer.

Watts: It seems to me it's inadvisable for anybody to say I will never do this because frequently you wind up doing just what you said you would never do. I can assure you that we won't be settling without it, without a strike, unless whatever appears that I can't even imagine at the moment, is so much better that it would be obvious to you. Now I do not expect that we are going to settle short of a strike, without a COLA. I have doubts that a difficult strike will be required to get it. On the other hand, I'm not promising you that we are going to get one.

Local Vice President, Ronnie Renfro whispered to me, the members think he promised COLA.

I nodded.

Question: We need more than a cost-of-living; we need a raise.

Watts: Well, we normally get a wage increase at what we call the go down, and a cost-of-living raise at each anniversary. I would expect any contract we ultimately produce would have more than the rejected agreement. (Applause) That's why you rejected the agreement.

Question: Can you explain how a COLA works?

Watts: Ideally if you were making a hundred dollars

a week and inflation went up 10 percent you would receive ten dollars in a cost-of-living raise. Most COLAs are not built that way. They provide a basic wage increase of perhaps 3 percent, which is normally related to national productivity, which is about that rate. In addition you would get a cost-of-living increase on top of the 3 percent: a formula of perhaps 50 cents for every one percent in the cost-of-living, plus 6 tenths of one percent of your salary. Normally when these pieces are put together you manage to come out ahead of the cost-of-living until inflation reached about 15 percent. Most cost-of-living formulas don't reach that level, however.

We've laid out our proposals and it's hard to get the Company to agree. I'm sure we will be striking in order to get them to agree, and as they do agree they can come back with a counter proposal which I'm sure will be a design we don't like. Then we will negotiate to get the design changed to the point that both sides will accept it. That's what bargaining is about. We start with our objectives and they with theirs. We work and work and finally come together in the middle, with an agreement. (No applause).

Question: Can we settle our grievances since the Company has cancelled the grievance procedure?

Watts: The Company is trying to scare you. They are required by law to negotiate grievances with us. Even though we can't arbitrate. We are not going to buckle because of cancellation of the grievance procedure and dues check-off. Money is not important now. We will survive in very good fashion.

Question: We get built up every three years, and then let down with the agreement. We don't feel we get the support from the National Union. Why is this happening to us?

Watts: I've never yet found a local bargaining committee, person or staff, when they made a decision and reached an agreement, are totally satisfied. Negotiators often sit down and hold their heads they are so dissatisfied. But they feel they were making the best decision they could make under the particular circumstances. They usually are let down themselves because they did not get what they wanted. What I'm saying is, unless you have been on a bargaining committee or had that responsibility, I'm willing to bet that under the same circumstances you would have made the same decision. I've been there; I know the feeling. I've sat back as president and told staff what to do and that's always easy unless you are on the firing line, then it is different. (Applause).

Question: When will the defense fund begin?

Watts: We attempt to delay your payments where we can. Members who have cash to pay their bills should take care of them. But if bills can't be delayed, members in this situation will not lose their cars, homes, second car or boat for that matter. Some people will get more; some will get less. After 2 weeks we pay for food. After a month we look at those other areas to the extent that the defense fund will last, it will take care of home possessions, and from being hungry. I feel we can manage that for a very long period of time. I don't mean we will strike till hell freezes over if we have an offer and good reasonable people know we should settle.

Question: What should we do with the wage increase the Company has placed into effect?

Watts: I'm glad they did. Don't give it back.

I looked at Mendoza, who had taken exception to the Company placing the increase into effect. I wondered what he was thinking.

As the questions ended Watts reminisced on how he had made ends meet while on strike. He told of CWA buying a telephone Company when the Union couldn't reach an agreement with the owners after going out on a strike. Watts complimented the Local and had knowledge of some of the good things the Local had done. A few months earlier, (at my suggestion) Darrell Freeman had been featured in the CWA News with a full-page article about the accomplishments of his Local).

President Watts received a standing ovation from the over 1000 members in attendance.

I took Watts to the plane and he headed for California. I took a plane to Birmingham to fill a commitment I had made, (teaching a leadership course at the University of Alabama in Birmingham.)

KINGSPORT TIMES
Letter to Editor -- September 19, 1979
At it Again
To United Telephone Co.:

Well, you're at it again wanting to increase our phone rates. What about what your subscribers want? We would like to be able to pick up our phones and use them, but they are either dead, full of static and buzzing, or have busy signals before we're through dialing, or bring in somebody tied into our private lines.

I have a business phone as 1 own a trailer court, and two-thirds of the time people can't get through to me because my phone won't ring when people call. My son in Morristown tried seven times today to get me; on the seventh try my phone barely rang. My neighbor has to go through the operator to get me most of the time.

We have reported this trouble three or four times, but our complaints have been ignored. When you send out your bills, you expect payment. When we want to use our phones, we expect them to be in working order. If we refuse to pay our bill, we would be cut off. Maybe we'd be better off with out phones and get better service from carrier pigeons.

Every United customer, who has a complaint about phone service, should refuse to pay their bills until they can get good service, and see how the Phone Company likes that.

Before I could mail this letter, a repairman came and checked my phone. He said he couldn't find anything wrong with my phone. After he left, I called my neighbor and there was so much static, we couldn't hear each other and had to hang up. This is a ridiculous situation that should be corrected before you have the nerve to raise our rates.

Mrs. Frank Bucca, Sr. & Mrs. Reuben Hinkle

Chapter 28: Media War Begins!

United of Tennessee had been notified that in my absence Local President Darrell Freeman had full authority to speak in the Union's behalf.

At 11:30 a.m. Monday, September 17, my leadership training class in Birmingham was interrupted with an urgent telephone message to call United's council and chief spokesman, Ed Norris. In my mind I knew he probably was playing games and, because I was out of town, would want a meeting.

At 12:45 p.m. I reached Norris at his office in Kingsport. He stated he had been trying to reach me all morning and wanted to set up a meeting for 10:30 a.m. Tuesday. I asked did the Company have anything new to offer. Norris responded no, they did not. I ask him was he trying to set a meeting just because I was out of town. Norris responded with a chuckle, "Now Calvin, I wouldn't do a thing like that."

I responded, "Well Ed, you've said that we are at an impasse and if you have nothing to offer I must agree with you. If you have no new proposals then there is no reason to meet. The Union stands ready to meet when there is something of substance to offer."

I suggested we meet on Thursday. Norris declined saying he had other commitments. The Company held a press conference.

The September 19th headlines read:

PHONE WORKERS, UNITED STILL IN STANDOFF

"United is standing by its final contract offer and prepared to operate should some 1200 employees strike September 30th, the Company's president said today.

"However, President W.W. Hill said telephone installation and routine repair work would be among several services that could suffer in the event of a work stoppage.

"Hills comments this morning to reporters assembled at United's Bristol headquarters indicated the Company and the Communications Workers Union remain far apart in the nearly three month old contract talks.

"Hill said neither the Union nor Company has indicated any progress in preparing new proposals for consideration. As a result, no plans have been made to resume negotiations. "The Company has made its final offer to Local 10871 of the Communications Workers of America and is ready to continue providing telephone service if a strike occurs."

"The Company and Union began negotiations in late June, and bargaining committees worked past expiration of the three-year contract and on August 24, reached a tentative agreement.

"But despite recommendations to accept the contract by the unions bargaining committee, workers rejected the proposal by a more than three to one margin.

"Local C.W.A. Representatives then consulted with Union leaders in Washington D.C. to set a strike date. Since the establishment last Friday of a midnight September 30 strike date, the Union and Company negotiators have been unable to renew talks.

"Local Union leaders have withdrawn their

sanction of the original agreement and reverted back to the Unions first contract demands. The Company has repeatedly called those terms unacceptable.

"Again today Hill pointed out the Union bargaining committee's original acceptance of the Company's August 24th offer and contended the Company can offer nothing better. He said the proposed three-year contract carries increases in wages and benefits of more than 25.5 percent. "These increases will cost United more that $4.1 million." He said, "To offer anything higher than that amount would not be in the best interest of the employees, the Company or United's customers." Hill added that granting similar wage and benefit increases to the Company's 900 non-union employees would place the cost of the settlement at about $7 million.

"The major point causing the impasse, Hill said, is the Union's insistence that any agreement include a cost-of-living adjustment. He said such an adjustment would guarantee employees wage increases as inflation rises, but the Company, with rates determined by governmental agencies, would have no guarantee of additional revenue to pay the increased wages.

"Hill said the proposed contract includes 9.5 percent increase in wages and benefits the first year. "In fact, we are already paying the wage increase to the employees who are now threatening to strike,"

While still in Birmingham, I responded to the Company's press conference.

The September 20 headlines read: UNITED OFFER "NOT ENOUGH" UNION'S SPOKESMAN SAYS

"A war of words continued yesterday as Company and Union officers continued their wrangling in the

United contract controversy. Shortly after United's President, W.W. Hill, told a press conference the Company could not budge on its wage offer, Communications Workers Union leader, Calvin Patrick, responded that, "employees have spoken loud and clear that it is not enough."

"The Union said it requested a meeting this afternoon but was told the "Company has other commitments." "We are therefore urging a meeting at the earliest possible date," Patrick said.

"Later Patrick said "hopefully" a session will be scheduled Monday. "We're waiting on the Company to make the next move."

"With 11 days remaining before the unions September 30 strike deadline, both sides are steadfastly defending their positions without any moves toward a compromise.

"Hill said federal mediators have been involved in the talks on occasion and may be called in again in coming days.

"Patrick responded to the Company's statements that the package would cost the Company 7 million dollars by pointing to the 10 percent rate increase recently allowed United by a court decision.

"The Company has not convinced us that the Public Service Commission will not grant increases that affect the cost of labor; historically the Public Service Commission has granted increases which include a cost-of-living formula for other telephone Company's in Tennessee including South Central Bell and Highland Telephone Co.

"As an example, in South Central Bell in August, 1979 top craft (employees) received a $38 per week increase including cost-of-living. The proposal we have on the table here in United would only produce

$26 per week.

"The Union feels that in the future the Company's ability to attract qualified craft persons will be affected due to the higher wages of all Companies surrounding the United territory.

"While the (Union) bargaining committee did not approve the agreement, the Company had said that this was all they were willing to give. Therefore, we made a good faith attempt to get it ratified.

"However, the employees have spoken loud and clear that it is not enough. We are responding to the members. It is their contract and they make the final decision." Patrick concluded.

The article concluded: "The Company had been critical of the Union leaders for agreeing to the tentative agreement and then blasting it as unacceptable after the workers voted last week."

I flew home Thursday and upon seeing the results of the two news articles felt we had won round one.

I immediately contacted Human Resources Director Jack Gaddis and requested a bargaining committee meeting as soon as possible.

At 3:25 p.m. Saturday, September 22, we met at the Ramada Inn in Kingsport. Company spokesman and Council, Ed Norris, opened the meeting. "We have a number of things to say. We believe the rejected agreement was excellent. Obviously you did too or you wouldn't have recommended it. Now the membership has rejected it 615 to 393.

"We would like to resolve the impasse that has existed since that time. As evidence of our good faith we are going to reinstate the check off of Union dues and the arbitration procedures.

"The Company is willing to reevaluate its total

position. We felt from the beginning that we couldn't negotiate a contract in the media. We are therefore asking that the parties agree to a black-out in the interest of reaching an agreement and avoiding a strike.

"We are prepared to reevaluate our position and the Company's offer if the Union will agree to a black-out on publicity. "If a black-out is acceptable we would like to meet with you privately Monday morning and the committee Monday afternoon", Norris concluded.

Patrick: "Is the Monday meeting conditioned on a black-out"?

Norris: "We are not making any conditions to a Monday meeting, but we feel a black-out would help us in reaching an agreement."

Patrick: "After the way you have abused me and the committee in the press there will never be another joint press release with this Company as long as I am here. You have tried to destroy this committee's credibility. I've talked to you and President Hill, yet it still pops up every day in the paper and on television. Destroying our credibility will keep us from reaching an agreement that the membership will accept."

Norris: "Can I talk to you in private?"

Patrick: "ok".

We walked outside the conference room.

Norris: "Calvin, I want to meet Monday and present a package that will make you and the committee look good. Ha. Ha. Ha."

Patrick: "Ed, if you have a package that does not have a COLA I won't even check it out with Washington. That is a strike issue. But we will agree to meet on Monday."

We reconvened.

Norris: "I suggest we recess until 3 p.m. Monday."

Patrick: Ok, see you Monday.

Chapter 29:   Must Have a Media Black-Out

At noon Monday, September 24, I had lunch with Ed Norris and Jack Gaddis. After a pleasant lunch and small talk Norris opened the conversation.

"Can we have an agreement on the suggested news black-out?

Patrick: "The Union is not going to black-out what is going on in bargaining, in fact we plan to expand our media coverage this week with ads in all newspapers and with television and radio spots. Too many people are looking at us for a pattern."

Norris: "Could you communicate within your organization but not in the papers? Just talk about the final offer that was rejected by the members, which has already been publicized.

My mind was racing wondering what Norris was up to. Had the Company gotten themselves in a bind in the media by their bad press conferences? Were they afraid to compete with us in the media? I knew if they were smart enough to capitalize on the fact that more was on the table than the Union was asking for in our earlier formula for COLA, they would confuse our members and possibly turn them against the bargaining committee.

I responded. "I don't know if we can agree on a black-out under these terms or not. I'll have to think about it and discuss it with others I am responsible to."

Norris: "Is there some way we can reach an agreement without a COLA formula?"

Patrick: "No way. A COLA formula is top priority. There is no need to negotiate if there is no COLA formula."

Jack Gaddis spoke up, "Calvin, the Company doesn't have the authority to grant a COLA."

Patrick: "Jack, I would suggest that you call Kansas City and tell them they had better change their mind or you are going to have a strike. I begged you to put a COLA on the table, you refused and now President Watts is calling the shots. I'm just a messenger boy. That message to you is without a COLA formula, we will have a strike."

As the luncheon broke up without an agreement I kidded Jack that I knew he was a leader and if he was forceful enough Kansas city would do what he requested.

I called President Watts and asked his view on the black- out. He said he must check with a couple of people and would get back to me.

3:00 p.m. The two bargaining committees met. Attorney Ed Norris opened the meeting.

"There are a few things I would like to say. I've told everyone in Tennessee that this is the best CWA committee in my experience. The Company team had no problems with your team. We have the highest regard for you individually and as a team. Both sides of the table have attempted to do what is best for all. We feel we've come a long way because of the leadership of the committees and Calvin Patrick in particular.

"We want the new relationship to continue and we hope our personal relationships continue no matter what happens in bargaining. "We have evaluated our position trying to analyze why the contract was turned down and what we can do to break the impasse between the parties.

"We had requested a blackout on media from the beginning of bargaining. I personally have never seen a contract negotiated in the media: the media thrives on confrontation; it sells papers.

"We recognize CWA's right and obligation to keep the membership informed and we have not and do not propose any restriction on internal communications to members or to any joint releases by the parties.

"As we discussed Saturday, the Company is willing to reevaluate its position with the assurance of a black-out of media publication on these negotiations, with the full recognition that if no contract is reached by September 30 the agreement would be off and both parties could use the media as they see fit.

"We want a contract -- we don't want a strike. We feel, with the same kind of spirit and attitude that was at the table on August 24 and before, we can reach an agreement. But we can't do it if both sides are constantly making charges and counter charges in the media.

"We are on the same plane, we will fly or crash together. No one wins in a strike. To do this the Company needs input, advice and help on what it will take to get an agreement. We need a meaningful list, without a COLA, that would help us resolve this dispute. We don't have time to go back to June 22," Norris concluded.

Patrick: "I have discussed your request for a black-out with President Watts. He hasn't given an answer. I'm expecting a call any time. "If we could agree on a black-out it would be under the following conditions.

1. CWA would continue its media advertising and comments to the press based upon the Company's final offer of August 24.
2. We would talk to the media in terms of no significant progress, not repeating any proposals offered across the table.
3. We would continue talking to the members through bulletin board notices, telephone recordings, and other methods we may choose and we will spell out details about progress. The media has the telephone recording numbers and may use the material as they have over the past weekend.
4. CWA would reserve the right to go public at any point we felt there was no alternative to a strike.
5. If there is a strike, both parties would have to agree now that no references to early offers would be made.

6. All information would be transmitted to other Union Officials, and there would be no assurance of what other United units may do with the information with regards to going public because of their own negotiations. "You can think about these conditions and if President Watts gives the go ahead I will get back to you.

Patrick continued "The Unions position on resolving the differences and reaching an agreement are:

    1. An uncapped COLA.

    2. Hospitalization paid 100 percent by the Company.

    3. A fully paid dental plan.

    4. The CWA savings plan check-off.

    5. Employees would have the opportunity to work the 6-day of any week before the Company hired outside contractors.

    6. The Company must agree to the Locals hardship fund Check-off.

    7. The CWA COPE check-off.

"Failure of the Company to come with a COLA formula would, in my opinion, make negotiations futile. If the Company has proposals we would like to see them, in order to properly evaluate your position," I concluded.

4:10 p.m. the Company requested a recess.

4:45 p.m. reconvened.

Patrick: "During the recess we have received an OK on the news blackout. It must be clear should a strike occur then all bets are off."

Norris: "With the understanding on a partial news black-out in the media the Company wants to make an offer to resolve all differences between the parties. This is a local contract, paid for by United of Tennessee. We can't go to Kansas City and ask for any more concessions. This offer is made in an effort to break the impasse now. We want a response from the Union no later than tomorrow. Because the proposal exceeds Presidential wage guidelines we will agree to place it into effect and not seek approval from the Presidents Council on Wage and Price Stability.

"The contract would be effective at 12:01 a.m. on August 24.

First year:
1. 9.3 percent general wage increase. Everything else remains as previously agreed.
2. First anniversary: 9.0 percent wage increase: 85 percent paid hospitalization: A Contributory dental plan which Company would pay 70 percent of the plan.
3. Second anniversary:

9.0 percent wage increase

90 percent of hospitalization paid by the Company

"All other economics previously agreed to would be the same"

On contract language:
1. Call-outs, we want to modify the agreed to proposal to pay only one hour if an employee was requested to work while he/she was still on the Company premises, otherwise we would pay two hours for a minimum callout.
2. Revert to the 1976 agreement on entry-level jobs, hiring from the street without regards to seniority.
3. Revert to no pay for the Local Vice President when meeting on grievances.
4. Revert from 24 months to 12 months on recall rights in case of layoff.
5. The Company withdraws the agreed to day-at-a-time vacation. "The Union must notify Jack Gaddis by tomorrow as to your position. The Company expects a counter proposal if this one is rejected."

Patrick: "Without checking with what my committee thinks my answer to Items 2, 3, 4, and 5 is NO!!! We won't agree, and that will be our recommendation to President Watts. I will pass your proposal on economics to President

Watts. I would like to set our next bargaining session."

Norris: "I had rather wait and get your response before we set another meeting." At 5:15 p.m. we recessed.

Chapter 30: May Not Go With COLA

On September 25 I advised Jack Gaddis that the Union had rejected the Company proposal. I requested a meeting for September 26. Gaddis agreed to meet.

For the remainder of the day the Union bargaining committee discussed our position and what kind of counter proposal we should offer since we had rejected the Company proposal.

I had discussed our position with National Director Mendoza. He was beginning to believe Kansas City might not go with a COLA. He suggested that since Kansas City was so sensitive about the term "COLA" that I should try a different approach calling it instead an "inflation protection plan".

At 11:20 a.m. September 26 The Federal Mediation and Conciliation Service met with the negotiators. All members of both Company and Union committees were present.

Company Council Ed Norris opened the meeting.

"Mr. Patrick it is obvious that negotiations are being coordinated among all the United bargaining units by the CWA in Washington."

Patrick, "I have no comment on that statement Ed."

Norris, "We can reach an agreement today if the Union is willing to negotiate without outsiders involving themselves in these proceedings."

Patrick, "Mr. Norris the Union is in a position to resolve the differences between the parties. I offer the following proposal to resolve our differences and reach an agreement.

1. The 9.3 percent on the table for the first year is ok if the Company would add an "Inflation Protection Plan".
2. The 9.0 percent at the first anniversary is ok provided we

add an "Inflation Protection Plan".
3. The 9.0 percent at the second anniversary will be ok provided there is an "Inflation Protection Plan".
4. The Company will pay 80 percent of the Hospitalization plan at the Go down.
a. Increase the hospitalization payment by the Company to 85 percent at the first anniversary.
b. Increase the Company hospitalization payment to 100 percent at the second anniversary.
5. Dental plan. The Company plan, where you offer to pay 70 percent of the premium, is inadequate. We will submit a counter proposal later.
6. Employees must be offered the sixth workday opportunity each week before contractors are hired.
7. The Local Hardship Fund deduction must be agreed to with the Company making a deduction once a year.
8. The Company must agree to make a CWA COPE deduction twice each year.
9. The date of the agreement would be the date the agreement is reached.
10. The Company must remove the retrogressive proposals placed on the table at the last meeting."

At the end of my presentation Jack Gaddis ask; "What the hell is an "inflation protection plan?"

Patrick, "Jack if inflation went above 9 percent at either the first or second anniversary, or at both anniversaries then the employees would be able to recover a portion of the inflation above 9 percent."

Gaddis, "Would it be based on local inflation or national inflation?"

Patrick, "As you are well aware government, industry, and labor uses the national consumer price index 1967 equals 100 percent. We would use that index which is statistically based on a national average."

Gaddis, "The consumer price index is not as high here as it is in the other parts of the nation."

Patrick, "The Union is willing to look at any reasonable counter proposal."

Norris, "If we can come with a fair and equitable settlement- ----?   We don't know where to go!!! --- we can't go with a COLA-----!!! May we recess?"

Patrick, "OK, lets take a 15 minute recess."

12:25 p.m. Reconvened. Norris, "Calvin we have studied your counter proposal. We are not optimistic. We will consider your counter proposal on the dental plan, but we reject the remainder of your proposal. We have stretched and stretched. Basically the ball is in your park. We have done the best we can. There is no way we can reach an agreement on your counter proposal. I suggest we adjourn subject to call by either party."

At 12:35 p.m. we agreed to adjourn subject to call.

3:05 p.m. I advised National Director Mendoza what had transpired at today's negotiations. He had no suggestions and said he would get back to me. I advised him I would be traveling to Chattanooga for the CWA Tennessee State Meeting and he could reach me there.

On September 27 while at the State Meeting President Watts' Assistant, John Carroll, who was to speak at the meeting, advised me that in United of Carolina the Company negotiators had raised the wage package to 9.0 percent at the go down and 8.5 percent at the first and second anniversary, for a 3 year agreement. We agreed we would wait and see what the other companies did around the Nation.

As if I did not have enough problems I received a message that the White House was trying to reach me. I called Jim Free at the White House. He advised me that there were problems between several political factions in Johnson City, Tennessee where First Lady Rosalynn Carter was to speak at a fundraiser. Free had received word that I was not going to attend the affair. I responded that I had real problems in negotiations with United of Tennessee and it would be difficult to turn loose.

Free asked me to get involved in the fund raiser and be sure the East Tennessee democrats were not embarrassed by the friction and therefore have a small turnout at the fund raiser and public appearance that was to follow. I agreed to do whatever was necessary and for him to have the advance team contact me and we would put it together.

As I hung up the phone, National Director Mendoza called and said that United of Tennessee must come with a different approach including some type of recognition of a COLA Principle. "If they refuse to do so President Watts will call the strike as planned."

Mendoza advised that he would be arriving in Kingsport Saturday, September 29, to supervise and coordinate bargaining nationwide, in all units.

Late on September 28 Local President Darrell Freeman and I drove back from Chattanooga and met with Ed Norris and Jim Gaddis. We brought them up to date on the Unions position as defined by Mendoza. We advised them that The National office was training defense fund directors in United of Carolina and we would be doing the same thing starting October 3. We then explained our counter proposal on the Dental plan.

Norris and Gaddis responded there was no way for the Company to pay 100 percent of the hospitalization plan during the life of the agreement.

A feeling of frustration, gloom, and sadness was evident in the four of us as we began to realize a strike was inevitable. Gaddis advised that if the strike came, employees would receive their pay on their regular payday and any earned vacation would be paid at the time it was scheduled, even if in the middle of the strike. He said employees would have to submit premiums for hospital and life insurance or the insurance would be terminated. Gaddis said that Employees must return all property such as keys, passes and equipment. He asked that we advise the employees we come in contact with of what they must do.

National Director Mendoza arrived at noon Saturday September 29. He asked that I press the Company to give me their bottom line to prevent a strike.

I called Jack Gaddis for a meeting. He advised the Company was not prepared to meet and suggested we meet at 2 p.m. Sunday September 30. We agreed.

A news reporter who had been fair to the Union during the negotiations had asked for an interview with some employees. His story would be on the human-interest side should a strike occur. I allowed the bargaining committee to be interviewed.

Chapter 31: Strike Inevitable

The Sunday September 30 headlines read:

PHONE STRIKE EXPECTED TO START TONIGHT

"It seems like a strike is inevitable," said Calvin Patrick, settling into his chair yesterday in the motel dining room.

"The countdown has reached the eleventh hour and Patrick, A Communications Workers Union leader is predicting nothing will be done to keep the 1,268 men and woman on their United Telephone Co. jobs past midnight tonight.

"The workers are ready to man picket lines at 78 Company locations in 14 Tennessee and Virginia counties. The present outlook is for a long strike past Thanksgiving, past Christmas and into 1980, Patrick said.

"At the same time some 3,000 Carolina Telephone workers in eastern North Carolina are preparing to walk off their jobs tonight.

"Before January 1, Union officers predict United Telephone of Indiana, United Telephone of Ohio, will become the third and fourth firms in the United system to be hit by strikes. United of New Jersey workers are already out.

"As salads and drinks were delivered around the dining room table, Patrick and his fellow Union negotiators talked of the issues that have brought the Company and workers to the confrontation point.

"Bob Brown, a telephone installer representing the plant and engineering employees on the Union bargaining committee, said the workers must have an annual cost-of-living wage increase to deal with inflation.

"For years, United employees have watched other telephone companies in the area get higher and higher wages than United until hourly rates became nearly $2.00 more per hour, Brown contends.

"Close behind the cost-of-living issue are demands for full hospitalization coverage, payroll deduction of voluntary worker contributions to a retirement fund and hardship fund, a dental plan and less hiring of out of state contractors for jobs Union members could perform.

"Brown is 35, married and the father of two high school age children. He said his wife recently had to get a job to help make ends meet. He said many other workers are finding themselves in the same position.

"Judy Graham, 31, a mother of one works as a telephone operator in Greenville, said the operators she represents on the bargaining committee have similar concerns.

"With inflation, we need something to keep up with the rest of the industries," she said.

"While Mrs. Graham is married she said a lot of the female United employees are the sole supporters of their families.

"Overall, the average age of the United work force is "pretty young," said Darrell Freeman CWA Local 10871 President. A "tremendous" turnover at United in the early 1970s brought in a lot of younger workers, he said. Only eight to 10 employees are eligible for retirement next year.

"Still it is the Veteran employees who are most concerned with inflation and the trials of trying to buy homes and meet other expenses.

"Freeman, 34, himself employed with United for

over 14 years, said he is in debt for hospital bills incurred by his wife last year. He said a trip to the emergency room for his young daughter cost $100 and he picked up nearly half the bill.

"It is situations like those that have the more than 1300 United workers here and thousands elsewhere, ready to stay off their jobs indefinitely, the Union officers said."

Chapter 32: COLA Or Strike!

At the Motel Mendoza advised the committee of the status of negotiations in the other bargaining units. The New Jersey strike - United in Kansas City has agreed to place 9.5 percent on the table but has not gotten United of New Jersey to agree to place it into effect yet.

United of Carolina - United is now offering 10 percent on wages at the go down; 9.0 percent at the first anniversary; 9.0 percent at the second anniversary; a dental plan. But there is no COLA formula on wages. Mendoza said that President Watts believes we are going to have a strike. "Watts wants you to modify our position on COLA in United of Tennessee and see if it will shake them loose."

At 2:15 p.m. Sunday September 30 the Union and Company committees met. After a few minutes of small talk I opened the meeting. The Union's position is as follows:

1. We are running tandem negotiations with United of Carolina. What is offered here must be offered in Carolina and vice versa.

2. We are modifying our COLA formula proposal. We are asking for a triggering mechanism to protect us from inflation. As an example; What ever wages we agree on, if inflation exceeds those wages by one percent, then the employees would get an eight tenths of one percent wage increase, for each one percent in rise in inflation.

3. Hospitalization 100 percent paid by the Company over the life of the agreement is a must.

4. The CWA savings fund check-off is a must item.

5. We will accept the Company's formula on the Dental plan.

6. The expiration date of the agreement will be September 30.

7. The local items we must have are:
   a. The hardship fund check-off
   b. The COPE check-off
   c. Sixth day work opportunity for our members before work is contracted out.
   d. Improve the board, lodging and travel allowances.
   e. Remove the retrogression placed on the table on September 24.

Norris: "My immediate reaction is, you are conditioning a settlement here on a settlement in Carolina and this is being done without your approval and consent. There have been statements at the bargaining table in New Jersey about bringing the United system to our knees in order to get a common termination date for all contracts. That is why you want September 30 as the date of the agreement. It is obvious President Watts is calling the shots by setting September 30 as the common date to strike."

Norris was at his best. As he leaned forward looking directly at me very intently his forehead was wrinkled, his face was becoming flushed, his voice became stronger: "The CWA has its own goals regardless of what the membership thinks. We have negotiated in good faith since June 22 in an attempt to reach an agreement. Tandem negotiations with other companies are illegal! The statements at the bargaining table in New Jersey are illegal; to tie this Company with what is happening in Carolina is illegal. We will not reach an agreement on an illegal basis."

Patrick: "Ed, these are separate negotiations. We know what is going on in the other units and will not put a contract out for ratification that has less for these members than what the corporation is offering in other units. That has been an issue since the beginning, parity with Carolina and other companies that surround us. We will make an independent judgment when our objectives are met at this bargaining table. It will be based upon the objectives as mandated by the membership of this local when they rejected the contract. What we are doing is not illegal and as an attorney you should know better."

In my mind I, too, felt the tandem negotiations were not legal but who am I to second-guess my Union who has expert attorneys to advise us in these matters. After all, United had said they could not violate President Carter's Wage guidelines and now say they won't even discuss the settlement with the Presidents Council on Wage and Price Stability. So they are no different than CWA. My thoughts were interrupted by Norris who by now was speaking in normal tones:

Norris:
- We are not willing to give a COLA.
- We are not in a position to pay 100 percent on the hospitalization.
- We have met your demand on the dental plan.
- We feel the savings fund is a worthy effort on your part but it would open the door for additional cost to the Company in the future, because you would ask us to contribute to it. Also it would be in competition with our credit union, therefore we reject it.
- We reject the cope and hardship fund check-offs.
- The proposed September 30 termination date is unacceptable.
- The Board and lodging is already substantial and is rejected.
- Working the sixth day before hiring contractors is unacceptable.
- The Items of retrogression are negotiable, we would like to have them."

Norris then restated the Company's position on wages as offered on September 24. He emphasized that the offer is not subject to the Wage Price guidelines and that the wages and benefits will be placed into effect without consulting with the Council on Wage and Price Stability.

Patrick: "Ed, your offer does not meet the objectives of this bargaining committee."

Norris, almost in disgust and sounding frustrated: "Basically our problem is you have reverted to the June 22 proposal. We have made you an offer and you have failed to respond."

Patrick, almost pleading to be understood: "We have responded to your proposal, Ed. Are we at an impasse or do you want to recess?"

Norris, suddenly at ease: "Lets recess subject to call. We are in room 102."

At 4:30 p.m. at Norris's request I met with him and Jack Gaddis in the breezeway of the motel. They gave me their bottom line.

1. They would move from 9.3 percent to 10 percent at the go down.
2. The First and second anniversary would stay at 9.0 percent.
3. The Company would go to 85 percent of the payment on hospitalization on January 1, 1980 instead of August 24, 1980.
4. They would pay 90 percent on the hospitalization effective October 1,1981 which was the same.
5. The Dental plan would be as we had agreed.
6. The Company would withdraw all retrogression.
7. The old termination date of August 23 would stay the same.
8. All items previously agreed to would be effective.

I responded that I really appreciated their movement and we would take their offer under advisement, but it looked like a strike.

I gave Mendoza an update of what had transpired. He in turn advised the Union committee that United of

Norfork, Virginia had come off retrogression on overtime and would pay double time after 50 hours. Wages in Carolina and Norfork were the same as United of Tennessee. New Jersey had agreed to the 9.5 percent increase in principle and since previously we had said that if New Jersey went to 9.5 percent it would meet our objectives. "We are in a position to reach agreement in New Jersey subject to it being placed on the Bargaining table by the Company" said Mendoza.

Mendoza reported that in Carolina the Company bargaining committee was saying there would be NO COLA---, NOW---, NEXT YEAR-- -, OR EVER!!!!

We checked out the value of the contract for United of Tennessee and the total Compensation over the life of the agreement was 31.8 percent.

Mendoza wanted to know where the United of Tennessee bargaining committee stood regarding striking. The committee went to my room. For an hour we discussed the situation:

    Our knowledge of the Company's financial condition,

    Their problems with the Public Service Commission,
The progress we had made in establishing a good relationship with the Company management team, including President Hill,
The 31.8 percent on the table, which was a lot more than the National Union had ever expected.

The contract was 9 percent above the average settlements in the nation.

One of our goals had been to help United of New Jersey end their long strike and that had been successful.

The fact that many operators had voted to strike because of a lack of knowledge about the new computerized scheduling which we knew from experience in other companies would be ok after some experience with it.

The bottom line based on all our conversations with

the Company both on and off the record was that we felt they would not come with a COLA formula regardless of how long a strike lasted.

We summarized our views on a sheet of paper and went back into the workroom and gave it to Mendoza. He read it silently.

1. The Bargaining committee feels the Company has bought a contract.
2. This agreement has produced more than President Watts was originally expecting even under a COLA formula.
3. We have reached the objectives of getting the Company to deal with us on the corporate level, as shown in the improvements in hospitalization and dental plan, which was a break through.
4. The Corporate system is dealing Corporate wide on wage concessions in all companies.
5. CWA has received a great deal of favorable publicity in the community, which can have a favorable impact on organizing.
6. We have the COLA issue to help us in negotiations in the future.
7. We have learned how to work together with other United Companies where we have contracts and delay contract terminations without striking.
8. If we strike the most we can hope for is an increase from 90 to 100 percent on hospitalization, and the principle of COLA.
9. The United of Carolina members may think they want to strike but they are only 70 percent organized and we wonder if they will be able to sustain a strike or effect Company operations based upon their recent history.
10. But in spite of our gut feelings, we will follow the leadership of the President. If he feels we need to strike, our local will sustain a strike.

As Mendoza finished reading a faint smile of satisfaction came across his face. He was going to get what he had wanted, United of Tennessee/Virginia to support a strike. The bargaining committee knew the answer without him saying a word. We would strike.

6:00 p.m. September 30. I called Vice President Brown and advised him of the Locals decision. He responded, "The Union couldn't find a Local anywhere that would have been more cooperative."

6:35 p.m. Mendoza gave us an update on his conversation with United headquarters in Kansas City.
1. "They are saying this agreement is more than CWA was looking for with a COLA formula and that a strike is foolish.
2 They said we may get a COLA if there is a strike but it won't produce these percentages of wage increases.
3, The Company acknowledges that there have been breakthroughs in negotiations with a dental plan and a 30 percent improvement on premium payments on hospitalization.
4. United of Kansas City is willing to look at an alternate package, a 2 year agreement with 10 percent at the go down and 9 percent at the first anniversary", Mendoza concluded.

7:05 p.m. President Watts called. Mendoza filled him in on where negotiations stand and what Kansas City was saying. Watts advised Mendoza that we could go for a two year agreement without a COLA to prevent a strike, provided all benefits were rolled into the first two years in all units.

Mendoza called United headquarters in Kansas City and gave them Watts message. He then instructed all bargaining committees to go for the two-year agreement.

I called Local President Freeman aside and told him that in my view United in Tennessee would accept a two year agreement because unlike the other bargaining units around the country all we had to do was move the agreed to increase in hospitalization forward from the first day of the third year to the last day of the second year of the two year agreement to comply with Mendoza's proposal. In fact to prevent a strike they may move it forward as much as 6 to 9 months. We knew that the other units were loaded with third year benefits and in my view this proposal would not fly except in United of Tennessee. Freeman agreed with my assessment.

I asked Freeman to go with me and help me explain the situation to Mendoza. I did not want to be hung out to dry again with a contract in Tennessee and no contract in the rest of the country after what Watts and Mendoza had been telling the employees all over the nation that "we would go out and come back together".

I gave my assessment to Mendoza as to how we felt. Mendoza said to offer the two-year agreement proposal.

My mind was racing; I could not believe what was going on. Why couldn't Mendoza understand the problem? Apparently he just didn't grasp what I was saying.

Did Mendoza deliberately want to get an agreement in Tennessee so that the other units would have to agree, without getting a COLA, or striking for it as he had promised? Or was he just screwing up as he had back in 1975 when he told General Telephone of Ohio, Indiana, and Kentucky to strike and General of Kentucky was the only one to strike? The other two units ratified the agreement and Kentucky stayed on strike for 5 months.

Time was running out and Mendoza was sabotaging his own strategy. Was he hoping I would make a mistake to take him off the hook? Would he blame me again for his failure to communicate, as he had prior to the first agreement, when he refused to get involved until after the agreement was reached?

If I presented the two year package and the Company in Tennessee accepted it, then, if the other units did not accept or could not afford to roll all benefits into a two year agreement, would Mendoza require me to back out of the agreement in

Tennessee? My integrity would be destroyed with United of Tennessee, which would mean all that the committee and I had worked for, during the last year, would go down the drain. United of Tennessee would have to strike along with the other units. It would also be an unfair labor practice against CWA, to back out of an agreement made in good faith especially on CWA's terms.

I made a conscious decision not to present the two-year package and to present another package we had been discussing. I would not tell Mendoza what I had done. If by some miracle the other bargaining units were able to obtain a two-year agreement we would then make the offer, but not before then. I called the Company and asked for a meeting.

8:05 p.m. I presented to the Company a counter proposal.
1. A 10 percent wage increase at the go down.
2. 9 percent at the first and second anniversary.
3. In addition, should inflation exceed the 9 percent wage increase in the second and third year by one percentage point, this would automatically trigger a wage re-opener in the second and third year of the agreement.
4. The Company must make the hospitalization premium increase to 90 percent effective January 1, 1981 (thus moving it forward 9 months from October 1,1981). The Termination date would be September 30.

I closed by saying, "Gentlemen, these small changes will get us an agreement. If inflation doesn't go above 10 percent in the second and third year the only additional cost to the Company is the additional 5 percent increase in hospital premiums for 9 months or about 100 thousand dollars. I suggest we recess subject to call by either party in order for you to study this proposal."

8:45 p. m. Norris and Gaddis called me to the breezeway again. They told me the Company was bleeding. Gaddis said in a pleading voice: "Calvin, believe me, we've done all this Company can afford to do. We don't know how we are going to be able to make a profit and live up to what we've committed to you already".

I advised them that we had put them on notice months ago.

"Gaddis still pleading said: "Calvin, you have challenged us to be leaders and take over this Company. We have shown you we intend for things to be different in the future. You have shown us that you too could be a leader when we reached the first agreement. We have a good package on the table, lets settle this thing and get on with handling the problems we have talked so much about."

I responded, "Jack you are right. All of us have shown leadership but I've had enough of it. I'm not going to have my ass chewed again and accused of selling out our members. Maybe Mendoza is right, only time will tell. If only you would have come with a COLA when I pleaded with you to do so back in July. The old hurricane has come in from Carolina just like I told you and has overtaken all of us, including the membership. "I'm sorry it has come to this but we are going to have a strike at midnight. I'll be available if you have anything new to offer or if there are any changes."

I walked away and went over and sat by the swimming pool. I knew from the hours I had talked to President Hill about low Company profits that indeed the Company was bleeding. Why had Kansas City been so stubborn back in July?

Random thoughts started through my head. I'm so tired. I've been in negotiations since April. In one contract Mendoza wrote a letter praising me for an outstanding job and here I've had Vice Presidents accuse me of selling out. It's so easy to second-guess a person at the bargaining table. Have we done the best we can? I believe we have, but maybe Mendoza is right. He gets around the country and has a feel for what is going on. Is Mendoza taking the militant attitude for political reasons to be reelected? Should I have placed the two-year offer on the table? What would Mendoza and President Watts reaction have been if United of Tennessee accepted the two-year offer and the other units turned it down? Would I be ridiculed again? Would I be fired? The load is heavy. If only the members understood the bargaining process. There is no way to involve them. When this is over I will be the villain in this local and will have to take the blame for everything that has happened.

Coming back to reality I said to myself, stop the self-pity, there is much work to do and if we strike tonight we must visit the picket lines and caution the members about violence and see how their morale is.

I went back to the workroom where the rest of the committee was discussing picket line assignments and Local President Freeman was checking with his picket captains.

11:10 p.m. Mendoza gave the Bargaining Committee a report from Kansas City.

The Company was telling him that the two-year package was too expensive to be rolled into a two-year agreement in all units except Tennessee.

United of New Jersey management is angry at Company Headquarters in Kansas City and is saying if everything is rolled into a 2 year agreement they will only place 8 percent in wages and they didn't care what Kansas City said.

He reemphasized that Kansas City had agreed to force New Jersey to place 9.5 percent in wages at the appropriate time.

11:30 p.m. President Watts called. Mendoza filled him in. Watts responded: "we are not going to leave New Jersey hanging out, there will be no agreement in any unit unless all units have a two-year agreement.

Thank God, I had not put the two-year package on the table. I then told Mendoza that the two-year package was not on the table in United of Tennessee; therefore, they could not accept it and cause the other units to be hung out. He fumbled for an answer. Finally he understood. I ask him what he wanted me to do. Mendoza advised me to go back to the Company and ask if we could continue negotiations in the morning.

11:52 p.m. I asked the Company had their position changed on my proposal. Norris emphasized that it had been rejected.

Patrick: "Well Ed we have a strike. Can we continue negotiations in the morning?" Norris's face was red. His brow and face was twisted into an agonizing frown. He said: "Calvin we have had a distinct understanding from our contact in Kansas City that you were coming with a proposal for a two-year contract. We can reach an agreement with that proposal. Why should we get caught up in these other peoples inability to reach an agreement?"

Patrick: "Ed. I have no two-year package to offer. My proposal is the same as at 8:05 p.m."

Norris: "Calvin, Mendoza has a different position than you are taking and has communicated it to Kansas City."

Patrick: "Ed, my position has not changed since 8:05 p.m. regardless of what you have been told."

Norris: "We will get back to you."

Chapter 33: CWA News "The Last Hours"

As the strike deadline loomed for United Intermountain and Carolina Telephone and Telegraph units, CWA President Glenn Watts and Independent Telephone Director Rudy Mendoza became personally involved in negotiations, along with the respective district Vice Presidents.

This is the story of the last minute attempt to avert the strike. Dave Kent of the National Union's Public Relations Staff was with Mendoza as he coordinated efforts to reach a settlement-Ed.

CWA H.Q. Staff- Internal Information
By David Kent

"Contract negotiations normally take place in well-lit meeting rooms of modern hotels and motels.

"In these negotiations there were meeting rooms to be sure, but there was also the phone booth along Route 11 E in the Tennessee hills. During the last days and hours, that broken-down phone booth became central to the drama that was taking place as the Company and the Union played their remaining cards. Thousands of CWA members in eastern North Carolina, Virginia and northeastern Tennessee would be affected by the outcome of the talks. These thousands would join about 180 other members, employed by United Telecommunications in New Jersey, on the picket lines if a strike occurred.

"As Friday, Sept. 28, dawned in Raleigh, N. C., CWA's Independent Telephone Director, Rudy Mendoza, met with the Union's bargaining committee representing members employed by Carolina Telephone and Telegraph Co., which includes the Norfolk and Carolina Telephone Co.

"After hours of meetings, Mendoza flew to the Tri-

Cities airport, serving Bristol, Kingsport and Johnson City, Tenn. He immediately went to the Ramada Inn in Kingsport for more meetings with the committee representing United Inter-Mountain employees.

"For both units, a strike deadline was approaching. Union President Glenn Watts had made it clear that if there wasn't an agreement at 12:01 a.m. on Oct. 1, CWA members would walk.

"Throughout Friday night and Saturday, Sept. 29, intermittent meetings had taken place between Union and Company negotiators, but these were not productive. Sunday morning at 1 o'clock, Mendoza left the Ramada Inn with Bob Brown, an area representative for Local 10871 and bargaining committee member. Mendoza needed to make a very private telephone call . . . away from the numerous "clicks" the Union people heard when they used the motel phones. He needed to confer with President Watts and Watts' Assistant in charge of collective bargaining, John Carroll.

"Brown and Mendoza drove 25 miles from the motel, to a pay telephone booth located on a pitch-black backroad somewhere deep in the recesses of the Tennessee hills near the town of Surgoinsville.

"It was an A.T.& T telephone booth, just beyond the United service district. The little light in the telephone booth that is supposed to light didn't work. The door that was supposed to glide shut was jammed half open. But the phone worked.

"Mendoza squeezed into the out of the way booth with his notes, written on a yellow legal sized pad. He couldn't see. Brown got in the car, turned on the engine, headed the car directly at the phone booth and turned on the headlights.

"Mendoza called Watts and Carroll and reviewed

the bargaining situation. It was after 2 a.m. when Mendoza and Brown got back to the Ramada Inn. ----

"Sunday afternoon, Sept. 30: bargaining committees are meeting . . . one in Carolina, another in Tennessee and a thousand miles away men and women are still walking picket lines in Flemington and Clinton, N. J

"Mendoza is in Local 10871's office in Bristol Tenn. checking his notes, ruminating over the various proposals and approving a press release that says, "The Strike is On" (The press release was never issued: as it turned out, there appeared, even as late as 11:30 that night, a slim, slender chance that there might be a settlement rather than a strike.)

"At 5 p.m., Mendoza is back in his motel room in Kingsport, talking to Calvin Patrick, CWA's East Tennessee-Kentucky Director, and chair of the bargaining committee, along with other members of the bargaining committee: Darrell Freeman, local president, Bob Brown and Judy Graham, both area representatives of Local 10871.

"He calls Delbert Gordon, CWA's North Carolina director and chair of the bargaining committee there. In Gordon's motel room are the elected members of CWA's bargaining committee: Rocky Barnes, the bargaining representative of Local 3680; Hugh Muse, vice president and bargaining representative of Local 3681; George Speight, bargaining representative of Local 3682, and Bobby Harris, bargaining representative and president of Local 3685.

"On Saturday, representatives from each local had come into Raleigh to count strike authorization ballots. Their tallies showed that 1,300 members had voted strike authority, as opposed to four "no" votes.

"Mendoza, with one bargaining committee at hand,

and the other in a motel room in Raleigh, is trying to sort out the various proposals, to check their subtle differences. Mendoza calls President Watts to discuss key issues in the Company proposals. Watts and Mendoza explore several possible recommendations: a two-year contract rather than a three-year contract, and the manner in which fringe benefits that would have begun in the third year could be fit into a two-year package. Watts tells Mendoza he wants at least an hour to consider these and other possibilities. Mendoza checks his watch. He will call Watts back at 9:30 p.m.

"Mendoza hasn't eaten all day, so he decides to drive back up the road and get a sandwich. But, first, he has to make three more calls to Vice Presidents Morton Bahr of District 1, R. Ben Porch of District 3, and Willard W. Brown of District 10. New Jersey is in District 1; North Carolina is in District 3, and Tennessee is in District 10. The vice presidents must be apprised of the situation. With 30 minutes left before the return call from the President he goes to eat a cheeseburger. While waiting for the sandwich, he begins making and checking notes. The sandwich is finally ready and Mendoza lays aside the notes long enough to eat and look around. He notices three burly teenagers, none of whom weighs less than 250 pounds.

"The teen-agers leave and Mendoza returns to his car shortly after. He drives back to the pay phone booth, points the car in the direction so the headlights will provide illumination, and starts to squeeze into the phone booth through the broken door. Suddenly, a car pulls up- - - with the three teen-agers in it. Mendoza pulls out of the phone booth. The teen-agers ask him if he wants "trouble." It turns out that they thought he was making notes about them while sitting in the restaurant. Suspicion runs high in those Tennessee hills where the manufacture of "moonshine" whisky is not a lost art.

"A companion with Mendoza talks to the teenagers . . . they talk about dirt track car racing and other interests, and the problems of finding a decent job. Eventually, the boys start the car and take off.

"Mendoza is on the telephone with Watts. Both agree there are still too many areas separating the Union and the Company. There is too little time left to resolve the many conflicts that remain. They hang up. ---A strike now seems inevitable.

"The Union cannot settle on the Company's terms-and the hour has grown very late: it is 10:45 p. m. with only 75 minutes left until midnight.

"Mendoza then calls Delbert Gordon in Raleigh, N. C. to tell him and the members of the Carolina Telephone and Telegraph Co. bargaining committee that the strike will start at 12:01 a.m. He calls the vice presidents again; telling them the strike is on.

"He drives rapidly to the motel in Kingsport where Local 10871's bargaining committee is meeting. It is about 11: 30 p.m., a half hour before the deadline. He repeats the news: CWA will strike. Bone-tired, unhappy that the strike had to be, at least Mendoza had the satisfaction of knowing that he and the Union had done everything humanly possible to try to get a settlement."

Chapter 34: The Strike Is On

12:00 midnight September 30th. The strike is on. 12:05 a.m. Mendoza called Watts to check our position. He told Watts that we want a COLA with a triggering mechanism to protect wages plus the other items we have talked about. Mendoza turned to our committee, commenting very strongly: "the System hasn't come with enough". Mendoza reconfirmed our position with our bargaining committee. I advised him that the position he had discussed with Watts was the proposal put on the table at 8:05 p.m. in United of Tennessee and was still there.

12:20 a.m. October 1st Norris and Gaddis asked to speak with Freeman and me in the breezeway of the hotel. Norris, with a very wrinkled brow and questions all over his face: What happened? We understood you were going to make a counter for a two-year contract."

Patrick: "Ed there are problems in the bigger world. There was an understanding with Kansas City but some of your people would not live up to it. Shall we meet at 9:00 a.m.?" Gaddis, resigned to the inevitable: "there is no need, everything we have is on the table.

AN AWKWARD POSITION

1:00 a.m. October 1 The Union Bargaining Committee started visiting picket lines. Spirits were high. National Director Mendoza flew to North Carolina.

The Headlines placed the Union in an awkward position.

LAST-MINUTE TALKS FAIL-PHONE WORKERS STRIKE
"A woman's voice, heard on a CWA phone recording from Bristol this morning, told inquiring strikers: "Your

CWA bargaining committee late last night reluctantly rejected the Company's offer which would have provided a 10 percent pay raise immediately and nine percent pay raises on the first and second anniversaries, in addition to substantial dental and hospital improvements. "While that may sound like a good offer to some people, we know it doesn't provide the kind of wage insurance we need to prevent the erosion of our paychecks," the unidentified woman said.

W.W. Hill, Company President, in a news release, said supervisory personnel and non-striking employees had been assigned to various jobs vacated by the striking employees. "We regret that Union represented employees have decided to leave their jobs, but we will do everything possible to maintain adequate telephone services," Hill said. "We hope for the customers understanding and patience during this difficult period." The Company asked customers for their cooperation in curtailing the use of operators and directory assistance as much as possible. Telephone repairs and new telephone installations will be made on an emergency basis only, they said.

10:00 a.m. I contacted Attorney Norris and Jack Gaddis to see how things were going with the Company. Gaddis said there had been no problems. Everyone seemed to be conducting themselves in a proper manner. The Company was operating but it would be a couple of days before everyone got adjusted. The Company was still concerned as to why the agreement for a two-year contract had fallen through. I jokingly reminded them of the hurricane that started last June. "I believe you now understand what I meant." I advised them I would be incapacitated for two or three days but that Local President Freeman had full authority to act on my behalf. The conversation ended with each of us pledging to keep in contact and keep each other abreast of any new developments.

Freeman and I visited work locations until 2:00 p.m. and held a press conference. I then admitted myself into the hospital because of pain I had been experiencing for two months. At 10:00 p.m. I received a call about a disturbance at the main office of the Telephone Company in Johnson City, which was one block from the hospital. I slipped on my cloths and hurried over. A deputy sheriff was hassling the strikers who had set up a large army squad tent on what appeared to be private property. As I walked up the deputy was threatening to put the strikers in jail. The deputy recognized me as I had been the Democratic Party Chairman and had run a candidate against his boss, the republican sheriff. I intervened rather forcefully. Standing toe to toe, I told him he wasn't arresting anyone and the minimum he had better do is check his facts or I would see that by this time tomorrow he would not have a job. He reluctantly backed off. The next day the strikers received an apology from the sheriff and a pledge of cooperation.

October 2, 3, and 4 passed with only routine problems and my personal problem was diagnosed as exhaustion and stress and that I should take a week to rest. After a day in the office, I was back in fighting form by Friday. The Company was complaining that striking members were harassing contractors even though the Company had set up separate doors for the contractors, which was legal. I visited several work locations where there had been complaints. The strikers readily admitted talking to the contractors who were, in the eyes of the strikers, scabbing across the picket lines. The strikers said they were simply telling the contractors that the work they were doing belonged to the strikers and in response the contractors freely agreed to go home and not work.

Chapter 35: Meeting with Advance Team from White House

I met with First Lady Rosalynn Carter's advance team lead by Ruth Berry. We discussed the logistics of Mrs. Carter's trip to Johnson City on Friday, October 9th. Who should be invited, protocol, getting a good turnout for the $50 per plate luncheon, and a public meeting dedicating the Johnson City transit system.

In planning the receiving line at the Tri-Cities airport for Mrs. Carter, I placed Local President Freeman and two Central Labor Counsel presidents at the end of the receiving line, behind 24 dignitaries chosen for this honor. The receiving line was transmitted to Washington and much to my surprise the White House pushed the three labor leaders up to numbers 12, 13, and 14. I was informed that labor had worked hard for President Carter and deserved better recognition.

There were no negotiations going on in any of the United units so we held a series of 4 meetings to boost the moral of members and bring them up to date as to where we were. At these meetings I urged the members to show up at Mrs. Carter's dedication of the transit system and we would have a place of honor for them.

The October 5 headlines read:

OPTIMISM FADES FOR QUICK END TO PHONE STRIKE

"Hope for an early end to the five-day-old strike of United of Tennessee is beginning to fade. Company and Union negotiators remain absent from the bargaining table. Each waiting shifts in the others positions that could justify a resumption of contract talks. Spokesman for both sides said no negotiation sessions are on the horizon. Richard Lawson, Public Relations Officer for United said, "Overall, both striking and none striking employees are handling themselves in a very professional manner." There had been about a half-dozen reports of minor picket line incidents in the Tri-Cities area. Only one involved violence, while others appeared to be indications of normal strike tensions. The one violent incident involved the injury of a CWA officer in Bristol. The Union officer alleges the husband of a striking employee swerved his vehicle at him brushing his hand with the side-view mirror."

On October 6 at 2:00 a.m. a cable carrying federal aviation circuits for the FAA, which controlled commercial and military air traffic, was shot causing a serious service outage. United seized upon this incident to start parlaying all cable troubles as acts of vandalism.

The October 7 headlines read:

PHONE WORKERS DENY CABLE VANDALISM LINKED TO STRIKE

"Strike-torn United Telephone Co. Continued to be plagued by vandalism yesterday, with cables in Kingsport and Churchill the latest targets of gunfire. Five incidents of vandalism have caused damage to cables Friday night and yesterday. The latest incidents brought to twelve the number of damaged cables found since early Friday morning. Gunshots have been responsible for nearly all of the damage, according to

John Brooks, United's public relations manager.

"CWA Union officers have denied any involvement in the vandalism by striking employees. "This goes on every day of the year", said CWA leader Calvin Patrick. "You've got wet cables, you've got cables shot, dug up by farmers, bulldozers, residents putting up fences, etc. This is part of the wear and tear of being a Telephone Company." Brooks said yesterday the Company posted a $500 reward for information leading to the arrest and conviction of "those responsible for the damage to the FAA cable." 'According to Brooks United formally requested the Union stop picketing designated contractor gates to Company buildings. The Union's code-a-phone Friday informed members of the request, saying the strikers "must stop" picketing the designated contractors gates. The tape concludes: "Let's continue to have a peaceful strike and we will be successful."

Chapter 36: Political Involvement Helps Cause

October 9: Everything went well at Rosalynn Carter's airport reception. The luncheon was a sell out with 900 democrats including 200 members of labor, many from CWA.

When we rode the metro bus system to the dedication ceremony, much to my delight, thousands were waiting for the First Lady. Over 150 CWA members, all with yellow CWA caps, were up front just to the left of the speaker's stand. After the dedication, First Lady Rosalynn Carter went directly to them, shaking a sea of out stretched hands. The T V cameras were rolling. The Speaker of the House in the Tennessee Legislature[15] and I rode the twenty-five minute trip back to the airport with Mrs. Carter. When she departed, the Speaker looked at me and chuckled because there was so much visibility for CWA. We congratulated each other on such a good day for East Tennessee democrats. Many local, mostly republican politicians however, had raised eyebrows as to how CWA was able to have a roped off area for striking employees in front of the Speaker rostrum. They had better seats than the politicians, especially in light of the dedication ceremony logistics being under the control of the Republicans. No one ever told them how it happened.

We had scored a public relations victory.

---

[15] Later Tennessee Governor Ned McWherter 1987-1995

Chapter 37: Can't Allow the Company to Win Media War!

Headlines on October 8th read:

VANDALS SHOOT CABLE

October 9: After returning from the airport it was back to business. I was determined not to let the Company win the war in the media although in my experiences it had never been done. I convinced Local 10871's Executive Board to match United's reward by posting a $500 reward for information leading to the arrest and conviction of the persons responsible for shooting the FAA cable. A press release was issued and received good coverage in the media, but the headlines kept coming.

October 10, 1979   Kingsport Times Editorial

Phone Strike and the Economy
"The telephone strike is heating up, and the two sides seem stalemated in their negotiations. Unless there is a breakthrough soon, it could be several months before a settlement is reached. This does not bode well for the region's economy for several reasons, including the primary need to maintain critical telephone service.
To understand the dispute, one needs to know where the two sides stand.
United Inter-Mountain has proposed wage increases of 9.3 percent in the first year, 8 percent in the second and 8.35 percent in the third. This offer exceeds anti-inflation guidelines established by President Carter, and would cost the Company $1.3 million in the

first year of the new contract.

The Union has rejected the offer and is asking for an additional cost-of-living factor that would come into play if the consumer price index rose one percent above the Company's offer. The Union is asking for a 0.8 percent rise for every one percent rise in consumer prices. The Company has said it will not incorporate a cost-of-living factor in a settlement.

Leaders of the Union say they would have accepted lower base wage increases (within Mr. Carter's guidelines) if a cost-of-living factor had been included to provide "protection" for the workers. Now, of course, they are demanding the cost-of-living guarantees plus the Company's higher wage offers.

It would be wrong to choose sides on the wage issue alone, however, for there are more parts to the package as it rests on the table.

For example, the Company has agreed to pay 85 percent of a complete medical insurance package instead of 75 percent. The Union wants 100 percent Company sponsorship. Automobile mileage allowances would rise from 12 cents a mile to 15 cents in the first year of the pact, and 16 cents in the second year.

The time of employment needed to qualify for various levels of vacation would be dropped by a year (four weeks after 17 years at the top end). Life insurance for each employee would rise 75 percent to $14,000 from $8,000.

Employees also receive a "commuting allowance" that is paid when a worker must travel from his primary city of employment (say, Kingsport) to another city (say, Bristol). That would rise to $12 from $8 a day. The Company also pays a meal allowance if an employee has to work during the day in another city, and that would rise to $12 from $10.

Finally, the Company has offered to pay 50 percent of each employee's local phone bill instead of the present 40 percent.

The payroll for the striking workers has been running about $15 million a year. This means the Company is saving $1.25 million a month while the strike continues. Even with added overtime costs for hourly workers who are not striking, the Company is saving a bundle while the strike continues.

By far the most difficult factor in this strike for customers in this region to swallow is the fact that the Communication Workers of America indirectly tie this strike by 1,200 workers here to another strike against a United Company in New Jersey. In that strike, some 80 employees are involved. Union leaders here acknowledged, "A settlement there could lead to movement here." This "solidarity for our brothers and sisters" gambit is ludicrous and should be dropped.

The Union's differences are with this United Company, and the issues should be settled here.

It also is important for the Company to reject the Union contention that while the contract proposals advanced by the Company already may provide terms far superior to what most employees in this area receive, they are not equal to what CWA workers receive elsewhere. Yet the CWA has members in places like New York and Chicago, where wage agreements are astronomical. To compare those agreements with one sought in this region is not appropriate. Finally, there is the question of violence and harassment. Already there have been cables shot out, tires slashed and other incidents. Union leaders say on one hand that this sort of thing happens all year. Yet on the other hand they say that the Union members are Company employees, as if to blame the Company. Both arguments are spurious and lack credibility.

As the strike drags on, it is imperative that Union leaders make it clear to their members that violence cannot be tolerated. After all it is not the Company being hurt by these acts it is the community. Telephone service is a vital link in our society and disruption cannot be tolerated simply to make a bargaining point.

It would appear that the Company has offered a fair package and should be a basis for settlement. The public must remember that the cost of any settlement will ultimately be passed along in rate increases, so a fair and just settlement is in the public's interest.

The cost-of-living issue also is critical to the public because it would build in more inflation, which is what this country does not need. Hopefully, the final package accepted by the Union will recognize this."

The October 10 headlines read

CABLES DAMAGED BY VANDALS

It is a normal routine during telephone strikes for a Company to list all telephone outages and give the press a list of troubles on a daily basis. If there has been damage where the cause is not immediately known or a cable has been shot it is automatically vandalism. After one report of vandalism then the press plays up the vandalism. I was determined to stop this type of reporting. I called a Company representative and ask them to stop giving press releases about vandalism unless they knew that members were causing the damage. If they did not stop, I was going to be forced to say some things I preferred not to say because it may cause harm later and we had to live together when this strike was over.

The October 11 headline read:
PHONE CABLES THE TARGETS OF VANDALS

The article did mention both Company and Union rewards if the vandals were caught.

October 12: Jeff Lowe, a CWA member, responded in "letters to editor" "---The causes of cable damages are many from storms to deliberate destruction. The implication of CWA is an easy answer. The correct and hard answer has rarely made headlines. I personally average repairing two gunshot cables per week during hunting season."---

The Company had serious maintenance problems. There were letters to the editors every week criticizing them. I believed we could get public support turned our way. I decided I was going to respond with a press release.

The headlines kept coming:
VANDALS USE FIRE TO DESTROY MORE PHONE COMPANY LINES

The paper dutifully reported the Company's account of the previous days vandalism and then turned to my response.

"In a related development Calvin Patrick East Tennessee Director of CWA commended United "for advising the public of so-called acts of vandalism. It is unfortunate that they chose the time when there is a labor dispute to began making these matters public." Patrick said, "The Company has started a program the public should demand they continue on a regular basis and expand to include the number of outages of five telephones or more caused by rain, lightning or equipment failure. "I believe by doing this public service the public will see many of their problems are reoccurring and there should be a way for the Company to make permanent repairs."

A Company spokesman responded; "It has always been Company policy to publicize service outages of any significance to make the public aware of why they are having trouble."

There were no more press releases by the Company about vandalism.

Chapter 38: "Settle Before United of Indiana Contract Terminates."

On October 12th Mendoza advised me to set up a meeting with the Company. He wanted to settle the strike before the United of Indiana contract terminated at midnight October 14th.

I contacted Jack Gaddis and requested a meeting. After checking with other Company officials Gaddis advised me the Company could not meet before Monday, October 15th because Company spokesman, Attorney Ed Norris, was out of town.

I called Mendoza and advised him of the Company's answer and suggested that if we were going to have a meeting it would have to be forced by United Headquarters in Kansas City. I advised Mendoza that, in my view, United of Tennessee would not take kindly to Kansas City forcing them to meet, but if President Watts wanted the meeting I was sure he could have it arranged.

October 13: Mendoza called and said: "Kansas City is telling President Watts that a COLA is not in the picture this year. President Watts has modified our position and wants us back at the bargaining table today." Officials in Kansas City had already advised Mendoza that Watts had not moved much.

I called Jack Gaddis requesting a meeting. After checking he advised that the Company committee would be unavailable until Monday October 15th. I called Mendoza and advised him that the Company could not meet. I reminded him that Watts had given our position to Kansas City and to me it was a sign of weakness to push for an early meeting just because the contract was terminating in Indiana. Mendoza agreed stating: "the ball is in Kansas Cities court".

2:00 p.m. Sunday October 14 Mendoza called and gave me a new negotiation position. (The second change without a response from Kansas City.) He had talked to officials in Kansas City and they wanted me to get with United of Tennessee informally and make a modified offer to "soften them up."

Jack Gaddis agreed to meet me at a restaurant. We had coffee and discussed what had been going on. He said, "we should write a book when this strike is over. I responded, "There had been a lot of unusual twist that I had never before experienced." We made a lighthearted commitment that we would write the book when we were not in a position of being fired.

I then advised him I would place a modified proposal on the table if problems could be worked out in the other United units.

1. A 24-month contract.
2. 10 percent wages at the go-down.
3. 9 percent at the first anniversary.
4. If the Cost-of-living exceeds 12 percent at the first anniversary, we want a wage re-opener.
5. The agreed-to dental plan must be effective at the go-down.
6. Hospitalization
　　80 percent of premium paid by the Company at the go-down.
　　85 percent paid effective January 1, 1980
　　90 percent paid effective September 30, 1980.
7. Savings fund check-off. We would agree that we would not ask the Company to make a contribution to the fund in future negotiations.
8. All negotiated benefits that were to be effective in the third year must be within the life of the two-year agreement.
9. September 30,1981 would be the termination date.

Gaddis said he would give me a response on Monday.

At 7:20 p.m. I received a call from the Unions chief negotiator in United of Indiana, Grover Cantrell. Cantrell said he was waiting on United of Norfork, Tennessee, Carolina, and New Jersey to set the pattern. It was his understanding that Indiana was to strike but he had not been told to pull the plug yet.

Cantrell wanted to know how the strike was going. I advised him that in Tennessee we had 90 percent membership when we went out and it had now increased to 96 percent. In Carolina it wasn't going as well. Over 1000 out of 3200 employees were crossing the picket lines.

Cantrell wished us well saying he was waiting on Mendoza to make a decision regarding Indiana striking.

At 12 midnight, President Watts extended the Indiana contract for one day.

On October 15, at 10:15 a.m. Jack Gaddis called me. He advised that the Company had reviewed our proposal and rejects it as totally unacceptable. He said, "United in Kansas City was standing by their final offer".

At 12:15 p.m. I advised Mendoza that United of Tennessee had rejected the Union's proposal. He said he would get back to me.

At 6:15 p.m. Mendoza called and said that President Watts was very upset because we were not negotiating over the weekend. "Watts was saying that the Company must make some change that is different from the offer on the table when the strike was called. Otherwise we strike in Indiana."

Mendoza said he was going to make another modified offer to Kansas City. He would delete the reference to the wage re-opener and modify the hospitalization insurance proposal as to when each increase would kick in. The savings fund and dental plan could be delayed but still had to be implemented within the life of the two-year agreement. He said that if Kansas City would agree to this modified proposal, then the Union would drop its request for a wage re-opener, and any reference to a COLA. He would also extend the contract in Indiana. If Kansas City refused this offer then Indiana would strike.

I said to myself, this is the third change without a response from Kansas City. They don't have to be too smart to know the Union is showing a sign of weakness.

10:30 p.m. Mendoza called and advised he had made the offer to Kansas City. They had requested that we extend the contract in Indiana for 24 hours so that they could study the offer. Mendoza was very firm saying: "If there is no progress within the next twenty-four hours we will strike in Indiana." Mendoza felt there were good vibrations coming from Kansas City regarding the offer and said: "there may be movement".

Tuesday, October 16,
Newspapers summed up the status of negotiations.

"An attempt to re-open contract talks between United of Tennessee and CWA failed yesterday when the Company's personnel director rejected a revised contract proposal offered by the Union.

Calvin Patrick, CWA Director for East Tennessee, and Jack Gaddis, United's Human Resources Director, met informally Sunday to discuss the Unions latest proposal. It marked the first change in either side's bargaining position since September 30, the last day negotiations were held. Patrick said the proposal could lead to an agreement if the Company agreed to its terms.

"Gaddis rejected the proposal as "totally unacceptable" at noon yesterday. Patrick would not comment on the Unions offer except to say it was "a substantial change from our original bargaining position. "I don't think it would be conducive to the collective bargaining process to say how I felt," he said.

At 5:00 p.m. October 16, Delbert Gordon, the Unions chief negotiator in United of Carolina, called. He said he had several items in the third year of the agreement that he could not get Carolina to move into the second year. He said the Company was hanging tough.

At 8:30 p.m. Mendoza called, advising me that Indiana was in a position to reach a 2-year agreement. He told Kansas City that we must have everything compressed into a two-year agreement in Norfork, Tennessee, and Carolina by midnight tomorrow or Indiana is going to strike, even though they are in a position to settle.

Mendoza said he was sure Kansas City had conveyed this message to Jack Gaddis in Tennessee and that I should be getting a call soon.

11:00 p.m. I called Mendoza and advised him I had not received a call from Gaddis. He said he would call Kansas City.

11:45 p.m. Gaddis called me and requested we meet at 8:30 a.m. He said he was meeting only because Kansas City had requested it and he was telling me up front: "I'm not very happy being forced to meet."

THE COMPANY STONEWALLS

At 8:30 a.m. October 17 Gaddis and I met at a cafe for breakfast. Gaddis expressed concern about the "old man" being very upset about Mendoza's tactics. I kidded him again about the hurricane and the fact that no one believed me. With a sarcastic chuckle Gaddis said: You S.O.B. Gaddis then made an offer for a two-year agreement:
1. A 10 percent wage increase at the go-down.
2. A nine percent increase at the first anniversary.

3. Hospitalization; 80 percent of the premium paid by the Company at the go-down, 85 percent effective January 1,1980. The Company would not go to 90 percent during the two-year agreement.

4. The dental plan would take effect at the first anniversary.

5. No CWA savings fund check off.

6. The Company must take back the five language items they previously agreed to. (This would really anger the bargaining committee)

    a. Call-outs, pay would be limited to one hour.

    b. Entry level jobs: The Company wanted to be able to hire from the street without considering present employees for those jobs in 7 Job categories.

    c. There would be no pay for the Local vice president while handling grievances. (Had previously been agreed to)

    d. Revert to allowing seniority for only 12 months for recall purposes when an employee was on layoff. (We had agreed to 24 months.)

    e. The Company was withdrawing the agreement that allowed employees with 15 or more years of service to take vacation a day at a time.

    I advised Gaddis that as far as I was concerned we could not reach agreement with the Company taking back the agreement we had reached on the 5 language items I expressed my dismay that he was trying to take his anger out on the members when they had nothing to do with placing the parties in the position we were now in, but I would pass his offer on to Washington.

    Gaddis said that he and President Hill were leaving immediately for a telephone association meeting in Virginia. This was a four-hour drive. They were planning on being away for two or three days. Gaddis said he would contact me later as to where they could be reached. At 9:40 a.m. the meeting ended.

    I notified Mendoza in Washington of the contract

offer. Mendoza said our position had not changed.

COMPANY SCORES A KNOCK-DOWN

At 11:45 a.m. Bob Carlton of WJHL-TV called and said that United of Tennessee had issued a press release that was a very strong story and he did not feel CWA would want to ignore it, especially since there are wage price controls and the Company is saying that they have over 31 percent on the table.

I told Carlton I would get back to him. After several telephone calls I confirmed that the Company had communicated to the employees and the public about the final offer of September 30. The Company statement read:

> October 17, 1979 "It is indeed unfortunate that CWA has a package worth over 31 percent on the table but has refused to allow the members to vote on it and has forced them to the street."

It was now very obvious why Gaddis had been so negative and had placed the retrogressive proposals on the table. They were being forced to the table by CWA and Kansas City and now they were angry at both Kansas City and CWA in Washington.

We had mutiny within the bargaining unit. The members exploded against the Union for not putting the package out for a ratification vote. The Company had scored a knockdown.

4:00 p.m. No word from Gaddis. He wasn't going to call.

I had no choice but to hit the Company hard in the media. I started hitting 5 television stations, called 15 radio stations, and gave interviews to three daily newspapers and the wire services.

Television and the newspapers carried my statement.

"Since United of Tennessee has chosen to exploit the rejected agreement with the public, the Company must answer some questions. Our members were told prior to the agreement that if the Company were honest they would place the last nickel on the table to prevent a strike; therefore a strike would be useless. The Company told us "the last nickel was in the bucket."

"Kansas City dictated to this Company that they must hold back to save money, but when our members voted to strike, Kansas City tried to buy our members vote by putting more money in the bucket.

"Forbes Magazine says that United Telecommunications has more profit per employee than A.T.& T. $6,000 as compared to $5,400 for A.T.& T. Based on the above the Company must explain why our members have fewer dollars in benefits on the table than our brothers and sisters in United of Carolina and Indiana. As examples, more holidays, better vacations, improved pensions, and a savings plan check off that cost the Company nothing.

"United of Tennessee must explain to the public what is happening to all that revenue. Is Kansas City skimming the cream? Why are telephone bills higher here than in neighboring telephone companies? Also, why are our members making 75 cents to one dollar per hour less than the neighboring companies employees?"

While I was in the mood I responded with a "letter to the editor", to an October 10 editorial in the Kingsport Times-News, where they had devoted 26 inches of editorial space criticizing CWA for our strike against United when the Company's offer exceeded President Carter's Wage guidelines and "CWA continues to insist on a (COLA)", cost-of-living allowance. They raised a number of issues that were misleading and my letter addressed them

8:00 p.m. No word from Gaddis. Mendoza called

and said that United of Carolina is in a position to reach an agreement and is waiting on Tennessee.

Mendoza again advised that even though we were in a position to settle in Indiana we would strike tonight unless an agreement is reached everywhere.

11:00 p.m. The Unions chief negotiator in Indiana, Grover Cantrell, called me saying he had not heard from anyone since yesterday and was wondering "what the hell was going on", as he was scheduled to strike at 6:00 a.m.

11:45 p.m. Mendoza called. He said that Kansas City wants to extend the Indiana contract for another 24 hours and President Watts has agreed to extend until midnight October 18th. Mendoza said; "there will be no more extensions after that because the members in Indiana are anxious, not knowing what is going on in negotiations and are saying they want a contract or strike."

12:00 midnight. No word from Gaddis.

7:00 a.m. October 18th. Mendoza called and advised that President Watts was upset that we were not meeting with United in Tennessee at this critical moment. Indiana was being advised that we would strike tonight at midnight unless an agreement is reached in all other locations. Mendoza said I was supposed to hear from Gaddis soon.

1:45 p.m. Mendoza called Kansas City again and asked them to have Gaddis call me. Mendoza said he was getting twitchy and was afraid that someone would let the cat out of the bag that COLA was not an issue any more. (The membership had been told nothing and felt this was still the stumbling block in reaching an agreement.)

The pressure had now switched to United in Tennessee and me. New Jersey, Norfork, Indiana, and Carolina were now waiting on us and Mendoza had become concerned.

Anger and frustration was building in the United of Tennessee bargaining committee. Our committee had advised Mendoza on October 30th that they felt the Company had bought a contract, but they would follow the Union leadership in seeking a COLA. Now there was no possibility of a COLA and every bargaining unit but United of Tennessee was ready to reach agreement. To add to the insult, United of Tennessee was angry with CWA in Washington and United in Kansas City. "They now are trying to take from the members what we had agreed to before the strike started".

THE COMPANY: "WE'VE GOT TO HAVE THOSE LANGUAGE ITEMS!"

2:35 p.m. Jack Gaddis called. There was no small talk, straight to business. "We must have those 5 language items if we are going to reach an agreement". He said very briskly.

Patrick: "Jack, the only one of the five items that you have given a legitimate business reason for changing is in reducing the call-out from 2 hours to 1 hour, in the event an employee is still on Company premises and you ask them to return to work. That makes enough business sense that we will reluctantly agree to modify that item. But with the other 4 items, you haven't given us a reason for changing your position."

Gaddis: "Bargaining is a two way street. It's give and take, and we have given and given and given."

In my mind I was concerned that our members were on the street fighting for a COLA and we were not even discussing it. The bargaining committee was frustrated because of the real problems since the Company had exploited the offer that was on the table when we struck. I was thankful that the Company had waited so long. If I had been in their shoes I would have gone public the first day of the strike communicating with the members driving a wedge deep between them and CWA. President Hill in United of Tennessee was angry at the way Kansas City was pushing him. Everyone was ready to settle but us. Should we continue to hold out or modify our proposal to make Hill feel better about getting something out of bargaining and possibly keep from loosing the members if the Company kept up the pressure? I made a decision it would be in the best interest of the members, that if we had to, we would modify our proposal to some extent to get the members back to work.

Patrick: "Jack, we have come too far to let these 4 items previously agreed to, stand in the way of reaching an agreement.

Gaddis: "What has the Company gotten from negotiations?"

Patrick: "If you've got a good productive labor force that feels good about their employer you've got a hell of a lot out of it. I've taken a lot of flack, even during this strike, telling the employees things are changing for the better in this Company. That doesn't make me popular and I get criticized for it from many members. Now I feel you are attacking me trying to renege on the 4 items."

Gaddis: "It's not an attack on you."

Patrick: "Then who are you retaliating against? Is it President Watts?"

Gaddis: "No."

Patrick: "Then it's an attack on the members."

Gaddis: "We agreed to those 5 items after a lot of sole searching, but now it is a new ball game."

Patrick: "Jack, it is not fair to take away pay for the Vice President when he is meeting on grievances, because this Local, after so many years, is working with me to build a responsible relationship with this Company. Local President Freeman told me two weeks ago, since the strike started, he would never have believed we could have come so far, with the maturity and mutual respect these two committees have for each other.

Gaddis: "I believe that."

Patrick: "I had to sell them as much as I had to sell the

Company committee. Now you want to gut me and the bargaining committee. We've come too far to go backwards."

Gaddis: "We've got to have something."

Patrick: "Jack, the entire country is waiting on us to reach an agreement. For the sake of all the employees in every bargaining unit without consulting with anyone I'll take the responsibility of one more compromise. I'll add to the modified call-out, the withdrawal of the day-at-a-time vacation since the use of this section is under your discretion as to when an employee can get the vacation day. But Jack, this is an advantage to you as well as the employee. I ask you not to take it, but if it will save your pride, your foolish pride, I'll withdraw that agreement."

Gaddis: "The Company is putting a lot of money in this contract."

Patrick: "Jack, it's just your foolish pride. What you want is not based on sound business principles."

Gaddis: "It's like this, if we are going to get an agreement we are going to have something in return. If, however, you will accept a 3-year agreement, then these items would not be an issue.

Patrick: "Jack, I have no choice. Everyone in the nation is ready to sign off on a 2-year agreement except us."

Gaddis: "Well, I've been telling you about that petition that is circulating. The employees wanted to vote on the last offer that we made before the strike began. We can wait until the petition reaches Watts. The longer this strike goes on the employees are going to get tired of Washington telling them what to do. They will get tired of striking for Carolina and New Jersey. Some are tired already."

(*I thought to myself, If only our members knew how they frustrate the bargaining process and undercut themselves by doing such things. But then too, they have a right to be angry.*)

Patrick: "Jack, you've been out of pocket. New Jersey, Norfork, Carolina and Indiana are waiting for us to settle. They are in a position to reach a 2-year agreement. That is why I'm willing to offer you the two language items to settle."

Gaddis: "No, they are not ready to settle."

Patrick: "Jack, you better check with your people. Tennessee is now dragging hind tit. At 1:45 p.m. this afternoon it was again confirmed to me, everyone is ready to settle but us."

Gaddis: "Today?"

Patrick: "Yes. The only problems are here in Tennessee. All other units are ready to reach an agreement."

Gaddis: "Then let's get an agreement."

Patrick: "Jack, do you remember that hurricane? It doesn't work that way anymore."

Gaddis:" You and your dam hurricane!! Ha, ha."

Patrick: "Jack, you better look at the number of employees who have crossed the picket line. You know we only have 90 percent membership but 96 percent of the employees are honoring the picket lines."

Gaddis: "What will it take to settle the strike?"

Patrick: "Modify your proposal of October 17th at 8:30 a.m. by:
1. Granting the CWA savings plan check off.
2. Paying 90 percent of the hospital premium within 18 months.
3. Withdraw the retrogression by granting the 3 language items
   previously agreed to:
a. Payment for the Vice President meeting on grievances.
b. Maintain the agreed to restrictions on entrance level jobs. (Hiring from the street.)
c. Employees will have return rights for recall after layoffs for 24 months.

In return we will give up the modified call-out and the day at a time vacation."

Gaddis. "Will you come off the November 30th termination date?" Patrick: "I have no control over that item. Whatever Washington decides, let's see what is happening in the other Companies."

Gaddis: "Calvin you've got to give me some of these language items. My people feel very strong about them."

Patrick: "Jack, I've offered to give up two items of language, but that is the bottom line."

Gaddis: "Let's go to 18 months on recall after layoff."

Patrick: "Dam it Jack, we are not going to do that!!"

Gaddis: Well hell!! That is a compromise, and at the next negotiations we can improve it some more."

There was a long pause---------.

Gaddis: "The next time, before negotiations start, you and I are going to hold a meeting with your boys in Washington and my guys in Kansas City and tell them to stay the hell out of our business."

Patrick: "Jack, I told you on June 22nd to be a leader. You did not lead. I told you a hurricane was coming. Had you listened to me and come with the package we asked for we would have an agreement but----"

Gaddis: "Yea, I know."

We both chuckled.

Gaddis: "Could we modify the entrance level jobs and place some of those we removed back as entrance level."

A long discussion ensued and in an effort to reach an agreement I agreed to modify the entrance level proposal provided the bargaining committee would agree.

Gaddis: "Will the Union give me the assurance that you will work to cut grievances in half?"

Patrick: "Jack, we will do our best. Freeman wants to train his stewards and officers on the contract. I will give that commitment. However, we are going to process every grievance that has merit and, by the way, your supervisors have total control over grievances depending on how they conduct themselves. So you have most of the control of grievances. You've been talking about what the Union was giving up. Now lets talk about what the Union is getting in return." The CWA savings fund check-off.

Gaddis: "Wait a minute!! Wait a minute!! We've got a legal problem. I don't know if I can sell the Boss or not, and even if I can, you will have to provide a "hold harmless clause". I'm going to be trying. He hasn't agreed to the 90 percent payment of the hospital premium either."

Patrick: "These items are a must. The bottom line, we are going to have them."

Gaddis: "I know where you are coming from."

Patrick: "We have the dental plan, 10 percent in wages at the go-down, and 9 percent at the first anniversary."

Gaddis: "The wages would be effective upon ratification with no retro-activity. We told you that early on."

Patrick: "We don't believe a damn thing you say after you told us you had the last nickel on the table on September 24th."

Gaddis: "You son of a bitch!!!!"

Patrick: "Ha, Ha, Ha. And another thing, you placed the 9.3 percent raise into effect so we don't need your retro-activity since the members are on strike and it would only go to the scabs."

Gaddis: "Where is that relationship you wanted to build? That is a hell of a way to destroy it."

We both got a good laugh.

Gaddis: "You and I are going to write a book when this is over."

Patrick: "There will be no penalty for strike activity regarding benefits and seniority because the members have been so good."

Gaddis: "I'm going to have problems with this one."

Patrick: "Now Jack, as much as we have done since you've been here in Tennessee, we've come a long way since December 4, 1978; the famous day when we started removing the cancer: Our helping get the vice president of public relations moved. Boy, that was a mistake the way you have been trying to beat us in the news media and the demotion of the human resources director and the others that we have sidetracked. All these problems are now out of our way to a better relationship. Jack, you owe it to us not to punish the members by taking away their seniority and benefits for the strike period."
Gaddis: "Jesus Christ!!!!!!!"
Patrick: "We've come a long way, Jack."
Gaddis: "Yes, we've come a long way."
Patrick: "Jack, I wish you had been here two and a half years ago. You just can't realize the turmoil we've been through and how far we have come. The restoral of the employees' seniority should be a gift from President Hill. I know he doesn't have an obligation to do this but this will be a signal to the employees. I believe Mr. Hill will do it, and I will commit to tell the employees what I've said."
Gaddis: "That is a commitment from you?"
Patrick: "Yes it is."
Gaddis: "OK. Well I've got to get with President Hill. He is upset at how we've been forced to the table. I'll try to get back with you before 5:00 p.m."
Patrick: "Jack, we are very close. Let's wrap this up tonight."
Gaddis: "I'll call you."

Chapter 39 : Ups and Downs of Continued Negotiations

I called Mendoza and brought him up to date. Mendoza responded rather indignantly "they want their pound of flesh and that pisses me off". Mendoza instructed me to go back to the normal termination date of August 23rd, if this would keep from holding up an agreement.

I said to myself, "well, there goes Mendoza's strategy of dragging contracts to seek a common termination date."

Mendoza said that President Watts wanted to know if we felt there would be problems with the committees in agreeing to go back to work. If so, he was going to call a meeting in Washington of all bargaining committees in all companies.

I responded that the United of Tennessee committee went out because the President asked them to and I was sure they would do what was best for the members. I did not see the need for a meeting as far as we were concerned.

Mendoza said that it looked good. The other units were holding, waiting on Tennessee. He said, "I'll update them and get back to you before 6:00 p.m."

I felt badly about modifying the two Items of language and giving up one of the other items. But my greater concern was the Union's position and the repercussions it would cause should the members realize where Mendoza had led them, especially in light of the Company's publicizing the 31 percent package that had never been presented to the members.

I discussed our position with the bargaining committee. They were reluctant to go with giving up the one language item and modifying the other two. They said it would mean going back to work with less than they had when the strike started. Yet they realized Indiana would be striking for Tennessee if we didn't reach an agreement.

Reluctantly they agreed to go along since we were holding up the Nation.

At 4:55 p.m. Jack Gaddis called from Virginia. "Calvin, the old man is tough to negotiate with but he is coming around. Everything is OK, including the savings fund check-off but it will not go into effect until the 23rd month of the agreement. He will give seniority credit for the strikers but he won't pay for the Vice President meeting on grievances. With that exception, my friend, we have an agreement. We can put these people back to work and start doing the things we need to do."

I responded, "ain't that the truth. Well, I'll have to get back to you after I talk to my committee, I don't think the committee will accept no pay for the Vice President. I am very negative about it myself but will let them decide. Where can I reach you?"

"At the Landmark Hotel."

At 5:00 p.m. I called Mendoza and gave him the Company's position.

Mendoza said, "So he wants to extract more blood by not paying the Vice President for handling grievances?"

I responded, "Yes, and in my view we should not let him have it. We've bent over backwards to reach an agreement but enough is enough."

Mendoza said, "He may blow this agreement out of the water." I responded, "I want to tell him that we don't have an agreement."

Mendoza said: "OK, tell him he's blowing everything out of the water."

MISUNDERSTANDING CAUSES CONFUSION

After I touched bases with the bargaining committee I called Gaddis, "Damn you Jack, we are going to blow it. You have pushed and pushed and pushed. We've got to have the

Local Vice Presidents pay and the CWA savings fund check off must come in the first 12 months of the agreement. We've both compromised and have come a long way."

Gaddis responded, "Well!! You are right; we both have come a long way. Ok is that all that is holding us up."

I said: "Yes. Jack lets get this thing wrapped up tonight so that I can have some good sleep for the first time in 3 months. Jack, its time to be a leader, damn it."

You just don't know. You just don't know. Let me think about it and get back to you. Where can I reach you?" "I'll be with the bargaining committee here at the Ramada Inn."

Gaddis, "I'll get back."

5:35 p.m. I called Mendoza and advised him I felt the Company would come on the Vice Presidents pay handling grievances and the CWA savings fund check off.

Mendoza said, "We are so close I don't think Indiana should strike tonight."

7:15 p.m. Gaddis called. "We are holding firm on the savings fund check off kicking it in on the twenty-third month of the agreement. Calvin I think we are there!"

I asked, "You are going with me on the Vice Presidents pay handling grievances."

Gaddis exclaimed. "Wait a minute!! Wait a minute!!"

"Damn you Jack, don't start backing up.

Gaddis responded, "I'm not backing up. When you came to me at 5:25 p.m., the only issue was the savings fund. I assumed you had come off the Vice Presidents pay."

I said, "Jack I told you we had two issues. The Vice Presidents pay and the CWA savings fund check off."

Gaddis, very firmly: "No.-- Nope that is not my understanding."

"Jack, damn it, that's the way it is. I'm looking at my notes."

"Calvin I'm looking at my notes too. At 4:55 p.m. I

told you, no deal, on the Vice Presidents pay."

"Jack that is true, but when I responded just before hanging up at 5:00 p.m. I told you I would let the committee make the decision on agreeing with your 4:55 p.m. proposal. I'll be dammed."

Gaddis responded, "I'll be dammed to. Unless I'm completely deaf, I had a note there was only the savings fund check off."

"No! Hell no!! That's not true. You had your mind on what you told me and apparently did not listen very well. Well it's still on the table and we are going to have it."
Gaddis responded. "Ok then it's on the table and we reject it and we are at an impasse. We aren't going to pay for the Local Vice President meeting on grievances. We've given to dam much."

I said. "I suggest we start repeating ourselves. You are holding firm for the savings fund check off to kick in the twenty-third month."

"Right".

"You haven't said anything else?"

Gaddis, "I've responded to the item we had hanging."

"Jack, you stated your position on the Local Vice Presidents pay at 4:55 p.m., even IF I had been silent I did not concede the Vice Presidents pay. Therefore, it was never taken from the table even under your understanding of what had transpired since 4:55 p.m."
Gaddis "Ok! Ok! If you want to correct it, fine, it's on the table."
Patrick "Well it's on the table and a bone of contention."
Gaddis: "So we have two issues the Local Vice Presidents pay while handling grievances and the savings check off." I responded. "Right and I'll get back to you."

I reported to Mendoza on the misunderstanding and the position we were taking. The bargaining committee was very upset because of the Company's insistence on not paying the Vice President for meeting on grievances. I told Mendoza there is no way we can give in on this item as a matter of principle.

Mendoza said we might have to live with the savings plan kicking in on the twenty-third month. I was relieved when he agreed that we must have the Vice Presidents pay when handling grievances.

Mendoza, thinking the Company would give in on the Vice Presidents pay during grievance meetings, made plans for all bargaining committees to go to Washington to work out a back to work agreement. When he called back to advise of the arrangements he said he did not believe Watts would hold up the agreement to get the Company to grant the Local Vice Presidents pay. It was with great difficulty that I kept my composure.

I responded. "This Local committee is very upset. We've conceded more than we should have, trying to reach an agreement because we knew how President Watts felt and the fact that every other bargaining table is waiting on us. Maybe the Company has taken our concern as a sign of weakness. Now the local committee is saying to hell with the SOB's. They are trying to take advantage of us. I agree with the Local. We went out because you and the President wanted a COLA and contracts to have a common termination dates. Well those issues are down the drain but this committee, including me, is asking President Watts to support us now. Otherwise we are going back to work with a lot less than we had when the strike started."

Mendoza had nothing helpful to say.

I attempted to call Gaddis several times. He and President Hill had left the hotel with their wives and had a leisure dinner and drank a bottle of champagne, toasting the new agreement, as they knew we would give in on the Vice Presidents pay.

NO MORE BLOOD!! THAT'S IT!!

10:50 p.m. Gaddis called and asked where we stood.
I responded. "Everyone is inflamed over the Local Vice Presidents pay including Local President Freeman."
Gaddis. "Freeman has got to understand it's a new ball game."
"Jack, by God it's not a new ball game."
Gaddis. We've stretched and stretched and it's a give and take proposition."
"Give and take hell!!! You know very well we would have had an agreement way back if you had come with what's on the table now."
Gaddis. "I wasn't in a position to come then."
I said. "You talk about being stretched, I believed you on August 24th and look where it has taken us."
Gaddis. "And so have I. You know if it had been left to me I would have come with more."
"Then lets quit talking about being stretched and get this strike over." At that point the long distance circuit went very noisy.
Gaddis. "Dammed telephone Co!! Why don't you come up here and organize them."
Patrick. "Hell, I'm tired man. I don't like organizing and having to put up with problems like you."
Gaddis. "I've rejected the Vice Presidents pay, its not going to fly. I'm telling you we need all five of those language items."
In anger I said. "Jack, I've offered you four-fifths of the candy bar, but like a greedy child you want it all. You ain't going to get any more blood from me. That's it."
Gaddis: "I'm---
"That's it Jack, you ain't going to get any of the candy bar. We are going to keep all 5 of the language items. This strike won't be settled until we have all 5. You don't want a

responsible relationship. You want blood but you have had all the blood you will ever get from me."

Gaddis: "I don't want blood."

"I've tried to give you more than any reasonable man would and now you come back and want more blood, and dam it, it's not there. You screwed up on August 24th and now you've screwed up again."

Gaddis: "Fine so you are saying the Vice Presidents pay is holding up an agreement?"

"No, I'm saying you aren't going to get a damn one of the 5 items of language. Jack, you have done it to yourself. Your Company did it to you. God knows I've gone out on a limb to be fair."

Gaddis: "We could have a dammed good relationship. I think you and Freeman are going to see it."

"Jack, I'm through talking. Here is Freeman, talk to him."

Freeman: "Jack, what the hell are you trying to do to me. I've gone the extra mile. It's the same old cancer we've been telling you about. It's still there."

Gaddis, "No, it's not. The cancer is out of the picture."

Freeman, "Then we shouldn't have the problem because these items were agreed to once."

Gaddis, "Bargaining is a two-way street. Since August 24th we have made several moves. My god man what more do you want?"

Freeman, "It took me a long time to get serious about a responsible relationship. I've had it stuck up my ass so much. I didn't believe the Company was serious. I've trusted you and Dan Luethke, and god dang it now somebody is sticking it right back where it was. I'm getting screwed anyway I go, by the Company and the Union."

Gaddis, "That's where I put the blame. If CWA Washington had stayed out of our business we would have a good contract."

Freeman, "We tried to tell you. You had more there but

didn't put it on the table."

Gaddis, "Now damn it Darrell, I didn't. You have got to believe me. If I had had more it would have been on the table."

Freeman, "How can I go to my executive board and tell them you've gone back on the agreement?"

Gaddis, "What the hell does the stewards care about the Vice President getting paid?"

Freeman, " The executive board, the stewards and the members care. They are very touchy on the Vice Presidents pay. I want to tell you. It took Calvin Patrick a long time to convince the bargaining committee that you were serious about a better relationship."

Gaddis, "We are serious. You don't know what I've been through convincing our people to go with the CWA savings fund."

Freeman, "You have got to come with the Vice Presidents pay."

Gaddis, "We can't do it, we've gone as far as we can."

Freeman, "Its a shame!"

Gaddis, "We are so close to an agreement. Those people could come back to work----Is Calvin there."

Freeman, "No he left."

Gaddis, "Ok we will leave it at that, see you later, bye."

I had had enough. My desire to get the members back to work had apparently been taken as a sign of weakness by Gaddis. I was concerned as to whether President Watts would back me, based on Mendoza's earlier statement that Watts wouldn't continue the strike for the one outstanding item. Now there were 5 items as far as I was concerned. I felt we were in a solid position to ask for continued support of the President since the Company had once agreed to these Items.

11:25 p.m. I called Mendoza and told him the agreement had fallen through. I advised him I would do as I was instructed, but in my view if we let this Company get away with taking back these 5 language items this local would be getting screwed by the Union and the Company.

Mendoza talked to Freeman, suggesting we had made some breakthroughs.

Freeman responded, not in this Local. All we have is retrogression. I say we strike the mothers until it's off the table.

Mendoza did not sound favorable, and said all the bargaining committees would be coming to Washington tomorrow.

7:00 p.m. October 19th: The bargaining committees and CWA staff representing Indiana, Norfork, New Jersey, Carolina, and Tennessee met in the CWA Executive Board room in Washington D.C.

Mendoza opened the meeting by saying he hoped everyone recognized this was a difficult corporation to deal with. "We have made some significant inroads and changed attitudes of people who make the decisions. We've demonstrated that when we put our minds to it we can work in concert with unity and discipline."

President Watts remarked that this getting together was different than the other times we were together. "Being here this evening under these circumstances, one would have to agree, began in Kansas City in June.

"We have reached a point where, in my view, we are in a position to settle the strike. Everything is not cleared up in terms of what I would say is absolutely acceptable, but we are at a point where decisions have to be made.

"I've had the opportunity to meet with a large portion of the Tennessee group before we got into this phase of negotiations and talked about the situation we were confronted with. We understood clearly from that group as well as the others what the objectives were. I pointed out that we wouldn't lead them down a primrose path and be jumping off cliffs. In my opinion we have run out of string in reaching the one objective we all had been searching for: That being an escalator clause or COLA. In my opinion it's not possible to achieve that objective in this round of negotiations; no matter how long we keep the strike underway or how many other groups we parlay in to the strike.

"While it's a difficult decision, once I became convinced in my own mind as we have proceeded, we've looked at what would be acceptable and permit us to reach an agreement that would improve on the benefits that were rejected by the Tennessee group and was in access of what most other units had anticipated, without strike action. Obviously, there have been significant improvements with a two-year contract.

Watts continued, "I'm convinced that the process has brought us to the point that during the next round of negotiations we are going to be able to go a bit further than this time.

"We need to see what is left hanging in each unit and decide what process we are going to use as we go from here."

Frank Cummings, bargaining committee member from Indiana, wanted to know whether commitments had been made with the System to terminate the strike.

Watts responded that there had been no commitments made. "We are in a position now, to clean up the outstanding items. It is in the best interest of our members to terminate the strike. All units are ready to settle except Tennessee."

A two-hour discussion ensued regarding shooting for a common termination date for all contracts, as this had been a very high priority in calling the strike. Questions were raised about the fact that no progress had been made as a result of the strike except to reach for a two-year agreement instead of a 3-year agreement.

Vice President Porch, over North Carolina, emphasized the fact that although "we did not get a COLA we would be back a year sooner and can get a catch-up raise." Porch said that "2 locals in Carolina were beginning to hurt and in another week we will be hurting a lot more. A month from now we will be crawling back and I don't want to see us in that position. The two other Georgia locals are still looking good. We won't be holding up a month from now."

Frank Cummings felt that Indiana had not had their opportunity to pay their way by participating in the strike along with their brothers and sisters.

Each chief negotiator stated that they felt they were in a position to settle.

All during the session of almost 3 hours the Tennessee delegation had remained silent. At this point I laid out our problems and then asked each of the bargaining committee members to give their feelings.

Local President Darrell Freeman, "With the retrogression on the table all I can tell our members is that the strike has cost them 3 to 4 weeks. The Local has lost 8 to 10 thousand dollars a year that it will cost us to pay the Vice president in grievances meetings."

Bob Brown and Judy Graham made it clear the members would not appreciate going back to work for less than they had when we came out.

President Watts then summed up the Unions position. "The 5 items previously agreed to by United of Tennessee must be placed back in the contract."

Mendoza asked Watts whether we must have a contract in all units or no agreement in any unit.

Watts said we must have agreements in all units, but once agreements were reached in all units and sent out for ratification, under the law each bargaining unit must vote on their own contract. If all but one unit ratifies, then that one unit will be on its own.

The Local President from New Jersey thanked everyone for their help. "Without you we would still be hopelessly out there". The 25 negotiators present gave him a very warm round of applause.

The Tennessee delegation headed for the Mayflower hotel feeling good knowing the Union would support us.

That evening in the Washington Mayflower Hotel dining room the Tennessee committee had dinner at the table next to the Carolina committee. During the course of the evening the Chief negotiator for North Carolina criticized me very heavily, saying that I had reached an agreement without approval and now when everyone else was ready to reach an agreement, that I couldn't get an agreement. Now Tennessee was holding everyone up. I did not respond.

In my mind I was thinking of Vice President Porch's remarks just an hour earlier about the two Carolina locals being in trouble and would be crawling back to work in a month and he did not want to see that happen.

At 6:30 p.m. October 20th we were back in Tennessee. Darrell Freeman and I met with Jim Gaddis and Dan Luethke at the Holiday Inn. I laid out our position. The five items were back on the table and keeping us from reaching an agreement.

Gaddis responded, "I got pissed off when you placed the Vice Presidents pay back on the table after I had rejected it. We are willing to settle on the basis of paying the Vice President, as that was all that was outstanding. That's all we are willing to give. "Kansas City ain't going to call this shot. Your proposal on reinstating all 5 items is rejected."

Dan Luethke suggested we break off for an hour or so and then get back together.

9:30 p.m. we reconvened.

Jack Gaddis, "apparently Mr. Watts is playing games. Kansas City is telling us that the only issue is the Vice Presidents pay."
Patrick, "Jack, that is not true, all 5 items are on the table."
Gaddis, "Then we are far apart."
Patrick, Then there is nothing further to discuss on that issue."

"Jack, there is another issue I need to put you on board about. Back on the 17th of October when the Company went public about the 31 percent wage increase being on the table and the members did not have an opportunity to vote on it, I wrote a letter to the editor on the same subject in response to an editorial. I want to stop that letter because it hits the Company real hard, but am unwilling to do so unless the strike can be terminated." I advised him the letter might have adverse effects on the Company when the Public Service Commission holds the hearing on their rate increase on October 30th. "In addition, if the strike is not ended I will be seeking permission to testify before the commission about service deteriorating needlessly due to the Companies reneging on previously agreed to language items." I assured Gaddis this was not a threat but a fact of life. "We are in a life and death struggle and that doesn't make sense because there are no issues between us that haven't been resolved at one time or another." I concluded.

We separated in gloom but determined to hold the Unions position.

11:25 p.m. Mendoza called and said that Kansas City had talked to Gaddis and that Gaddis was upset with Kansas City. He asked that I have no more meetings except with Gaddis and myself. "Kansas City wants to nudge Gaddis into a meeting.

At 12:20 p.m. on October 21st Gaddis called me and requested a meeting at 2:00 p.m. "Don't tell anyone we are meeting", he said.

Gaddis wanted to modify the entrance level job requirement to allow the Company to hire from the street in two additional titles, cable helper and line worker. I called Freeman and asked for his view. Since this was part of an agreement made in these negotiations we agreed to modify our proposal in order to show movement on our part. I advised Gaddis that we would do this.

I again advised Gaddis about stopping the letter to the editor as it was coming out in the afternoon paper on the twenty-second; but again emphasized we must know we have an agreement before I made that move.

Gaddis didn't respond to my request but felt good about the modification of our position and said he was going over to see Mr. Hill and try to sell him on the package and would call me at 6:00 p.m.

I contacted Mendoza and advised him of our changed position. He shared with me the conversation he had had with Kansas City as to what the problem was. According to Kansas City, Gaddis had become aggravated over the events of yesterday. He felt he is in the middle. President Hill is ticked off, whether at CWA or Kansas City they do not know. It started last week when the agreement fell through. Hill thought there was an agreement and had celebrated, only to find we had placed all 5 items back on the table. Hill felt very strongly that once those issues had been withdrawn they should not be back on the table, and this has Hill bent out of shape.

Kansas City was saying a compromise has got to be worked out before we can reach an agreement. They feel at least 2 of the items must be withdrawn.

7:15 p.m. Gaddis called and said he had not made much progress with Hill. "We will just have to sit on it a day or two."

I ask Gaddis was the problem connected to the

agreement falling through last Thursday. He said that was part of it but there were other factors too. I asked whether it would help if I talked to Hill.

Gaddis responded, "Let me work it out in my own way."

I again reminded Gaddis of the letter to the editor hitting the paper tomorrow and that I wished we could have prevented it.

Gaddis said, "Let's keep in touch".

In reporting to Mendoza, he wanted to know what he should do to help. I responded that he could tell Kansas City in confidence that I believe I have an agreement with Gaddis, but it will take a couple of days to bring Hill around.

President Hill had all kinds of pressures building and was apparently reacting to them. Kansas City was pressuring him to make an agreement in which it was questionable whether the Company could afford because of very low earnings. The Public Service Commission had denied a rate increase over 15 months ago and had gone to court to fight the increase. Local President Freeman and his legislative chairman Johnny Thompson had gone to the Public Service Commission on behalf of the Company and requested that they not appeal the Court of Appeals decision which had been rendered in August, and to allow a hearing on the rate increase and either grant or deny the increase. The PSC had agreed to have the hearing and President Hill was getting prepared to testify.

Company Attorney John Hoffman was advising President Hill that CWA had nothing to do with the granting of the hearing by the PSC. Hoffman had in the last several days prepared a document criticizing the PSC and asking one of the commissioners to remove himself from the upcoming hearing because of the commissioner's statements to the press during his election campaign. President Hill had signed the document and it had been delivered to the

PSC. Because of these problems President Hill was apparently fighting back at everyone.

Chapter 40: Building Up Strikers Spirits

On October 22nd to get spirits up we scheduled seven Union meetings covering 250 miles in one day. I opened the first meeting.

" Last Wednesday and Thursday when the Company sent you a letter saying the Union had a 31 percent package on the table and the Union had refused to allow you to vote on it, your spirits went to zero.

"The Company had been telling us you had a petition circulating asking the Union to allow you to vote on the package. Many members started criticizing the Union leadership. There was bickering among yourselves. Your bargaining committee's spirits dropped because we were losing your trust. Many on the picket lines were talking in front of Company guards complaining, and the guards reported your feelings to the Company

"Just by accident we have come across a teletype status report from the Company for those days. The report contains data on the number of calls completed by supervisors and scabs, the number of trouble reports received, etc. Then the report turns to the employees: Attitude of striking employees-poor: Attitude of working employee--excellent. You know, they were right. By talking to the Company guards and supervisors you were destroying your position as strikers and solidifying the Company's. So they in turn took a more firm position against us at the bargaining table.

"If we are to win this battle, you need to be telling the Company guards and the Company managers that we will be out here until hell freezes over or until the Company removes the retrogression from the table.

"We have had calls from many of you. Many, many of you made the mistake of calling the Company and asking why you had not been allowed to vote on the 31 percent package. Because of your questions, the Company decided to exploit the 31 percent offer by going public hoping to get the public, which has been supportive of our strike, to switch in favor of the Company. We had made them look like the bad guys when we continually said we were negotiating within the Wage price guidelines. But with 31 percent on the table obviously we would lose the public support. So I went public with a press release saying the Company must answer some questions. By doing so the public and employees have come back to supporting the Union.

"I also advised you through the press release that we were increasing the food allowance by 50 percent. This too helped your spirits.

"At my lowest point, two members, a man and his wife, both janitors, came by my office. They were upbeat saying, "We've had to suffer all our lives. This is just a little more. If we are going to have anything in life we are going to have to sacrifice."

"I really needed that positive attitude from those two strikers. My spirits picked up and although tired and exhausted your bargaining committee and I have spent 18 hours a day visiting the picket lines.

"After you received a letter from us and digested the good press we received, spirits began shooting up again. On the picket lines we saw R.Vs, tents, horse trailers and all had plenty of food. At one location on Sunday a group had their musical instruments, singing and playing. Now that's upbeat. What do you think the Company felt when they saw that sight?" (Prolonged laughter) A person yelled-- did they have tin cups? (Laughter)

"One group told us a story of how they had gone by a certain food store and gotten food so often they felt guilty. So for a couple of days they decided not to go back. When they got up enough courage to go back the store had several sacks of food waiting and the members were told, "we thought you guys didn't need any more food."

"At another location a restaurant was supplying hot meals. At another, a mobile home dealer had supplied a 25-foot mobile home. At another location a Company supplied electricity, at another a phone. On and on went the good reports. It was obvious the public was supporting us.

"The other night in Bristol the men were supplying coffee to the women. You have gotten to know and trust each other. (Someone yelled I hope not too much--laughter). And Brobeck will you please quit looking in the Company window at Jack Gaddis!! (Brobeck yelled--what's wrong with it--laughter). I don't know but Gaddis told me he did not like it

"One of our members, Sam Hardwick, had a broken bridge when the strike started. His dentist was on the third floor of one of the buildings we were picketing. This guy knows how to get publicity. He rented a crane, which lifted him the 3 floors to the dentist office, and the dentist leaned out the window and fitted Sam's bridge. By coincidence a photographer got a picture and the story and picture made the wire services and ABC national news. Stand up Sam." Sam received a prolong applause.

"We are now at a very critical point in negotiations. I can't go into the details except to say that New Jersey, Carolina, Norfolk and Indiana have been waiting for a week for us to reach an agreement.

"The problem is here in Tennessee. It's an attitude problem caused by, I believe, a misunderstanding and personal pride. They won't tell me. We must be very careful as to what we say or do and not upset negotiations during this critical period. If a cable is cut, and egg thrown, a confrontation on the picket line, it may upset the delicate negotiations.

"I know some of you do not support the United Way. Local President Freeman is opposed to United Way because of a personal experience. I believe in United Way and we now have an opportunity to change an attitude and possibly resolve this strike. If nothing else we will get some good publicity and do what many of you would do if you were on the job. I have received a letter from Don York, chair of the United Way services division. Don has said that if the striking employees would sign their pledge cards, it would put the United Way over its goal. President Watts is Chair of the Board of Governors of United Way, the National organization, and he would appreciate your pledging by signing your pledge cards."

The Johnson City Press Chronicle reported the story:

"Calvin Patrick was milling around the crowd of strikers in front of United Telephone's North Roan Street office with a press release, with him was Don York, Chairman of the United Way services division and Vice President of First Tennessee Bank. He too had a press release

"Yesterday's event, a departure from the usual incidents of the 22-day-old strike, was neatly capsulated in both news releases. Over 600 CWA members in the region of Local 10871 signed, or pledged to sign United Way pledge cards. According to York's release the United Way Service Division was several hundred dollars short of reaching its goal until the United employees made their pledges.

"Over the weekend Patrick met with Glenn Watts, National President of the CWA, in Washington D.C. Watts, according to the release, commended the workers for supporting United Way, even in their time of need. Watts is chairman of the Executive Committee of the Board of Governors of United Way."

An editorial in the Johnson City Press Chronicle stated:

"Members of the striking Communications Workers of America are not so caught up in their own situation that they cannot recognize real needs elsewhere. Union members this week have been filling out pledge cards for the Johnson City United Way campaign. CWA's national president put it this way: "Our members still care for others, even when they are having difficulties of their own, and this reaffirms our national slogan, "we are the community minded Union. The Communications Workers, on strike though they may be, have set a good example for the entire community."

I wondered if my trip with the editor to the White House for a briefing on the Panama Canal had made the difference.
That afternoon, October 22nd, my letter to the editor hit the news. They had made the letter into a guest editorial with large headlines.

Kingsport Times News
Commentary
The CWA Position
By: Calvin Patrick

"I feel compelled to respond to your editorial of Oct. 10 and agree with you totally "to understand the dispute one needs to know where the two sides stand." I do not believe you understand the position of the Communications Workers of America.
1. You stated that the issues are with this Company

(United) and should be settled within this Company. I agree, but United Telecommunications in Kansas City is telling United Inter-Mountain Telephone what they can offer and cannot offer. Therefore, the Corporation has made the issue larger than United Inter-Mountain Telephone Company.

2. Since the United Telephone System in Kansas City is involved, it is only fair for the public to know that United Telecommunications, the third largest telecommunications system outside the Bell System and General Telephone and Electronics, has the highest profit per employee of the three major telephone companies, according to the May issue of Forbes Magazine. Profit per employee in United Telecommunications is $6,100. General Telephone and Electronics, the second largest, has a profit per employee of $2,900. A.T.&T., the largest system, has a profit per employee of $5,400.

Therefore, based on the above profits, I think United Telecommunications owes more to their employees, and a lot of answers to the public as to why the wages in United Inter-Mountain Telephone are the lowest in the United System. From the public's reaction in your newspaper, the service is apparently the worst in the United System.

3. The employees of this Company, because of inequities in the past, rejected the Company's offer by an almost two-to-one majority. Had the Company listened to the Union bargaining committee, we would probably have had a contract today. As I told the Company immediately after agreeing to the tentative agreement, which was rejected, this was the first time that I have ever felt let down after negotiating a contract because I knew the employees would reject it. But the Company had said, "that's the bottom of the

barrel - the barrel's empty."

4. The most important factor in labor relations between union and management is credibility. On Aug. 7, I advised our members, as I always do in any contract negotiations, that if a Company has credibility, they will put every last penny in the final wage offer, and if it is rejected, the Company knows the Union will strike, and the member knows if he/she votes to strike, the Company is willing to take on a strike. This is necessary in order for both parties not to play games with each other.

United apparently was playing games. They came to the media and talked about the Company's "highest, best and final offer." But after the members voted to strike, the Company changed their position and offered a dental plan and additional improvements in hospitalization, plus an additional 1.65 percent increase in wages.

To say the least, the Company's credibility is shot, and I am sorry to say that because of this, the membership will have a difficult time believing the Company when they say it's the Company's highest, best and final offer, and that, my dear editor, could cause another strike at the next contract.

5. In comparing wages, you inferred that we were comparing our wages with New York and Chicago. Nothing could be further from the truth. We compared our wages with our fellow CWA members in the Chesapeake and Potomac Telephone Company that joins United just over the Virginia line; with our fellow CWA members in South Central Bell which joins our territory just west of Mosheim, Tennessee, and with our fellow CWA members in Southern Bell that joins this Company just south at the North Carolina line. These fellow CWA members, while doing the

same work, have fully Company-paid dental plans, fully Company-paid hospitalization, superior pension plans, and wages as much as 75 cents per hour more for operators and $1 per hour more than Installers in United.

6. At the same time that our members are receiving so much less than those described above, the telephone service is cheaper in those areas than in United. In light of this, how can United Telecommunications, the richest telephone system based upon return per employee, according to Forbes, justify the poor treatment of its employees and the public?

7. Another very important factor, as it affects service, is that the Company should be concerned with paying adequate wages in order to attract higher qualified people. It is my understanding that two employees who recently completed a nine-month Company school have found better jobs and will not be coming back to work after the strike. This is a tremendous investment for the Company to lose.

8. Contrary to your statement, New Jersey will not be a bar to getting a contract here in United.

In conclusion, our Country was founded on sacrifice. The signers of the Declaration of Independence were willing to sacrifice their life, liberty and pursuit of happiness for freedom. Those in labor have bled and many have died for labor justice. Our members are the ones who are cold, hungry and suffer, but willing to continue to sacrifice for equity."

The letter made an impact.

Even though the contents of the article were similar to the press release on October 17th, the Public Service Commission hearing was only a week away. The letter made an impact.

At 8:30 p.m. that evening I delivered a copy of the prepared dental plan the parties had been working on to Jack Gaddis. Gaddis said he wished the letter had not been printed so close to the PSC hearing date. I again explained my position and that I had been given no choice.

I asked Gaddis for a meeting and let's settle this thing. He responded we might have been close to a meeting if the letter had not appeared.

Chapter 41: Company Criminally Immoral

During the day CWA local Legislative Chair Johnny Thompson had talked to the PSC and had been told that President Hill was criminally immoral because of a document he had sent to the PSC regarding the hearing scheduled for Monday October 30th. I asked Thompson and President Freeman to drive the 560 miles round trip to Nashville and discuss the issue with their PSC sources. They arranged a meeting for the 24th.

At 12:30 a.m. on October 23rd after hearing the Company bargaining tape, I called Jack Gaddis. "Jack, I'm tired and have had all I'm going to take. Every time the Company issues a press release it takes me 5 hours to respond to it and you know damn well I will die in my tracks before I let your group get the upper hand with the media. If we don't resolve this thing I'm going to get as mean as hell and the letter to the editor will be like Ned in the primer. I just can't take much more emotionally or physically. You've got to do something to settle this strike."

Gaddis said he would get back to me.

10:00 a.m. Gaddis called and asked that we meet with the committees at 6:00 p.m.

2:00 p.m. Mendoza called and said Kansas City is reporting that Gaddis is very upset about the article in the paper. I advised Mendoza that Gaddis had agreed to a meeting and we may be back on tract.

6:00 p.m. All members of both committees were present. Attorney Norris advised us that the Company had not changed their positions.

I responded; We haven't changed our positions either. Tell me why if these 5 language items were the right thing to do on August 24th why aren't they the right thing to do today, and end this strike?

Norris: We only gave them to reach an agreement late on August 24th.

I responded, Then why aren't they reasonable now to end the strike? You've gone back on an agreement that at one time was said to be fair and equitable.

Norris, I have never gone back on my word.

I said, when you told us on August 24th that the last nickel was on the table and then after the employees rejected the contract you found a gold mine. Freeman even told you how he had changed his mind about the Company, but is now saying he was wrong to trust you because the Company is now trying to punish the local membership because of the National Union.

I could tell the Company wanted to reach agreement and were obviously upset because they were not being allowed to do so. Consequently, they would not respond to my continued probing. This was intuition and I needed some answers, not intuition.

I continued talking about the upcoming consolidation of traffic operators within the next two years but apparently you don't care for the operators. If they are laid off they never will return to work without our extending the recall rights. Bob Nicar, General Traffic Manager over Operator Services and a member of the bargaining committee, was a very compassionate and caring man, but he remained silent looking toward me.

I turned to Gaddis and talked about how hard we had worked and almost had an agreement. That I had compromised and compromised but Gaddis wanted the whole candy bar, the whole 5 items of language and that I decided I liked candy too and by damn I would keep all of it. Now the Company was taking it out on the members.

Finally Dan Luethke broke the silence. "The problem is not taking it out on the members. It's the National items that have kept us from reaching an agreement. The

Company wanted to put the three-year agreement out for ratification but the Union wouldn't allow it."

Gaddis opened up by saying, "The Local had nothing to do with getting the Public Service Commission not to appeal the court ruling and getting the Commission to set up the hearing on the Company rate increase."

Well we were at least finding what their real problems were and maybe we could find a way to resolve the issues.

I responded to Gaddis that he was wrong about the Local and the PSC hearing. Jack, for your information, every time a Public Service Commission member comes to this area, a local officer of this local picks him up at the airport and stays with him until he leaves. Neither you nor anyone in the Company apparently knows what is going on.

I knew Gaddis had opened up an unnecessary can of worms with this Local and probably would pay for that remark many times in the future. The Local had gone to a lot of expense and time and effort to get the hearing set for the Company.

At 7:41 p.m. the meeting adjourned with the Company saying there was no need to set another meeting date unless the Union changed its position.

On October 24th Local President Freeman and Legislative chair Johnny Thompson drove to Nashville to find out what had caused the PSC to say that President Hill was criminally immoral.

At 12:00 noon I listened to the Company bargaining tape message. They stated that they had filed an injunction against CWA. They apparently had found a judge favorable to the Company to hear the case.

At 6:30 p.m. Mendoza advised that Kansas City was saying they will settle but they want 2 of the language items withdrawn. Kansas City was also saying that while the strike is strong in Tennessee, it was softening in North Carolina with over 1000 employees crossing the picket lines. Also, United in Tennessee was bent out of shape over the letter to the editor. They say they will compromise but will not capitulate.

I advised Mendoza to just hang loose; I was fixing to get the knockout punch to end the strike if my information was correct.

Chapter 42: The Knock-Out Punch

At 2:00 a.m. I received a call from President Freeman. He was returning from Nashville and wanted to meet me at 3:00 a.m. He had a bomb!!

At 9:00 a.m. I called the Federal Mediation and Conciliation Service and requested they set up a meeting and suggested they recommend to the Company that we settle on the basis of my understanding with Gaddis on Monday. By having the FMCS make the recommendation it may make it easier for the Company to accept.

I reread the 13-page bomb prepared by Company in-house attorney John Hoffman:

PRE-HEARING MOTION TO RECUSE (disqualify) COMMISSIONER

"Petitioner does not make this request lightly or frivolously: It clearly recognizes that public servants, like all other citizens, enjoy the Constitutional right of free speech and as politicians are often called upon to publicly express their opinions. However, it is apparent that this action is necessary to protect the petitioners rights to a fair and impartial hearing on substantial record of evidence under the laws of Tennessee."

The document then attacked Commissioner Keith Bissell directly and Commissioner Frank Cochran by association, by quoting excerpts from newspapers:

"I was shocked to learn that telephone services are the same as 8 years ago---"

"The Company says they need more money. We say they have enough money---"

"We've had a problem with the Telephone Company for decades---"

"I'm amazed that the telephone management makes statements that they can't improve service unless they have adequate rates---"

"If it's a management problem, then you know that presents serious questions as to whether this particular Company ought to be operated under its present owners----"

"----We may consider cancellation of the franchise---"

The Company went on to make their own statements of opinion of the commissioner:

"Commissioner Bissell seems willing to discuss petitioners rate cases anywhere, anytime and with anyone except at a hearing---"

This was heavy stuff for a Company that was asking the commission for a rate increase within a week.

At 9:30 a.m. I called the Companys' in house council John Hoffman and requested that he meet me at my office as soon as possible as it was very urgent.

At 11:30 a.m. I opened the conversation

"John I've been hearing that you have been advising President Hill and other officers of United Telephone that CWA and this Local doesn't have any input to the PSC in Nashville. This came across the bargaining table yesterday that the Local had not helped in getting the hearing set that is scheduled for next Monday, October 30th.

For your information we received a call from the Commission on the 22nd saying that President Hill was criminally immoral. Yesterday Local President Freeman and Legislative Chair Johnny Thompson spent the day with the commissioners and they are very angry. Here is what they are angry about."

Hoffman had turned white and was shaking.

I continued, "Rather than accomplishing your objective if this document reaches the public, these commissioners will be heroes by taking the publics side against a giant corporation. That is how they were elected. I am seriously considering turning this document over to the media."

Hoffman tried to shift the blame to President Hill saying he had not wanted to prepare the document but President Hill had insisted on it.

I suggested to Hoffman that he talk to the persons he had been giving incorrect advise to, straighten out that advise, including his remarks that the Union has no input with the commission, and get the strike settled before the PSC hearing next Monday. In addition, if he was very smart and wanted to keep his job, that 13 page Motion must be withdrawn today.

At 1:00 p.m. the Federal Mediation Service Representative called. He had had discussions with the Company and made the offer I had suggested. The Company was willing to meet tomorrow, provided the Union will come to an agreement without outside interference from the CWA in Washington or pressure through Kansas City. I advised him that we had the authority to settle the dispute but that President Watts must be in agreement to any settlement we reach.

At 2:45 p.m. Mendoza reported that Kansas City was concerned that negotiations were not going on in Tennessee. They wanted to resolve the strike but were still insisting that we compromise and give up two of the language items.

This seemed rather strange to be repeating the request for compromise a second time after President Watts had said the Company must agree on these items. Was it the Company: Watts: or Mendoza wanting to do this? I had my hunches.

I asked Mendoza to hold on a minute and turned to Freeman. "Mendoza apparently wants us to compromise on two of the language items. I feel we can't in good conscience do it. How does the committee feel"?

Freeman responded, "That SOB wants to sell us out, just like he has in other companies. We said he would do it!! I'm with you.

Rather than ask Mendoza was I being instructed to compromise our existing position and then be locked into a position if Mendoza said yes, I responded, "the local officers and bargaining committee are very angry at the Company's belittling their efforts with the PSC and are not willing to move." Mendoza responded that we should maintain our position.

At 3:30 p.m. I received a call from Company bargaining committee member Dan Luethke. He said that a call to Gaddis might pay off if I called. Gaddis was unwilling to call me.

I called Gaddis and suggested that we meet... Gaddis was up beat and said he would like to meet and suggested we meet in my office.

At 4:30 p.m. in my office I suggested to Gaddis that we settle on the basis of our conversation of last Monday. Although we must have all five items, we would compromise on the entrance level jobs as he and I had discussed on Monday.

Gaddis responded that this sounded good to him. He would have to talk to President Hill but felt Hill would feel favorable. If it was possible, Gaddis wanted to wrap up the agreement. He asked if the Local would help with the PSC. I responded they were very angry now but in time it would work out, in my view.

Gaddis then asked, if we reach an agreement, would I have dinner with President Hill, in-house chief counsel John Hoffman and him tomorrow night. They would like to talk to me about the upcoming PSC hearing scheduled for Monday. I agreed to the dinner meeting if the strike was settled and committed that CWA would help open up channels of communication with the PSC.

At 9:30.p.m. Gaddis called and said we had an agreement, provided we will help with the PSC. I checked with Local President Freeman and he responded that no one could help the Company unless they were willing to make changes, especially in their attitude. I passed this on to Gaddis and he said he would be working in this area and felt we would see changes.

At 10:30 a.m. October 26th we met formally with all members of both committees present and started going over the agreement.

At noon we recessed and Mendoza had a conference call with all chief negotiators to check out every Company and locals' position. All were in a position to reach an agreement. Mendoza gave his last directive: "Everyone sign off."

At 3:35 p.m. Jack Gaddis and I shook hands across the table. We had an agreement. The strike was over.

That evening President Hill, Jack Gaddis and Company Chief Counsel John Hoffman and I had dinner. We discussed the Company's need for the rate increase and how the Company could improve its relationship with the PSC. We complimented each other; how our relationship had improved during the last six months in spite of all the adversity and all looked forward to working together in the future.

Company chief counsel, Attorney John Hoffman, sat silent all evening and could not eat. As the evening ended, Hoffman asked to speak to me in private. Very nervously Hoffman asked me to intercede and help him save his job. I said I would see what I could do.

As I drove away, I wondered if President Hill deliberately made Hoffman come to dinner. He was a shrewd fellow. I bet he did. [16]

---

[16] 16   *In 1985 a committee from Local 10871 wrote a letter to the Vice President of District 10 requesting that Patrick come back to East Tennessee and bargain the contract with United Intermountain. The committee stated that the 1979 agreement was the best contract*

they ever had. Other CWA staff were now responsible for United and it was not appropriate to honor their request.

Election CWA Vice President District 10

On January 1, 1980, District 10 Vice President, W.W. Brown, promoted East Tennessee/Kentucky Director, Calvin Patrick, to an Administrative Assistant job in the District 10 Office in Birmingham, Alabama. In Tennessee/Kentucky Patrick had 12 locals that he had to keep happy, handle their grievances, administer their contracts and in some cases negotiate their contracts. He developed personal relationships in each local and the job was manageable. [17]

In Birmingham the world was a very large and a different universe. There were competing loyalties, many staff that had different agendas, and competitive relationships. There were 70 locals with 4 to 10 officers in each, and 4000 stewards from all the locals. They represented 50,000 employees, mostly in the South Central Bell Telephone Company. Each local had its own priority. Some were involved in Public Politics along with the normal responsibilities of contract administration, training and politicking to be reelected in their own local's. Other locals

---

[17] *Patrick had been responsible for workers from; South Central Bell, Knoxville, TN and Eastern Kentucky United Telephone...............Bristol, Tenn./Virginia Southern Electronics Company, Greeneville, Tenn. Wright & Lopez, Inc.,..........Bristol, Tenn. Sammons Communications, Bristol and Morristown, Tenn. Highland Telephone Cooperative...Sun Bright, Tenn. Star Construction Company, Inc, Knoxville, Tenn. North Electric Company........Johnson City, Tenn. General Telephone...............Lexington and Ashville, Kentucky Involved in Politics, Patrick was Washington County Democratic Party Chairman and Liaison Secretary for The Democratic Party in 13 counties in East Tennessee. He was Jimmy Carter's State coordinator for East Tennessee.*

were very interested in Union Politics and used their membership as leverage in the administration of their goals within the Union.

This was the environment Calvin Patrick stepped into and immediately found himself in the middle of controversy.

A group of local Presidents led by Pete Walker of Jackson, Tn. Were determined to have a candidate run against CWA District 10 Vice President Willard Brown in the next election in June of 1980. As early as October of 1979 in a meeting of Tennessee Local Presidents, Walker stated that in the up coming election "we have to have a new Vice President, Vice President Brown was senile and could no longer function." Walkers view was that staff of the Union should not be involved in the election process.

Vice President Brown was responsible for 5 States: Alabama, Kentucky, Mississippi, Louisiana and Tennessee. This was the same territory that composed South Central Bell Telephone and Telegraph Co. (SCB). SCB with forty eight thousand bargaining unit employees was the largest contract CWA administered in the District.

Brown had confided to his inner circle staff that he would not be a candidate for reelection during the June 1980 elections. He had committed to CWA President Glenn Watts not to make the announcement until after CWA's Executive Board meeting in Bal-Harbor, Florida in February 1980. The hope was to minimize the affects of politics on the members if the campaign could be kept short.

Brown was going to support his Administrative Assistant, T.J. Volk, as his successor. The plan, until the Executive Board meeting was over, was to say publicly that Volk would run if Brown chose not to run. South Louisiana Director Harry Swaim was also thinking of running and knew of Brown's pending retirement. He was also saying he would run only if Brown did not run.

Local President Walker was looking for a candidate who had the courage to announce publicly that he would run against Brown. The word kept circulating that Brown was senile. Patrick spoke to T.J. Volk about these statements saying that he hoped Brown did not hear about them since he would be retiring and there was no use hurting him with insinuations that were in no way true. Volk responded he felt Brown should know what was being said about him and was going to tell him.

Without consulting with Brown, Volk made an announcement that he was going to run regardless of who was in the race.

The anti Brown forces, not knowing of Brown's plan to announce his retirement in February, felt that Volk was being tough running against Brown. After mailing his letter of announcement, Volk approached Brown and advised him of the letter. Brown responded, you mean you are going to run against me? The stage was set for the campaign to start in earnest.

Brown had the district to run and had other problems, including a need to go into the hospital with a heart problem. His assistant was retiring and South Central Bell bargaining was to commence in June. He asked Patrick to be his new assistant. Patrick asked him "let me think about it".

In preparation for the upcoming negotiations, Brown had scheduled a South Central Bell bargaining unit meeting to begin on January 23,1980. He felt betrayed because of Volk's announcement to run. Being a very proud man, he backed out of supporting Volk and decided to support Harry Swaim. Earlier he had hoped Swaim would withdraw in support of Volk. All these issues were adding to the pressure of the job and his health problems.[18] He was

---

[18] *In Union politics, health issues were very secretive as they could effect a*

also being affected because of the senile issue being used against him.

The SCB bargaining unit meeting started on January 23rd as planned. Even though Brown had decided to support Swaim, he did not allow politics to interfere into the selection of the bargaining committee. He announced that T. J. Volk would be chair of the SCB bargaining committee and Calvin Patrick would be Co-chair.

Early in the meeting, rumors started circulating that Brown was not running for Vice President and that Brown was supporting Swaim. Rumor had it that Patrick was to be made Brown's assistant. Swaim was allegedly saying he would keep Patrick as his assistant should he be elected.

The Swaim forces were saying that CWA representative Jack Baccari was to be Volk's assistant if he were elected. Baccari was not from the telephone industry; therefore, there was much resistance to his having such an important position.

CWA Representative Mitchell Roshto was responsible for special assignments and had been dealing with South Central Bell for several years handling grievances. Roshto, a hard working man of fifty-one years of age, had said in private conversations that he would have to run for vice president soon or it would be too late for him.

Roshto had come on staff in 1972. He and Patrick had worked together in organizing campaigns. Patrick had praise for Roshto and said that he was a hard working union representative. In the last two years, Roshto had been having conflict with his supervisor and had become disenchanted with Brown as a result of this and other issues.

Roshto was now supporting Volk. It had been reported as early as June 1979, at the CWA National Convention, that Roshto had started building support for Volk. He had been credited as starting the senile issue

persons electability.

against Brown.

Rumors were flying at the bargaining conference about Jack Baccari becoming Volk's assistant. Roshto perceived that he might be left out of a Volk administration. On January 25, 1980 after the regular business had ended, Roshto requested the opportunity to talk to the three hundred delegates. Everyone stayed.

He started a rambling speech by saying he had made a decision he had been thinking about for a long time. He said he was not a candidate for District 10 Vice President. He said that he was a Christian but that word was misused sometimes. He stated that he had been used as a political pawn in this election. Volk had told him that he would be used on grievances and arbitrations if Volk were elected. Harry Swaim had also been telling inquirers the same thing if he was elected. Roshto went on, " if I have any talent it is in the area of grievances and arbitration." (Roshto should have felt comfortable knowing both candidates respected his work. There was no doubt about where he would be working.)

He complained that grievances was the last thing the administration thought about, and about his being sent to Louisiana to clear up a backlog of grievances "get some seasoning, you know, for better things to come". He complained of being sent to Kentucky and Alabama to handle grievances and said he did not know what the state directors were doing in those states.

Roshto told of Vice President Brown asking him to take a job in North Alabama and asking him to move to Mississippi as the North Mississippi Director. He did not want either job, yet he was being very critical of the Mississippi Director.

He said he was the only staff in the CWA staff Union that did not scab during the seventy-six day strike of the CWA Clerical Employees in 1976. Then Roshto said, " What

I'm getting to is this, I don't like deals, yet there is a deal coming down. Calvin Patrick is going to be Brown's assistant.[19] He continued that he had gotten Volk to run for vice president. He had been advising Volk in his own way, as he thought he should. He said that Volk was his own man and did not always listen to him. "I don't like to be used, I'm not going to be used, and I don't want nothing out of this. Hell I'd put it in writing. I want to work on grievances, arbitration and bargaining." He then started condemning the 1977 agreement with South Central Bell, complaining about employee's expenses under article 9:10 of the agreement. He criticized the Union for allowing South Central Bell to offer pen and pencil sets and Mickey Mouse tee shirts as prizes. He talked about the District 10 policy of not allowing staff to return telephone calls unless they were collect calls and how he had disregarded that policy. He ended his 45 minutes of rambling and criticizing the Union, its staff, and the contract by saying; "Well all those things worry me, and you know Volk might not want me on his campaign after this, but I'm still going to be voting for him".

As the bargaining unit meeting ended, feelings were running high. Roshto had taken on the entire Union as

---

[19] *Roshto had no knowledge that Brown would offer Patrick the assistant's job. However, after seeing that Patrick was made co-chair of the 1980 bargaining committee it would have been a reasonable assumption that Patrick would be appointed. His assumption was correct. Patrick had started working with CWA on a temporary assignment in May of 1973 organizing General Telephone and Electronics in Huntsville, Alabama. Roshto was in charge of the organizing campaign and Patrick had worked for him. Roshto had been very helpful to Patrick, a former local president from Jackson, MS. After CWA won the election in Huntsville, Vice President W.W. Brown ask Roshto to write a recommendation as to whether he should offer Patrick a CWA staff job. Roshto was to point out all the good and bad points that he had developed on Patrick.*

working against the member. His appeal had been personal, and from the delegates' viewpoint, he was looking out for their interest while the rest of the Union did not care. They also felt he had been mistreated by his employer, the Union.

Patrick had asked Brown to let him think about accepting the assistant's assignment, knowing with the upcoming election if he accepted he would become a political football in the campaign. He discussed the negative aspects with his family and several colleagues he could confide in. All gave him counsel that it would be a very serious mistake to accept the assignment with the election only a few months away.

Patrick went to Brown and asked him to allow him to assume the duties and relieve some of the workload. Brown responded in his authoritative way that he would not allow an Administrative Assistant to supervise other supervisors of the same rank. He said he would just have to do the best he could.

By this time Brown was fed up with the way events were turning and said he wasn't going to any more meetings. He would just sit out the rest of his term. Patrick asked what would happen to him if he accepted the assistant's assignment and the incoming vice president didn't want to continue him in the office. He wanted to know where would he be assigned? Could he get his present title back?

Brown suggested that Patrick fly to Miami and talk to President Watts, who was attending the AFL-CIO winter meeting.

On February 18th, Patrick flew to Miami and discussed with Watts the situation in the District 10 office and how Vice President Brown was reacting. He informed Watts that Brown wanted to promote him to his assistant. Patrick expressed his reluctance because of the upcoming election. He explained his concern for the District and even though it may not be in his own best interest personally, he was willing to accept the assistant's job for the members.

Watts committed that regardless of who won the election for vice president, Patrick would not be moved out of Birmingham. If the new vice president wanted someone else as his assistant, Patrick would be allowed to return to his present title as an Administrative Assistant.

Upon returning to Birmingham, Patrick advised Vice President Brown that he would accept the assistant's job. Brown promoted him effective February 16, 1980.

On February 22, 1980 Roshto announced in a letter to all CWA local officers in District 10, that he "was a candidate for Vice President. "It has been very distressing to me to see staff lose credibility with local officers and members to the point it has almost become an "us versus them" situation". He laid out a program of improvements that in his view were much needed. He was well aware that there had been no money to accomplish his objectives.

He stated that there was a void in communications and he was going to start a monthly newsletter. He was going to restructure the staff in the District, placing two staff in each state.
He promised that he was going to remove Calvin Patrick as the Assistant to the Vice President. He made promises to stop the diminishment of seniority rights when South Central employees were laid off due to lack of work.

Local President David Alexander from Covington Louisiana announced, he too was running for vice president.

During the next three months Roshto worked on getting local leaders, who had previously committed to Volk through his efforts, to switch their allegiance to him.

In his speech he had said that he didn't want Volk to make deals and did not like deal making. Now, in several states, he was promising local officers staff jobs if elected.

He was saying that if elected he would make Volk his assistant. His strategy was softening up Volk's support and they were switching their allegiance to Roshto.

Patrick was supporting Harry Swaim, the Louisiana State Director. While he was busy with his new job and not directly involved in the campaign, it was obvious Swaim, with Browns support, would get the greatest number of votes on a first ballot, and he must win on the first ballot.

Patrick had also concluded that he was a big liability to Swaim's campaign and suggested that Swaim make it known that Patrick would not stay in the assistants job. Swaim refused to follow this advice.

Upon reaching the Convention on June 13th, local delegates who had been committed to Volk were now wearing Roshto buttons. Most notable was the Birmingham local which had almost thirty-seven hundred votes. All of the Birmingham officers had given generously to Volk's campaign. Now they were on Roshto's team. There was a very strong rumor that the Birmingham local president had been offered a staff job.

Momentum was on Roshto's side. Volk was losing ground and Swaim's campaign seemed to be stalled but not losing any votes. Swaim kept saying he had a win on the first ballot.

At the convention Vice President Brown called the District meeting to order for the election and turned the meeting over to the auditing firm of Ernst and Whiney, who conducted the election.

According to the CWA Convention rules, if a district election took longer than two hours to vote and count the ballots, the voted results were to remain with the auditor and the District meeting would recess for two hours while other elections were held that required the attendance and vote of some of the district's members.

At the end of the two-hour period District 10 had not

received word from the auditor of the election results. Vice President Brown was a rule follower and did not want to do anything to jeopardize the election. He went to the podium at two minutes after the hour and said "the meeting is in recess for two hours in accordance with the rules of the convention".

At this moment the auditor came into the room to deliver the vote results. Brown advised that the hour had passed and we would reconvene in two hours. There were screams of no! No! Lets get it over with! It was already 9:30 p.m. The delegates were tired and wanted to go to the hotel, as it had been a long day. Brown refused to change his ruling.

Brown and Patrick left the podium to go and have dinner during the recess. As they passed through the empty auditorium going to their waiting car, a female delegate approached them telling them the results of the election.

Knowing that only the auditors should know the results of the election, Patrick ask her and the two other delegates with her to go dinner with him and Brown, as the results of the election was not supposed to be public information. They declined the dinner invitation. Brown then asked them not to divulge what they had heard as it had not been released to the delegates.

After dinner and upon returning to the meeting room lobby, Patrick was deluged with angry delegates asking, "why did you withhold the election results from Volk and Roshto?" They accused both Brown and Patrick of giving Swaim an unfair advantage in order for him to campaign during the two-hour recess. Everyone already knew the results of the election.

At the appointed time the auditor gave the results of the Election:

Swaim   16,912 votes
Roshto   13,218 votes

Volk   13,206 votes
Alexander   4,836 votes

Patrick was in a state of disbelief. He was being accused of attempting to rig an election. He was concerned about what kind of effect the premature disclosure of the election results by the three delegates could have on the final outcome of the run off, in the second round of voting. Would there be grounds for asking for a new election?

As the auditor conducted the runoff election, Patrick attempted to reach President Watts on the phone. He was told that Watts was away from his suite and no one knew where he could be reached. After several attempts, Patrick advised Watts' assistant, "I don't care where he is or who he is with I need him to call me immediately." Patrick stood by the public phone just outside the voting room.

Roshto was busy making deals with delegates. Local President David Alexander was asked for his support in the runoff. Alexander told Roshto that he would support him in the runoff if Roshto would promise to bust Patrick back to a CWA Representative.[20] Roshto agreed to Alexander's request.

President Watts had been kept abreast of the campaign and was aware of Roshto's rambling speech on January 25th having heard a tape of the speech that Roshto had made and provided to anyone who asked for one. Watts had commented that the speech was rambling and incoherent. He had volunteered that something must be done once the campaign was over.

Watts returned Patrick's call and was filled in on what

---

[20] *Two years after the 1980 election Local President David Alexandra from Covington, La. told Patrick of Roshto's, agreement to demote Patrick to a CWA Representative in exchange for his vote. He was sure Roshto attempted to fulfill that promise, but failed.*

was happening.

Watts seemed concerned but not upset. He asked Patrick who did he feel would win. Patrick advised him that Volk's supporters did not like Brown and that most would switch and vote for Roshto. Watts responded that he hoped not.

At that moment the election results were announced and a shout went up. Watts ask what was that. Patrick responded, "Someone just won the election. Let me get the results."

      Roshto   27,988 votes
      Swaim   20,184 votes

Watts said: Oh my God.

Roshto's face was pail, his eyes were in a stare, and he was in a state of shock. He couldn't believe it. His supporters were jumping all over him yelling and screaming with joy. They had accomplished the impossible.

There were irregularities in the election that could be challenged by Volk, and could require a new election. There is no doubt that although Swaim had come in second, in a new election with Volk back in the election Swaim's delegates would switch to Volk because of his experience and Volk would become the vice president.

Volk chose to accept the decision of the members and not contest the election.

Before Roshto was sworn in he had fired Mississippi Director Mary Bryant and had threatened Kentucky Director, Nelle Horlander.

Patrick called President Watts early the following morning and made an appointment. He expressed his concern for the staff and informed Watts what had transpired regarding Bryant and Horlander. Watts responded, "Maybe they weren't doing their job." Patrick told him of working side-by-side with Horlander for 3 years and the kind of job she was doing. He responded, "Maybe you do not know all the facts." Suddenly Patrick realized there had been a changing of the guard. We have a new Vice President. Watts' expression of "Oh, my God," the evening before was only a human expression of disappointment. Today, as President, he was responding to the mandate of the members. Patrick excused himself.

Later that day Roshto presided at his first District meeting. The CWA staff located in the five states of the District, were scattered throughout the meeting room. He directed them to come down and sit directly in front of the podium. His first announcement was that President Watts had agreed to let Vice President Brown be an adviser to the bargaining committee. Someone whispered: "He said Brown was senile."

Roshto talked about his "lengthy and emotional speech" in January. He stated that many of the things he had said had upset staff. He had only been giving his opinion of a scab as it related to the 1976 CWA Clerical Strike. (Kentucky Director Nelle Horlander had been so upset at the time about the scab remark that she had stated she would rather be called a whore than a scab).

Roshto went on to say, "we will always have our differences and disagreements, they (the staff) truly believe in their hearts they did the right thing (about the strike). I want to publicly apologize to all the staff who are present."

Roshto then went to his letter of February 22, 1980 to all local officers reinforcing his promises. He asked the delegates to tell him, in all honesty, whom they felt would make the best staff. He said he would give every consideration to what they said.

At various points he would ask for a show of hands. If the delegates agreed with his statement, Union Staff were instructed that this was the way it was going to be. Instructions on handling the Union's problems were given to staff in a threatening and demeaning tone.

The delegates applauded several of Roshto's commitments. It became so embarrassing that Volk walked out. Patrick had wanted to accept Roshto's apology but felt the way it was worded he must be insincere. His demeaning remarks toward staff reinforced that belief.

During the previous evening Patrick had continued to seek out how the vote count leak had come about. He solicited the help of Local President Pete Walker of Tennessee, who had been the first local president to come out for someone to run against Brown the previous October. He was one of Volk's most avid supporters. Pete had switched and voted for Roshto in the runoff. Patrick knew he was an honest person and if we could find the truth he would support it. Several delegates were interviewed during the night.

Just prior to Roshto's first District meeting the next morning, Walker and Patrick had a meeting with about 10 delegates to put all their findings together.

The facts were that the three delegates, who knew the election results when they saw Patrick and Brown the previous evening, had by chance, passed by the auditor's booth and over heard the auditors reporting the results of the election to the Union's Secretary Treasurers office. These three delegates did not know that the District meeting had been recessed and the results not given to the delegates.

After they had left Brown and Patrick, they had related their story of the election results to some delegates. A rumor of a conspiracy against Roshto and Volk spread like fire.

During the District Meeting's, "good and welfare" portion of the meeting, Walker went to the mike and made this observation. "Last night rumors were flying, accusations were made, integrity was challenged. We have made an investigation that took most of the night. As a result of this investigation I want to state publicly Calvin Patrick's name has been vindicated. Willard Brown's name has been vindicated. If I owe them an apology I offer it to them." In a spirit of unity Patrick stood and said: "The integrity of the election process has been vindicated. That's important for all of us to know. The election is over. We should put aside any personal ambition we may have and support Vice President Roshto. If I do an outstanding job it will make him look good, that's the way the system works. That's the way it ought to be. He should have the credit. Let's leave here and move forward and make our Union great".

Patrick went home knowing that he would be demoted but felt President Watts would keep his commitment. He would remain in Birmingham as an administrative assistant. Roshto needed help and Patrick was willing to do his part. [21]

---

[21] *In the spring with the campaign for vice president of District 10 going strong, assistant to Vice President Brown, Calvin Patrick, started planning for Brown's retirement party. Plans were coordinated with the National office and invitations sent to Union colleagues and all local officers in the District. CWA President Glenn Watts and many officers from throughout the nation were present at his retirement, along with the District 10 staff and the local presidents. Vice President Brown was an avid and excellent Ham Radio Operator and could receive International Morris Code at 25 words per minute. Desktop computers were just coming on the market and Brown was anxious to obtain one. The guest at his retirement gave him over $7,000 dollars, which covered the cost of the computer and printer. In spite of the political rhetoric against him, all the candidates running for his job were there, showing their respect. He ended the very successful and upbeat dinner by reciting his most favored Poem "The Road Not Taken By Robert Frost. --------
" Two roads diverged in a wood, and I ---- I took the one less traveled by, and that has made a difference."* Calvin Patrick: "That was the kind of man he was. I have been

Three Years of Frustration and Uncertainty

Volk turned down Roshto's offer to become The Assistant to the Vice President. (Patrick's job under Brown.) After two days of uncertainty, Volk recommended to Roshto that he offer the assistant's job to George Werner who was looking forward to retirement in about 4 years. Werner accepted.

Back in Birmingham negotiations with South Central Bell started. Roshto decided to keep Volk as Chair and Patrick as co-chair of the Union's bargaining committee. Brown had appointed a committee of 5 local leaders, to the bargaining committee, one from each state of the South Central territory, . Roshto kept them on the bargaining committee also.

Although Roshto kept the bargaining committee appointed by Brown, he perceived that everyone was against him. He could not understand that the contract being negotiated affected these local leaders and their members. He felt they would do anything to hurt him. So he appointed Margaret Smith, the secretary of a small local, to the bargaining committee. She was his friend and had supported him. She would keep him informed.

After each day's session Smith reported to Roshto. She had never handled grievances, did not know the details of the contract, therefore was handicapped, except as it affected her own job classification. There was no way she could explain the complex language and problems in an in-depth way to Roshto. Roshto conferred with Volk or Patrick

privileged to meet Presidents, many cabinet members, senators, chief executives, pastors and others but I have only known two men in my life that I hold or held in awe. Willard W. Brown was one of those two."

only twice during the entire period of bargaining which lasted for two months.

Roshto remained hostile toward the bargaining committee. At one point he even invited them to go home. Tears were shed on several occasions.

During the final day of bargaining, Volk and Patrick were meeting with the Company chair and co-chair of the committee. They called a recess early and would not come back to the table.

Volk felt the Company was stalling. This did not make sense, as there had been slow but steady progress. Finally, the Company chair called and advised Volk that Roshto was negotiating with the Vice President of Personnel. This vice president had no detailed knowledge of the contract. Never before in the history of negotiations between CWA and South Central Bell (SCB) had this happened. Usually, the vice presidents of CWA and SCB were very aware of what was going on in their respective committees who filled them in each day. Since Roshto was communicating through Ms. Smith, who was not in any of the reduced group sessions Volk and Patrick were in, there was no way for him to know where the Union had made progress. This gave the Company a huge advantage in Roshto's private negotiations.

On the day the contracted terminated, Roshto walked into the Union's conference room at about 9 p.m. and said. "We have a contract. Are y'all going to accept it?" The next hour and a half was spent with the committee wanting an explanation of how the contract had been negotiated and what was in the agreement. They just kept asking questions. Roshto was impatient and kept yelling at the committee. A strike was to commence at midnight if an agreement had not been reached.

Roshto was not aware or apparently concerned about many of the items Volk and Patrick had been working on and Roshto was now leaving them on the table; items that the Union needed. Volk, in frustration, called the Company chairman.

They agreed to go back to the bargaining table. Volk and Patrick left Roshto with the committee, still arguing and pressing for the committee to agree with him.

As midnight approached, Volk and Patrick had captured several items where there had been close to agreement, but time ran out.

In the absence of Volk and Patrick, former Vice President Brown, who had been advising the committee and had been silent during Roshto's comments, observed that in his view CWA had a good contract. The 5 Union bargaining committee members finally relented. But the problems were not over.

A cover letter had to be prepared that would go to all members along with an explanation of the new contract language. It was customary for the bargaining committee to sign the cover letter in support of the contract.

The next morning Roshto said that he understood the committee had had a meeting and decided not to sign the cover letter. He assigned Patrick to go to the hotel and talk to the bargaining committee and insure that all signed the cover letter.

Smith was in the conference room. The other five members were in the room used for refreshments. Patrick went in and spent 90 minutes trying to encourage them as to why they should sign the cover letter supporting the contract. They did not appreciate Roshto who was now wanting their support by signing the agreement cover letter when he had never consulted with them, had not met with them, had not eaten a meal with them and had treated them badly, often to the point of tears. At some point Smith had come into the room. Patrick knew she would sign the cover letter so he had not spent any time with her. Finally the five said they would sign the cover letter. (One member later went to Patrick and asked would she be punished if she did not sign. Patrick told her to his knowledge she wouldn't, whereupon she declined to sign.)

This had been a very emotional time; Patrick went to each of them and embraced them. When he came to Smith, she recoiled and would have nothing to do with him. She then went into a long emotional discourse on how the other five-committee members had boycotted her. The committee gave numerous occasions they had tried to include her. All of this was to no avail.

She said the committee had accused her of having an affair with Roshto. She knew this was so because on the first day she came to the hotel to join the bargaining committee she walked into the hotel with Roshto. G.I. Jackson had looked at her and then looked at Roshto. "I knew what he was thinking, but Calvin Patrick had been in the lobby when I registered, he knew better". Patrick conveyed to Smith that what she did in her private life had nothing to do with these negotiations. She would not stop, accusing Patrick of trying to keep the bargaining committee from signing the agreement, rather than getting them to sign.

The committee now understood why Roshto had been so hostile. Throughout negotiations he had been seeing the bargaining committee through Smith's eyes.

Roshto had failed in his promises to change the expense plan. The Company had gained language where they could now give trips worth hundreds of dollars or other gifts, regardless of price, plus the pen and pencil sets and Mickey Mouse tee-shirts that Roshto had complained about so bitterly.

Employees who had never been required to sell Company products now could be forced to sell; if they refused they could be disciplined. The Company also got a provision requiring "threshold test" before an employee could exercise his /her seniority and bid on a better job. This test greatly eroded seniority, which Roshto had vowed to protect. Had he worked with Volk and had the background of what had been going on in negotiations, the threshold requirements would have been watered down to only two jobs. Now it applied to all jobs.

Later, Patrick commented to the committee: If you were the South Central Vice President and knew very little about the contract and was thrust into negotiations; if you knew your adversary had lots of knowledge about the contract, how many of your opponents proposals would you agree to not knowing how your decision would affect the Company? That's what Roshto was up against.

Overall the contract was a good package. Six million dollars was available for job upgrades and other improvements. A substantial wage increase and a COLA (Cost-of-living Adjustment) had been negotiated at the national bargaining table. The members ratified the contract overwhelmingly.

Watts Kept His Commitment. Almost!!!

President Glenn Watts had allowed Roshto to remove Patrick as his assistant, which was customary, but would not allow him to demote Patrick lower than an administrative assistant or remove him from the District Office.

In 1979 just before Roshto was elected, the Union had a dues increase that "had solved our financial needs for the foreseeable future". Roshto, like Patrick, was a poor boy from a large family. Now as Vice President, he had money coming out of his ears and was able to hire 4 new staff immediately. He chose 3 local presidents who had been supporting Volk before Roshto became a candidate in the race for vice president. They had switched and supported Roshto and this was the payoff. Ms. Smith, the elected secretary of a small local, with no experience in union problems, was also appointed. Complaints began to surface that Roshto did not take the recommendations seriously that he had solicited. The persons hired were, with one exception, not qualified.

During the next three years several thousand employees lost their jobs due to Technological change in the workplace and consolidation of telephone offices. Roshto did a credible job in handling these very complex problems. His failure was dealing fairly with his subordinates and local officers. He had lowered staffs self esteem to the point they just did their job and tried to stay out of trouble. Roshto continued to harass Kentucky Director Nelle Horlander. The Union settled Mississippi Director Mary Bryant's case before it went to arbitration. She was reinstated with back pay, but agreed to go through another two-year probation period.

It was not unusual for Roshto to have public confrontations with local officers. His first was early in his administration when he criticized a local president from Louisiana for filing too many non-meritorious grievances. While his motives were right his demeaning a local president in front of one hundred delegates, including several from the presidents own local, had negative vibrations that started unrest that would never be contained.

Since Watts would not allow Roshto to demote Patrick below his former title or remove him from the district office, Roshto immediately started keeping detailed notes on Patrick, taping many of their conversations.

The first of many encounters that lead to Patrick's demotion and transfer to New Orleans came immediately after negotiations. Patrick was assigned the responsibility of carrying the new agreement to Kansas City where the

CWA's printer was to print and mail the bargaining report for the South Central Bell contract to all of CWA's members in the South Central bargaining unit.

The morning Patrick was to leave for Kansas City the local presidents had been summoned to Birmingham for an overview of the contract. Prior to that meeting starting, Patrick drove by the hotel, planning to have coffee with some of the local presidents. He saw a picket line put up by the International Brotherhood of Electrical Workers who had a dispute with the hotel. Remembering Roshto's speech before the election complaining that staff had crossed a picket line, Patrick decided he would not go into the hotel as planned and he headed for the airport and to Kansas City. The local presidents had spent the night in the hotel where the overview of the new contract was to take place. Roshto crossed the picket line and convened the meeting. The local presidents were unaware of the picket line but when they were made aware, the Montgomery, Alabama president made a motion, which was passed unanimously, for Roshto to find another facility for the meeting. The meeting was adjourned and arrangements were made to meet at another hotel where the contract was explained to the local officers.

Upon returning from Kansas City, Patrick was called into Roshto's office and told that as management, "if I (Roshto) cross a picket line then you (Patrick) had better cross the picket line". Patrick attempted to explain that he was in route to the airport and did not plan to be at the meeting therefore his not crossing the picket line was a moot issue, and he did not understand the reason for the lecture. Roshto refused to believe his explanation even though Patrick had his plane ticket stub showing his flight takeoff time. Roshto's thought was that Patrick had tried to embarrass him.

Before their meeting ended, Patrick advised Roshto that while he was boss "Patrick really worked for the members and regardless of how you treat me, I will do the best job I know how."

A few days later at the Monday morning meeting of office staff, Roshto asked for a volunteer to edit the newly created District Steward News Letter which was to be sent to the 4000 local officers and stewards on a monthly basis.

As a communicator Patrick wanted to be the editor but he knew if he spoke up Roshto would think he had secret motives. No one volunteered. Several days passed and seeing that no one was going to volunteer, Patrick informed Roshto that "if you want me, I will be glad to edit the Newsletter". For two years the newsletter was lauded as outstanding. Patrick conducted editor workshops and 20 locals started newsletters.

Patrick was over union activities in Mississippi and Louisiana and reviewed grievances from these two states before sending them to Roshto's assistant whose job was handling grievances and arbitration for the entire five state region. Patrick was making as many grievance settlements as Roshto's assistant, working very hard for the members. In the absence of other staff, Patrick would arbitrate cases and had the only winning record among all staff with a win record of 80 percent.

Patrick was also disciplined for going to a Labor Day March on Washington, where he allegedly did not get permission to go. (This was a long bus ride to and from Washington and no fun time). Patrick had written a very detailed article for the District 10 Newsletter on this march. Things would not get any better.

Through Patrick's civic activities he had won the respect of several influential leaders in the business community in Birmingham. Through their efforts he was offered an appointment to a committee of communicators of fifteen of the largest firms in Birmingham. This was an honor that had never gone to a labor leader. Rather than accepting the appointment as he would any other civic assignment, Patrick sent Roshto a note asking his permission. Permission was denied without any discussion. Roshto recommended that the appointment be given to a newly appointed staff. No acknowledgement from the business community was ever received.

Campaign for Vice President 1983

At the Convention in July 1982 T.J. Volk let it be known that he would be a candidate for Vice President in the June 1983 election. In one of Volk's first letters to local officers he made the statement:

"The time is now to stop losing ground during contract negotiations, and start regaining some of the ground we have lost. "During bargaining (in 1980) with South Central Bell, the Union Bargaining Committees desires were ignored by the Vice President (Roshto), who used his authority to reach agreement over the objections of the committee. This was done during the afternoon and early evening on August 16, 1980 before bargaining pressure was really being felt by either side at the bargaining table. "The contract was to terminate at midnight. Agreement was reached about 8:30 p.m. by making concessions to the Company. I can stand pressure, I know how to bargain and I am not afraid to strike when necessary. Your vote for me will insure we get the job done correctly."

On May 24, 1982, Sue Cook, president of the 2400 vote Louisville, Kentucky Local, had approached Patrick. She said that if he would run for vice president, she would support him. Sue had served on the bargaining committee on two occasions and was one of the five members appointed by Vice President Brown to the 1980 bargaining committee and had gone through those chaotic negotiations. It was reassuring to know that even after Patrick had put a lot of pressure on the 1980 committee, to sign the bargaining report, she still felt his abilities good enough to be vice president.

On June 9, 1982 Gary Stanga, a vice president of the 500 member Covington local in Louisiana, had approached Patrick and said he was hearing some good words about Patrick and it may be possible to get the support of several Louisiana locals if he were to run. This was David Alexandra's local, who had run for vice president in 1980 and had worked to get Patrick demoted and transferred.

Joe Pearce, Vice President of a Western Electric Local in Jackson Mississippi, Patrick's hometown, talked to him about running. Pearce and Patrick went back 20 years working together. His comments were important to Patrick because more than anyone, Pearce knew him and Patricks' extended family in Mississippi.

Patrick continued to have people ask him to run. By July 19,1982 enough local officers had approached him that he realized he must make a statement if the door was to remain open without everyone making commitments to other candidates. Patrick also believed that by being in the race it would take some of the heat off Volk and he could pick up votes that would not go to Volk without a lot of cultivating. Patrick felt that should he not make the runoff election he could keep these votes in Volk's camp. Patrick decided that he would announce that he was considering running. This would keep the door open. The final decision could be made later. Patrick went to see Volk and advised him of his plans, assuring Volk that if he got in the race there would be no anti Volk talk. His bottom line was to defeat Roshto.

On July 29, 1982 Patrick sent a letter to all local officers in the district asking them to keep their options open and that he was considering running.

Later in the fall of 1982 Roshto stopped all travel by the Birmingham staff. His stated purpose: The budget was in the red and travel must be curtailed until the convention and a new budget goes into effect in June of 1983. He instructed staff not to return telephone calls unless they were collect. This was another switch from his campaign promises.

On November 10, 1982 Roshto called Patrick into his Birmingham office. He had his assistant George Werner and Executive Vice President M.E. Nichols who had flown in from The CWA Headquarters in Washington as his witnesses in the meeting. The meeting opened. "Calvin, this meeting is about you." Roshto spelled out 15 charges against Patrick. He then stated that Patrick was being demoted and transferred to New Orleans as a CWA Representative.
Knowing about discipline in the labor relations field and having conducted arbitrations, Patrick knew there was no merit in the charges but, because he was in management in the Union, he had no recourse except to appeal through the Union president and executive board and then if that was not successful he could appeal to the CWA Convention in June. But as for now he moved into the New Orleans CWA Office.

It had taken 2 years and 5 months of continuous complaints to President Watts by Roshto before Watts broke his commitment to Patrick and now agreed to the demotion and transfer. Roshto had also fulfilled on his campaign promise to Local President David Alexander, to demote and transfer Patrick.

As a result of his experience with Watts immediately after Roshto's election, Patrick knew that with power goes the spoils and he was now out in the cold with no one to turn to in the Union. He talked to attorneys in Washington and other locations and found there had been a Supreme Court decision issued on May 17, 1982, Finnegan v. Leu, which allowed an elected union officer to select his own union administrators which was in the Courts opinion an integral part of insuring a union administration's responsiveness to the mandate of the union election."

Under the National Labor Relations Act (Landrum Griffin law) this decision took away a union employees rights in situations such as Patrick's, short of being fired. It was interesting to find that the CWA legal counsel had given a legal opinion on Finnegan v. Leu to the CWA Executive Board seven days after the Supreme Court decision. Yet none of the staff were advised of it.

Patrick felt he may have an EEOC discrimination charge due to age or sex, but did not want to take my Union (CWA) to court. He did, however keep this options open.

Patrick announced he was running for Vice President by sending a 4 page announcement in the form of a news letter to all officers of the more than 70 locals in Alabama, Kentucky, Louisiana, Mississippi and Tennessee. A summery of that document states:

On December 29, 1982 he appealed Roshto's decision to President Watts. In a penned personal letter attached to the appeal Patrick requested that he be given the opportunity to meet and talk with Watts, informally, concerning his demotion.

On January 13th, Watts responded in writing to Patrick's appeal without addressing his personal letter, "The CWA Constitution does not apply to you as an employee of CWA" even though Patrick was a member in good standing. Watts further said; "Of course, as an employee of CWA you may wish to discuss your demotion with Vice President Roshto, Executive Vice President M. E. Nichols or myself. If you desire to do so, please let me know and arrangements will be made."

January 19, 1983, Patrick attempted to reach President Watts by telephone. On February 7th Patrick received a letter from Watts stating he had on several occasions tried to return Patrick's call and the letter was acknowledging his call. On February 9th Patrick called Watts and apologized for inconveniencing him. He related how disillusioned he was at what had happened; explaining that one of the charges was that he had written to Watts a confidential letter concerning a member who was to be offered a job as an organizer. Watts didn't even remember the letter. Watts responded: We in District 10 had never put politics behind us since 1980. Patrick responded to Watts saying that he had worked his buns off for Roshto and that you (Watts) must be getting your information from Roshto. He responded he had gotten it from others. It was obvious he was not interested in Patrick's views. The conversation ended by Watts saying he hoped we would get together and work for the members after this next election.

Patrick appealed Watts' Decision to the CWA Executive Committee, which was composed of five national officers in Washington including President Watts. Patrick received the same response as he had received from Watts "your appeal had no standing as an employee of CWA".

The CWA District 10 spring meeting was to be held in New Orleans on March 2-4, 1983. Watts was to be there. At the beginning of the meeting Roshto handed Patrick a note with Watts itinerary, including coming to New Orleans to our meeting. Roshto told Patrick to pick Watts up and return him to the airport. He sarcastically said, you will have your chance to talk to Watts. Patrick felt the decision on demoting and transferring him had been made and it was too late to talk to Watts now. As luck would have it, the candidates running for vice president were to speak to the

300 district delegates from all the district locals at about the time Watts plane was to land. Another staff picked up Watts for Patrick and apologized to him that Patrick was speaking to the delegates and could not make it.

The following morning Watts spoke to the delegates, participated in a reception and at the assigned time to leave for the airport Patrick carried Watt's luggage to the parking garage and asked for his staff car to be brought down. Watts and Patrick stood and talked about New Orleans, the weather, the Mardi Gras, and football. After 45 minutes and 3 inquires about the staff car, the parking attendant said he could not find Patrick's car. Watts left in a taxi with 40 minutes to travel the 10 miles and reach his plane.

Patrick appealed the Executive Committee's decision to the Executive Board of the Union, who responded on June 1, 1983, just 5 days before the annual CWA Convention was to start. Their decision stated, "The appropriate appeal procedure for Patrick would have been that adopted by the Executive Board in 1955 (see Pages 517 and 518 of the 1955 Executive Board minutes). However, that process required that an appeal "shall be made in writing not more that five days from the time the staff employee is notified of the initial decision. Patrick was notified on November 10, 1982 but did not (timely) appeal to President Watts until December 29, 1982. Therefore, his appeal is denied."

"Well halleluiah", after five months of appealing they "now acknowledged that Patrick did have rights under the Constitution, but did not file in a timely fashion. Hooray for justice. His rights were hidden back in 25 years of CWA's history. Not one of the National Officers even knew that these rights existed, yet they ignorantly espoused a decision that was totally unfounded and unconstitutional".

The CWA National Convention started on June 6. During the convention Patrick sought the opinion of one local president from another district who he knew and respected. He asked what the local president thought about his appealing the Executive Board's decision to the Convention if he was not successful in being elected vice president. This election would be held prior to the time set aside for appeals. The local president knew Patrick's background and what had happened, and why. It was his view that it would look like sour grapes if Patrick lost the election and then appealed.

Patrick's supporters felt it would detract from his campaign to appeal the Executive Board's decision to the convention. Union staff wasn't too popular anyway. Patrick knew if he appealed he would have support from 60 percent of the delegates in District 10 but not having discussed the issue outside the District no one else knew about it. The few CWA staff around the nation who knew about it were in some cases afraid to discuss it.

Patrick made the decision not to appeal to the Convention. Time limits on filing an age and sex discrimination charge with the Equal Employment Opportunity Commission or filing a charge with the National Labor Relations Board, which was required if Patrick was to sue the Union in hopes of returning to Birmingham, were also expiring. Very nervously Patrick decided to take his chances with the Union. CWA had been good to him. Patience had always worked in his favor. If he or Volk won the election he would be returned to Birmingham. If Roshto won the election he would stay in Louisiana as the Louisiana State Director and his family would have to move to be with him.

Back in January, coincidental with Patrick's transfer to New Orleans, Volk's assignment was changed to strictly office duty. Now Roshto had us both isolated from the members. All of a sudden it was O.K. for the staff to travel, except Volk and Patrick. Roshto's assistant, George Werner, was going to all the states. Roshto had spent the holidays visiting locals in Louisiana buying meals like they were going out of style, taking his in-laws and wives of officers to dinner. His campaign had started and nothing was to be spared for him if it could win a vote. He bought gifts for a marriage and charged it to the Union. He purchased flowers for funerals and sent them in his and his wife's name. The Union paid for these flowers as well as separate flowers sent in the name of CWA.

The District 10 spring meeting expenditures showed that during this meeting in New Orleans, Roshto had spent more than $8,500 for "booze" and charged it to the Union. This was an expense clearly not in line with Union policy. There was a hospitality fund, funded by the delegates, that hospitality expenses were usually paid from. We've got plenty of money was the rule until the election was over. (Except for servicing the members.)

While in New Orleans Volk and Patrick discussed the election until late in the night. It had become evident to them that if they played their cards right Roshto would not be re-elected. Volk's supporters wanted to be sure that his and Patrick's supporters were together in a runoff as neither Volk nor Patrick had near a majority of the votes. Volk felt he was in a much stronger position than Patrick. Patrick felt "we are running neck and neck". Patrick had been talking to his supporters as well as Volk's. His entire campaign had been, "if you can't support me support Volk". Patrick had 2000 votes that would go to Roshto in the runoff whether it was he or Volk. These 2000 votes were with Patrick only trying to keep Volk out of the runoff. Patrick was their second choice, after Roshto. He did not discuss this aspect of his campaign with Volk. Volk said he felt Roshto had done Patrick an injustice, "that my talents were too valuable to the Union to be stuck off in New Orleans". We understood that whichever of us was in the runoff the other would support him.

Roshto was trying to get a bandwagon going. He kept telling his contacts his lead was increasing. He would raise the figure each week to indicate an upward trend. Two days before the convention a CWA staff person, who had been supporting Patrick, encouraged one local to have the members of that local instruct their delegates to support Volk rather than Patrick. This was a switch of 449 votes. After this switch according to Patrick's calculations the votes were divided as follows:

                Roshto 18,000
                Volk   12,800
                Patrick 12,000

    Volk lost 324 votes in a credentials floor fight. On the eve of the election one of Patrick's supporters had a death in the family. His alternate, a Volk supporter, flew in to vote. This was a switch of 246 votes to Volk.

    The same auditors who conducted the 1980 election were back. While the first ballot votes were being counted Volk and Patrick exchanged campaign buttons. Patrick was wearing Volk's, and Volk was wearing Patrick's. For the first time the Roshto supporters realized that in fact the Volk and Patrick supporters had a pact to support each other. They began to panic. For 30 minutes both Volk and Patrick supporters were having a party. They knew when the votes were counted Volk or Patrick would be in the runoff and would win over Roshto.

The primary vote was:
                Roshto   17,549
                Volk   13,417
                Patrick   11,926

When order was restored and the second ballot taken and counted the count was:
                Volk   23,535

Roshto   19,357

Roshto was gracious in his concession speech. He said; "I'm reminded of and old saying, The Lord Giveth and the Lord Taketh away; Blessed be the name of the Lord."

He urged the members to put the past behind them. He said "I want every person that supported me to do what should have been done in 1980. I want you to pledge to me and pledge to the new Vice President that you will quit this bickering and fighting-- -It's so important that we all work together now more than ever before. I feel real proud of my supporters. I asked them to talk on high levels and thank the Lord they did. I'm going to show everyone in this room what a defeated candidate can do, who has his heart right. My heart is here, my Union is here and I'm not going to be out politicking. I guarantee you, if any one of you hear of me saying anything about Vice President Volk, tell me. I'm going to work with the Administration and hope you will. Thank you".

Vice President Volk immediately reversed several policies Roshto had implemented.

The nightmare was over!!!!.-----Not Quiet!!!!

Roshto Files Objections to the Election

Within a few days Roshto had changed his mind about working with the new administration, just as he had done in 1980. He filed objections to the election with President Watts. President Watts responded to his objection on July 18, 1983; "There is no constitutional provision or authority for an internal Union appeal to a convention election of officers; consequently, no internal action can be taken on your "complaint and objection".

Roshto appealed President Watts' answer to the Executive Committee of the Union. On July 30, 1983 he received a reply: "The Executive Committee concluded that there is no constitutional provision or authority for an internal appeal of a convention election of officers once a convention has ended."

Roshto stated later he had discouraged his supporters from challenging the election on the convention floor prior to its adjournment. Had he brought the issue to the convention floor, the convention could have required a new election had there been sufficient grounds. Roshto knew how to go about doing this as another election had been challenged on the convention floor in 1977.

On August 15, 1983 Roshto filed charges with the Labor Department who set aside the election and ordered a new one. Roshto had given the Labor Department information on delegates with 8,000 votes that had questions as to whether the local elections had been conducted in accordance with the stringent rules of the Labor Department.

When ballots are mailed to a member, the member is to receive a ballot, an unmarked envelope to place the ballot in, and a stamped envelope with a return address on it. The unmarked envelope is placed in the stamped self-addressed envelope to be sent to the local election committee. The member is required to place his name on the outside of the stamped envelope. When ballots are to be counted, the election committee looks at the name on the outside envelope, records that name (to insure no one votes twice). The Election Committee then removes the unmarked envelope with the ballot, from the outside stamped envelope and places all the unmarked envelopes with ballots, together for counting. This way no one knows how a member votes.

There are many kinds of unintentional irregularities in elections. Local unions operate their locals on a voluntary basis and have no experience in holding elections. In fact, elections conducted by the Labor Department its-self have been set aside. The election in this case was set aside for reasons such as, the local did not keep the outside envelope with the name on it as required. Ballots were counted when the voters name was not on the outside of the return envelope as is required. Some locals had rules requiring attendance at a certain number of meetings, without any exceptions, which was irregular. etc. They were conducting their elections as they had always done. It was the same rules Roshto was elected by in 1980. The same rules as in 1980, where Volk could have challenged the election when he lost to Roshto by 12 votes. For the good of the Union he chose not to challenge that election.

Another irony of the challenge to the election was that while Roshto was Vice President, a local president, Tommy Doty from Tupelo, Mississippi had brought up the issue of delegates being elected which were not in accordance with the rules of the CWA convention. Roshto had ruled him out of order. Doty had appealed Roshto's decision to President Watts who had ruled against Doty. Now Roshto was appealing the same rules that he had denied to Doty.

Watts Denies Vice President Volk's Request

Vice President Volk upon being elected on June 17, 1983, had gone to President Watts and requested two things. He wanted CWA Representative Stanly Powell, who was in Patrick's old job as East Tennessee/Kentucky Director, to be his assistant and he wanted Calvin Patrick returned to Birmingham "where his talents could be used for the Union." Watts ask about Roshto. Volk said he could not trust him and did not want him in the District. Watts said Roshto must have a job in the District. Since they could not agree on Roshto, Watts refused to grant Volk's two request.

In preparation for negotiating the 1983 contract with CWA and South Central Bell, Volk appointed Powell as Chair of the South Central Bell Bargaining Committee and Patrick was made co-chair. Neither knew what the future held with regards to their assignments after the negotiations were over.

Roshto's challenge to the election caused the Labor Department to set the new election for March 27, 1984 in Birmingham. The election was to be conducted by the Labor Department.

Roshto, trying to get delegate support in the new election, wrote a 4-page letter to all delegates about how he had been treated after the election.

In spite of several changes made by Volk immediately after winning the election over Roshto (stopping the District 10 Newsletter, stopping grievance reports to the local presidents, The CWA South Central Bell contract being negotiated involving a 22 day strike), Volk overwhelmed Roshto in the rerun election.

On September 1, 1984 after negotiations were complete, Watts and Volk settled their dispute with Powell becoming Volk's assistant, and Patrick was returned to Birmingham as an administrative assistant. Roshto was assigned to Patrick's old East Tennessee office as a CWA representative.

Roshto's Retirement University Inn-Birmingham
January 18, 1985

The nightmare was finally over.......

On January 18, 1985 Vice President Volk gave a retirement party for Roshto as was the custom for retirees. Norma Powell gave the invocation and later talked about her relationship with Roshto and how he had helped her as a black female in her very early and difficult years when she was appointed to the CWA staff in 1973. She said that with the climate as it was in Birmingham at that time it could have been very difficult for her had it not been for Roshto's helpfulness. She told of how they went to Kentucky to organize a company and while driving Roshto spent his time telling her about the NLRB. About how union busters operated, the kinds of tactics used by companies and what the unions campaign would be about. In spite of all the mistakes he had made, she was his friend and was eternally grateful. Former Vice President W. W. Brown spoke and started by saying although he had been retired for 5 years he could still climb to the podium without assistance; that he was not senile as many had said. He said he had hired Roshto in 1972 against the advise of many. He was very complimentary saying that no other person could have organized GTE-Automatic Electric in Huntsville, Alabama and an unnamed company in Louisiana. He told of Roshto's being able to get on top of a heavy grievance load "that all of his predecessors were unwilling or unable to do".

George Werner, Roshto's assistant, opened his remarks by saying that when Roshto was elected Vice President he did many things that upset the CWA staff and it even upset him. But he gave one example of how one man was to be laid off and had been denied a right to move to another city. He stated that Roshto had negotiated a new procedure that allowed this employee the right to transfer. This changed his mind about Roshto.

W.E. Reiser, Assistant Vice President of Personnel for South Central Bell, said when he looked back, the period of 1980-1983 during Roshto's vice presidency would be the highlight of his career. He stated that during this period of new technological changes, consolidations of offices and placing employees into large teams, had caused thousands of employees to be surplused. Many were relocated or laid off and the preparation for Divestiture caused a lot of pain and difficult times. He felt that under these circumstances Roshto had done an outstanding job.

The party had about 80 in attendance and had gone well. It had been put together by an administration that had defeated Roshto in his reelection bid and everything had been done to make it a good night for Roshto. By this point Patrick was feeling good, Roshto was retiring with dignity and his adversaries were treating him with kindness.

Roshto's response was good. There were small jokes. He said he was glad they had elected him Vice President because that high salary for three years had doubled his retirement benefits. He told of moving back home to Louisiana and building a log house, which he could not have done without that large pension. He was going into the antique business. He said he had left a lot of things undone for years and now he was going to make up for it by working for the Lord. He stopped just before breaking up.

During the evening Patrick thought back over the past, the number of times he had tried to be honest and fare to Roshto and the way his efforts had failed. Patrick's family had gone through some wrenching times as a result of his being forced to move to New Orleans, yet Patrick now felt good toward Roshto. He hoped Roshto would have a good retirement. Patrick felt with Roshto's emphasis on working for the Lord, it would also mean he would be willing to forgive and forget. Although it seemed forgiveness had been rejected seventy times seven, Patrick wanted to try and make amends once more.

When the program ended, Patrick went to the podium and extended his hand, grasp Roshto's arm and with tears in his eyes told Roshto that he wanted to be his friend. For a moment Patrick felt Roshto also had that need. He looked at Patrick and said, "Keep working for the Union, keep working for the Union." As Patrick left the podium he said a prayer to himself. He had forgiven Roshto. It felt like a burden had been lifted. Lord, give Roshto the inner peace he so desperately seeks.

Epilog

CWA President Glenn Watts actions and dialog throughout this book (including verbatim recordings of speeches and discussions) was of a seasoned intelligent leader, who allowed the rope to be played out by various leaders with different agendas, but he knew when to take charge and lead. He never learned of the internal clashes or behind the scene issues raised in this book or the issue that settled the strike between CWA and United Telecommunications (In East Tennessee/Virginia.)

Rudy Mendoza's efforts to lead the United Telecommunications Locals was vindicated in 1981 When The CWA Executive Board changed Union Policy placing The Independent Telephone Director in the process of Bargaining. Had he had this authority in 1979 there would have been no story to tell.

On January 1, 1984, through a court ordered divestiture, AT&T and its 23 operating companies including South Central and Southern Bell were broken up and the old Bell System was dead. In its place was a new AT&T and seven regional Bell operating companies, which included BellSouth, made up of South Central Bell and Southern Bell. This required CWA to consolidate also.

In 1985 for six months a team of Southern and South Central Bell managers and a team of CWA District 3 and 10 staff met in Anniston, Alabama in an effort to consolidate the two separate contracts into one Bellsouth-CWA Contract. The efforts were very successful with the consolidation of all but three articles that were resolved in the subsequent 1986 negotiations between the new CWA district 3 team where T.J. Volk's assistant, R. Stanley Powell, was chairman and Calvin Patrick was co-chairman of the unions committee.

At the end of T.J. Volk's 3-year term in 1986, he and Stanley Powell retired. Calvin Patrick continued as the Administrative Assistant in District 3 to Vice President Gene Russo. Patrick continued with the responsibility of grievances and arbitration and contract interpretation for the 5 states of old District 10. In 1989 and 1992 Patrick was on the CWA negotiation team with BellSouth and retired in September of 1992 after 44 years of service with AT&T and CWA. The old CWA District 10 office in Birmingham was closed, commensurate with Patrick's retirement. Patrick's papers are at ETSU in Johnson City, Tn and The University of Alabama in Tuscaloosa, Al.

CWA has continued to grow and expand its jurisdiction. CWA members now work in telecommunications, broadcasting, cable TV, journalism, publishing, manufacturing, airlines, customer service, government service, health care, education and other fields. While CWA has lost members due to industry consolidations, down sizing and the economy, its overall membership has grown and CWA now represents over 700,000 men and women across the United States, Canada and Puerto Rico. Six women now serve on the 19 member CWA Executive Board

* * * * *

Arbitration of Cases and Grievance Handling for Employees

By Calvin Patrick

Case #1 If the Member Could Only Be There!!!!

On February fourth 1986 South Central Bell advised CWA the Company was going to down grade the job of plant assigner cutting the wages in that job over $125.00 per week. They were also going to reduce the workforce by 242 employees. Many of the technicians in this title had worked most of their career to reach this prestigious and highest paying job within the crafts. The Company upon notifying the Union of this change was advised that the Union would be filing grievances challenging the Company's downgrade of the plant assigner job.

I received more letters on this issue than on any other change ever made by the Company. I requested that the Company set up a visit for me to visit a work location to learn more about the job functions. When we arrived at the Birmingham location, management answered our questions for over an hour. When we were ready to proceed into the work environment, I asked the manager to tell me the name of one of the CWA Job Stewards she had confidence in and that the employees also trusted. There was a former local president in the work group but she gave me the name of a job steward named Wayne Gilmore. As I did not know Wayne I asked the manager to introduce him to me. Wayne talked very frankly about the job, its difficulty and the training that went into it before a person could become proficient. It was explained to him how we would challenge the Company's decision. I left my CWA business card with Wayne and asked him to call me if he had any questions.

Later that afternoon Wayne called and said the plant assignors were meeting after work to discuss the downgrade issue. I asked could I come and maybe be of help. He felt that was a good Idea. For three hours that evening questions were answered. The contract was explained. The employees were told how we would approach challenging the Company's actions. From my observations the manager had been right. Wayne was the leader. He was very mild mannered, understood what the Union needed to challenge the Company's decision to down grade the plant assigner job, and agreed to lead a team in obtaining the needed information for CWA's challenge of the decision to down grade the job. I had a comfortable feeling that while the employees were not happy, they understood the problem and were satisfied with the way we were planning on challenging the Company.

The next morning the Company gave the employees an overview of what was going to happen. During that meeting Wayne asked would employees with more than 15 years service have their wages protected for three years as was provided by the contract. Either Wayne misunderstood the manager or she mislead him but his perception was that employees with 15 or more years service would not have their wages protected. In our meeting I had assured him these wages would be protected. The following day I called Wayne to get a report on how his group was coming in collecting the data that we needed to support our case. Wayne was very cold and distant. He was not putting anything together. I asked why. He said I had lied to him about the wage protection for employees with over 15 years service. For 10 minutes I attempted to explain that under no condition could the Company deny this contractual right. He finally in desperation said that the Company paid his wages and he believed them not the Union. The Union had lied before and that we were doing nothing to help the employees.

By then my frustration had turned to anger. I advised him that within an hour he would hear from the Company straightening this misunderstanding out. He responded he would believe it when he heard from the Company but not before then.

That day I had been meeting along with other Union and Company representatives in Anniston, Alabama in an ongoing joint Company and Union effort of merging the South Central and Southern Bell CWA contracts together. This process, which took 6 months, was necessary as a result of the AT&T divestiture in January of 1984 and the subsequent creation of Bell South from the former South Central Bell and Southern Bell Companies.

As I left my hotel room after talking to Wayne, my counterpart with South Central Bell, Henry Dawson, fell in stride with me as we headed back to the workroom. I vented my frustration and anger with Dawson of how could the Company create such an impossible misunderstanding. I ask Dawson to get on the phone and get this mess straightened out. Dawson put his arm over my shoulder as we walked and said he would make the call. I know he could feel the pain I was suffering knowing that it must be devastating when a steward rejects a man who is working his heart out for the members. An hour later I called Wayne. He was ok and ready to do his job. He never apologized but he now believed in his Union again. This was a lesson for me also. The Company had surplused over 10,000 employees in the last 4 years. 2300 of them were on layoff. I had talked to hundreds of them about their rights under the agreement. I had worked out many problems for them but with Wayne, for the first time, I really understood the feelings of a man who had given over 30 years of his life to the Company and Union and was now feeling that no one really cared about him or the other employees. He was as low emotionally as he could go, feeling desperate and helpless.

If he only knew how my heart went out for him and the others: If he could only sit in the meetings with management and union as we work together trying to find solutions to complex problems that the contract does not cover: If he could be there when in desperation we ask the Company to just give us their answer on a grievance and we will arbitrate the case: If he could be with the Union staff as we sit together and attempt to come up with alternative solutions that will protect the rights of all our members when there has never been a problem of this magnitude before: If he could only be there when I later call the Company to offer a possible alternative to the problem and be relieved that honorable men such as Henry Dawson are also working on an alternate plan based upon our previous conversations that we felt had been a failure: If he and our other members could only be there when we reach an agreement that both parties can live with that gives our members additional rights they never had and saves jobs also. But that's the life of a Union representative. The member only knows when he or she is in trouble and no one seems to care. When a solution is found they say that's why we pay our dues.

But deep inside the Union representative knows he or she has helped a group of employees that could not have individually helped themselves. It's not a job, it's a labor of love.

Case #2 Arbitrate or not to Arbitrate

"While many labor disputes are clearly suitable for arbitration, one of the potential hazards of labor arbitration has been said to be an "over optimistic estimate" of its effective scope, "which tends to consider it an all purpose tool or panacea for the resolution of any and all disputes where the parties fail to settle privately. Even if a dispute is of a type generally suitable for arbitration and is arbitral under the agreement, judgment must be exercised in deciding whether to arbitrate the particular dispute. Included among the factors to be considered are the merits of the case, the importance of the issue, the effect of winning or losing, the possibilities of settlement, internal policies and politics within the Union and the Company, psychological and face saving considerations, and the like." (How arbitration works 3rd edition Elkouri and Elkouri P-44)

Two basic principles most arbitrators use; they will not give to either party what the parties could not obtain (agree to) through the collective bargaining process. Usually on issues affecting management rights, unless the Union has clear unambiguous language supporting its position, the arbitrator will rule for the Company. If on the other hand the issue involves a discharge, the arbitrator will give any benefit of the doubt to the employee.

Ask any member about his/her grievance and each will tell you arbitrate their case, unless it is settled favorably. This is ok if they have been fired. In other cases arbitration may not be in his/her or the unions best interest although it is hard to explain to members in a way they will readily accept.

As an example, in BellSouth there is a four step discipline procedure; counsel, warn, suspend, and then termination. If an employee has been counseled and warned and then is given a suspension, should the case be arbitrated if there is a question of credibility?

The arbitrator usually will come down on the side of management unless it can be clearly demonstrated the grievant is in the right. Also, the arbitrator does not see a short suspension of a few days as a severe penalty. If a decision is made not to arbitrate then under the CWA contract with BellSouth, the Union can reject the Company statement of the facts and close the grievance. While the Union cannot later bring up that grievance and ask for pay (if it was a suspension), it can later have an arbitrator decide the merits of that suspension.

Let's assume an employee with 15 years service is suspended for 5 days for a motor vehicle accident where another vehicle hit him at an intersection. The Company has ruled it was a preventable accident. They say the employee should have used defensive driving techniques taught by the Company. When the facts are presented to the arbitrator he must decide who is right, the unions story or the Company's investigating committee. The grievant testifies that the intersection was in a curve. It was overcast with drizzling rain and visibility was low and grievant could not see clearly. Let's assume the arbitrator had some small doubt about the grievant's testimony and ruled for the Company. Let's assume the grievant later has a more severe accident. He was speeding and received a citation from the police for being at fault. The Company determines again that defensive driving techniques were not used and this too was a preventable accident. Let's assume he is a steward who "police's" the contract and his supervisor doesn't like him. Based on his overall record the Company decides to dismiss him.

The Company has followed progressive discipline. Based on all the facts. He had been counseled, warned, and then he was found guilty in the suspension arbitration case.

Probably there is nothing the Union can do about his discharge unless we find some technicality. We believe he was discharged in part because of his union activities but we have no proof. The grievant can testify about how the supervisor reacted when he filed grievances. Even if we arbitrated ----because of losing the suspension arbitration case and the severity of the last accident when the grievant was ticketed for speeding, we would lose the case.

If on the other hand the Union had "rejected" the Company's statement of the facts on the suspension grievance and had not arbitrated, we would have reserved the right to resolve the merits of that case later. We could now argue the suspension at the same time as we argue the discharge since discharge is the capitol punishment in the workplace. A higher standard of proof will be required of the Company in the discharge case. That was not true in the suspension case. The employee's long service of 15 years now works in his favor.

When the Union presents its case and talks about the suspension, the way the steward policed the contract, the way his supervisor reacted when a grievance was presented, when we talk about the weather and the accident happening in a curve just before dark and there is the question of visibility, doubts may be raised in the arbitrators mind. He will be thinking about how his decision will affect that employee and his family. He will lose not only his job but will have his retirement affected also. The arbitrator may decide, with regards to the suspension, that there were questions raised on credibility and he would give the employee the benefit of the doubt believing the employee told the truth and rule in favor of the employee.

We recently had a case similar to the one described. The Union felt it was a very difficult case. Even after the hearing we had doubts about winning. The arbitrator ruled the employee should be put back to work with a 30-day suspension. We have had other more severe cases where the arbitrator would place the employee back on the payroll with no back pay. At least he had a job and pension rights even though a lot of pay was lost.

Union representatives, rather than insist that all suspensions be arbitrated, should be sure they are acting in the best interest of the member. In my view, unless the evidence is clearly in favor of the grievant, it is better to fight the battle later and to win than to take a chance with a short suspension and lose.

Case #3 Scabs Have rights Too

Under the National Labor Relations Act unions are required to represent both the member and the non-member. The failure to represent a member or non-union member can subject the Union to a lawsuit. The non-member receives all the benefits of a Union but is not required to pay dues in twenty states. In the other thirty states, he is only required to pay a "dues equivalent", if the employer is willing to enter into that type of an agreement with the Union.

The following case is one that was tried before an arbitrator on behalf of a scab. The grievant allegedly indecently exposed himself to a female and her 3-year-old daughter. He vigorously denied the accusation and the Union did not have knowledge of a police report being filed. The grievant did not tell the Union, apparently thinking he could get by without this becoming public. This was an issue of creditability. Therefore, the Union had no choice except to believe the grievant. Testimony at arbitration showed the lady and her daughter were at a community children's wading pool. A car drove up and a man exposed himself, motioning for the lady and calling, "Come here". This activity went on for five minutes. She noticed the car had a rusty trunk and she took down the license number and gave the description of the car to the police and identified the grievant from among several men in street cloths at the police headquarters lineup.

The arbitrator noted she did not know the grievant prior to the incident. The record did not reflect she had a history of making baseless charges. In an embarrassing situation of this kind the easiest thing for her to do would have been to forget the matter. If she had done this, the arbitrator said she would not have been a responsible citizen.

"This arbitrator appreciates the vigorous defense that

the Union made for the grievant. He is also sympathetic to both the grievant and his family. There can be no question, however, that the evidence clearly shows that he did commit the offense in question. The only full court hearing conducted in this matter resulted in a finding that the grievant was guilty of the offenses charged. This Company, as a public utility, cannot retain employees who have committed such offenses and are likely to commit these same offenses again, as the grievant may be required in emergencies to go on the premises of customers.

"Medical authorities do recognize that exhibitionism of this nature is an illness. The grievant should undergo a course of psychiatric treatment. It is recommended that if the grievant presents a report that he is permanently cured and also makes available a competent psychiatrist to consult with the Company doctor, the Company should give some consideration to his reemployment, if the Company doctor is satisfied that the grievant has been completely cured of these tendencies. This can be only in the nature of a recommendation and is not a finding on the part of this arbitrator".

"Grievant was discharged for proper cause."

Case #4 The Hot Dog Case/Off Duty Sexual Activity

Most cases handled by the Union are of a very routine nature. There are four or five cases that stand out as unusual of the hundreds that are adjudicated. The Union does not condone these activities any more than the Company. However, we do have a responsibility to insure that the Company does not impose its own personal values on employees when they are off the job. In the following case the issue was off duty conduct. Arbitration history is full of cases that say an employee's off duty conduct is none of the employers business unless it would have an adverse public impact or publicity.

In this case the grievant was a male and worked as a telephone operator along with a large group of females in one large operating room. The grievant became sexually involved with one of the female operators. He had pulled a trick on her and the trick became the talk of the operating room. When the Company heard of it they confronted him and he gave a long written statement of the facts. The Company discharged him.

At the arbitration hearing it was disclosed from his statement that the female had taken the initiative in developing a social relationship. She quickly became the aggressor in frequently practicing unorthodox sex relations upon him in his automobile after work while simultaneously denying orthodox relations due to her fear of pregnancy. Her persistent refusal to submit to orthodox relations irked him, and his annoyance was aggravated by embarrassment and humiliation that he experienced from subsequent teasing at work by fellow employees to whom she had disclosed their relationship. He consequently reached the decision to get even with her by conceiving a plan, in his own words, "to make her feel lower than a dog."

The grievant procured two local motel rooms for the

night, telling her in substance that this night would constitute a special occasion. He took her to the motel room, having obtained as props a hotdog and mustard for the staging of the occasion. When his victim and his props were in place to suit his purpose, he turned on the light in the room, which constituted a pre-arranged signal to four fellow employees in the adjoining room to enter the room. They did so, viewing her in his language "looking like a fool." News of this episode spread rapidly among Company employees that resulted in the grievant's appearance before the Company security officers, his written statement and discharge. The arbitrator stated, "it is clear that the grievant's behavior which caused the Company to find him "unsuited for continued employment" constituted off-duty conduct on his own time and away from any Company facilities. The grievant's behavior further did not result in the filing of any criminal or civil charges against him. In addition, despite the obvious grapevine through which the news traveled within the Company, it is agreed that no media publicity of any nature occurred. Under these circumstances the three criteria cited by the Union, which normally support a discharge for off duty misconduct, do not exist in the present case. The Company has been unable to produce any evidence that the grievant's behavior brought actual or reasonably predictable harm to the Company's reputation or product, or rendered him unable to perform his job duties or to appear at work, or caused the refusal, reluctance or inability of other employees to work with him. Indeed the Company conceded at the hearing that the episode had no effect upon the Company's service and caused no discernible change in the level of its performance. "The grievant's behavior, however it may be characterized, was not job-related and the Company, consequently, lacked the contractual power to impose discipline because of such behavior.

"This opinion constitutes no defense or excuse for the grievant's conduct by the arbitrator. Similarly however, it serves no purpose to stress the Company's personal view that his conduct was "dehumanizing" to a fellow employee. The characterization of conduct by unpleasant names, however subjectively offensive that conduct may be, does not somehow inject "proper cause" into a termination action so unrelated to the job that the nature of the misconduct is essentially personal and therefore of no contractual consequence." (75-47-1051-SCB)

In another off duty case, an employee had participated in a live stag show and evidence was given where management and craft had attended many such shows. The arbitrator stated management can not be the guardian of its employees' morals. If a Company retained only the wholly rectitudinous, pious, self righteous on its payroll, it would have to part with the services of a surprising large number of people ranging from sweepers to executives. (Ref: 60-46-297k-SB)

While the principle of off duty conduct was decided in the two cases cited above, the first in 1960, many more were decided prior to and in later years, unions still must continue defending the employees rights depending upon what management morals are controlling on a given day. As an example in 1981 the South Central Bell, Mississippi Personnel Department imposed a suspension because a female employee had received seventy parking tickets over a period of about a year. The personnel manager's comment was "We cannot tolerate that type of morality with this Company."

Case #5 Morally Right/Legally Wrong-Fired

One of the most difficult problems in handling grievances is when our own values get in the way. Believe me this can happen to a Union representative too. A case in point was where a church deacon was a central office technician. In his job he was assigned to test circuits that required him to monitor a circuit momentarily to determine if it was in use. Many times when a circuit was busy he may momentarily hear a small portion of the conversation. Federal statutes do not allow a telephone employee to repeat or use any information he may hear to other persons. There are very serious penalties, fines, and jail sentences for violation of these statutes involving the "Secrecy of Communications". All telephone employees are aware of this law. In addition, periodically management will require employees to sign statements stating they have read a booklet entitled "A Personal Responsibility", or a similar document, which speaks to this and many other ethical or legal questions faced by employees on a daily basis. This particular deacon was working the evening shift maintaining the central office equipment. He happened to monitor a busy circuit in preparation of doing routine maintenance on it. He recognized his pastor and the organist talking about their private sex lives together. He was devastated. He wrote a note, but did not sign it, and placed it on the pastor's car telling him, we know about your involvement with the organist. The next evening he deliberately listened to the circuit again and heard them discussing the note. They said it was the deacon who placed the note on the car but he couldn't tell anyone about or he would get fired so don't worry. Daily he continued monitoring the circuit and the conversations continued. His threat was not even taken seriously. The deacon rigged up a circuit from the office to his home and had his wife place a tape recorder on the circuit and taped the conversations. He, then along with another deacon, confronted the pastor with the tape. The pastor refused to resign. Two years later the pastor moved to another church. Upon leaving he went to the Telephone Company and reported the deacon. The deacon confessed to everything and was fired.

I was responsible for making the decision to arbitrate. If I had been in the deacon's place, I may have responded the same way. It was a very personal and core value issue. I could empathize with him but had to make the decision to arbitrate or not arbitrate based on the facts. After reviewing the case with Union attorneys and other staff, the Union's collective view was that the law did not support the deacon's conduct; therefore the case could not be arbitrated.

The deacon had flagrantly violated the law on several occasions and unlawfully taped a private conversation. The local president still felt the deacon was right. He could not separate the immoral conduct of the pastor from the deacon's violating of the secrecy of communications law. He and a large majority of his members continued to believe the Union should have arbitrated the case.

Case #6 Pastor and Secretary Allegedly Involved in An Affair!

Another case involved a pastor, who was also president of a Chapter of the Moral Majority, and the church secretary.

Two telephone employees were members of the pastor's church. One, an operator, was the relief church secretary. The other employee, a service representative, handled inquires about customer telephone bills. There had been rumors that the church secretary and pastor were having an affair, but no proof. One day the relief secretary was working in the church office and observed from the church telephone bill that the pastor had made a 70-minute telephone call to the church secretary's home late at night while he was out of town. The service representative, who was a good friend of the relief secretary, happened to call the relief secretary to chat. The relief secretary told her about the telephone call. The service representative decided to pull up last months church telephone bill to check it. There was a similar call on that bill. Then the service representative decided to check on the church secretary's bill. She found a call from the secretary's home to the out of town hotel where the pastor was staying. This information became an issue at the church business meeting. The congregation sided with the pastor. Both employees were reported to telephone Company management. The relief secretary was suspended for 30 days and the service representative was fired.

The Telephone Industry jealously guards their customers' privacy. This service representative, in her normal activities, did not have the two accounts as her responsibility. Therefore, she would never have a reason to look at them. Yet she not only violated Company policy in looking at the bills, she discussed them with the relief secretary and the bills then became an issue in the church business meeting. While she may have felt there was hanky panky going on, there was no evidence. It is possible that the conversations were about the business of the church. Whatever the pastor may have been guilty of, it was a violation of the law for the service representative to discuss this information. We were able to get her a termination settlement of several thousand dollars.

Case #7 Information From Call Given to Police-Stops Crime

There is only one instance where a Telephone Company fired an employee for revealing information and the Union was able to win at arbitration. In that instance an employee overheard a conversation revealing a crime was to be committed. This information was passed on to the law enforcement officers and it stopped a crime.

Case #8 Employee Denies Sexual Encounter-Has Witnesses

(Some names have been changed.)

Leaving his office, Calvin Patrick headed north out of Johnson City, TN. A five-hour drive to Louisville, Kentucky lay ahead. Patrick was considering the dilemma he was in having to arbitrate a case dealing with Sammy Mason who had been accused of having sex in a Company vehicle on Company time with Jenny Withers, who was 23 years old and mentally challenged. The female staff representative assigned to Louisville felt very uncomfortable in arbitrating a sex case and Patrick was arbitrating the case for her. He would be the unions' council for this case.

As he drove, he reminisced on how he had come to this point in his life. He had been working for the Communications Workers of America (CWA) for ten years, and had gained the respect of his boss, Willard Brown, who was the CWA Vice President over District 10, which covered five states, Alabama, Kentucky, Tennessee, Louisiana and Mississippi. Willard Brown was a man of few words who could be very charming but would not play games. Brown expected his subordinates to earn the respect of the employers they interfaced with.

As he drove Patrick thought back on a great lesson from Brown on following orders. His first negotiations had been with a small electronics components manufacturer with 300 employees. After each session of negotiations, he would write a report to Brown on what transpired. Brown, after reading Patrick's report, would usually call him and they would discuss the next step to take. Patrick had mentioned in several of his reports that he was seeking a "successor clause" in the contract. This clause was very desirable and meant that if the Company was sold the successor Company would have to abide by the terms of the contract. The Company attorney in these negotiations had stated in several of the negotiating sessions that there was no condition under which he would agree to such language in the contract. Patrick had dutifully placed these remarks in his reports to Brown. Brown in turn had verbally told Patrick that under no condition should he continue to insist upon the "successor clause", as obviously we could not obtain it and it was delaying reaching an agreement, as negotiations had already been going on for six months.

Brown and Patrick both had private phones for their use in communicating with each other. After reporting on the successor clause in his next two reports he received a telegram from Brown.

"Respond immediately by telegram why you continue to disobey my direct orders "not to negotiate a "successor clause". "Brown."

Patrick knew he was in serious trouble and fretted for several hours over how to handle the problem. He did not want to send anything in writing, as he was sure it would wind up in his personnel file. Finally, at 3:00 p.m. he picked up his private phone and dialed Brown. Brown answered, "Brown".

For twenty minutes Patrick tried to assure Brown that he was and would continue to follow Brown's orders and how much he appreciated Brown's help on this contract. At the end of the conversation Patrick felt he had convinced Brown that everything was all right as Brown had said very little during the conversation. Patrick thanked Brown for listening and ended the conversation.

Twenty minutes later Patrick's secretary, Ann Greer, said Western Union was holding for him. He picked up the phone and Western Union stated "May I read a telegram to you"? Patrick, puzzled as to what the telegram could be about responded, Yes. Please read it.

"Please respond to my telegram of this a.m. signed "Brown".

As he crossed the Tennessee line, Patrick thought back on his childhood and how he had gone to church until he was twelve when his parents and he stopped. He soon became a boy scout and earned the rank of "Life". One of his passions had been to become an Eagle Scout, but it became impossible when his family moved into a rural town in the Mississippi hill country where there was no scouting program. He thought about how as a young man he became a scoutmaster leading his troop to excel in learning the Boy Scout motto and oath. They learned how to camp out and cook, how to tie knots, and canoe. At night they observed many of the constellations in the heavens and learned how to observe the stars and know directions at night. Swimming and life saving was taught to his troop.

As he drove north he remembered how desperately he wanted to play football while in the eight grade. His coach had promised that if he learned the more than 100 plays he would be given the opportunity to play. The next day he had all the plays memorized and reported to the coach who quizzed him in detail about the plays. Coach lived up to his promise and allowed him to play in a number of games that year at his small high school in Terry, MS. The first time coach sent him into a game he was so excited that he stumbled and fell in front of the bench. The team and stadium became alive with laughter.

As a young athlete, he had boxed in the Golden Gloves for four years as a 135-pound lightweight boxer. Twice he went to the State finals only to lose in the championship fight. He recalled how he had never deviated from the life long habit, taken up while boxing, of running five miles each morning no matter where he was or how busy his schedule.

Driving past Bowling Green, KY he thought how his

belief system had been formed; that his ethics had come from his experiences in church, as an athlete, and with the scouts based on the scout laws and oath. Now he was taking on a task that if the Company was right, went against all that he believed in. Why?

Sammy Mason had been terminated for allegedly having sex with Jenny Withers during working hours. Mason had claimed he was innocent and had two witnesses who would testify giving him an alibi. Under the circumstances the Union had no choice but to arbitrate his case.

The alleged victim, Jenny Withers, had moved from Louisville after the sexual allegation was made and could not be located for an interview by the Union. Without her testimony the Company would not be able to prove their case. The local Union was insisting that the case be arbitrated so that Sammy would get his job back.

Patrick was very uncomfortable handling the case but the Union had no choice as the evidence gave Sammy an alibi. Patrick's hope was that after interviewing all of his witnesses and putting the evidence together and discussing the case with the Company, they would withdraw the charges and return Sammy to his job.

He arrived in Louisville in mid-afternoon and the local officers and job stewards had Sammy, his wife and his witnesses at the hotel to be interviewed. At nine p.m. Patrick completed his interviews and felt comfortable that Sammy and his witnesses may be telling the truth. The officers and stewards too felt very good about the Union's chances of winning. The bottom line was that Jenny Withers and her mother had moved and there was no trace of them in Louisville either in telephone Company records or records of the Louisville Power and Light Company.

In instructing the witnesses about testifying in the arbitration case, Patrick had ask each to be sure and listen to the questions posed by the Company attorney. "If a question could be answered with a yes or no, then say yes or no, do not elaborate. If you elaborate you will get yourself in trouble as the Company counsel would challenge every statement that is made." Every Union witness said they felt comfortable with the questions the Union would ask and understood the Company would be trying to prove what Sammy had done with Jenny Withers.

Patrick addressed Sammy; "I do find it difficult to believe you would travel 5 miles from your job assignment to see a woman when you know the Company keeps a close tab on you. If the Union's evidence holds up, you will have your job back in two weeks, but if Jenny shows up and testifies, it will create a serious doubt as to your truthfulness. The arbitrator will view her as having no reason to lie and she would be a credible witness. You haven't given us any information that would refute her charges except that you were not there."

Christina Preston was an operations manager for South Central Bell working with the Company's chief legal council Marvin Thompson. She was new in the personnel department but had been a manager since she went to the work for the Company after college. She was now on the fast track for promotion to upper management. She had held a number of jobs over the years in four departments of the Company. In her jobs she had dealt with the local Union and was comfortable with them, having a good reputation of being honest. Forty-five years old, she weighted 115 pounds and was very attractive with her long blond hair resting on her shoulders. She wore very smart business suits and always drew the attention of men. Very confidant Christina knew she was moving up at a very fast pace. This new job in personnel was the highest position she had held and was going to give her a lot of exposure to top management of the Company. Over the years she had made very good impressions with higher management, getting promoted on an average of every eighteen months, and was looking forward to negotiations with the Union coming up in a year. Her plan was to be a key player on the management bargaining team. She was well prepared and understood the meanings and interpretations of the labor agreement that had been adjudicated between the Company and Union since 1941.

Christina had met Patrick for the first time the week before and was one of 3 Company managers that dealt with him on everyday problem solving. She was ready to do battle and had no qualms that this was a sex case.

The Company and Union officials were staying at the Louisville Holiday Inn where Professor C. Wallace McGehee would try the case. Professor McGehee had taught labor law at Ole Miss for 35 years. He was a friend of CWA and in 1970 had been the only professor in Mississippi who would accept scholarships the 15 CWA locals in Mississippi provided each year for students of working families. The climate for unions in the state of Mississippi had changed a lot over the years and CWA now had scholarships in several colleges in the state. Professor McGehee was very special to labor for taking a chance in accepting the Union's scholarships when no other college or university would. The AFL-CIO had honored him on several occasions and he had spoken at AFL-CIO conventions. McGehee had tried many cases between these two parties and was perceived to be fair by both Company and Union. The Company did not know how close the relationship with the Union had been.

After his morning run and a refreshing shower, Patrick went to breakfast in the hotel dining room. He felt ready for the day's challenge. The Company team was sitting over in the corner of the dining room in serious conversation. Patrick walked over and spoke to Christina and Marvin who introduced him to the local managers who would be testifying. Jenny Withers was not at the table. Patrick ask, "is there any information that you could share that could help us resolve this case before the hearing?" Marvin chuckled and said, "we shall see".

Patrick walked to the middle of the dining room and spoke to Professor McGehee who was eating by himself. Patrick said, "Prof. I would eat with you but it might look bad". McGehee responded, "I am comfortable, thank you anyway."

Patrick then went to the side opposite the Company team and had breakfast with Sammy Mason, his wife, and several local officers and stewards who had come to learn how the arbitration process works. Sammy's wife had spoken very strongly last night in support of Sammy and about his innocence.

The case went smoothly for the first hour with the Company laying out their case and putting on several witnesses who testified about the timing of the incident; the kind of vehicle Sammy was using in his job assignment and the location of the home of Jenny Withers and her mother.

After the Company laid out their allegations, Patrick put on the Union's case. Sammy's assignment was five miles on the other side of Louisville. He had not been in the area where Jenny Withers lived as testified by the Company. The Union's witnesses supported Sammy with an alibi saying during the period of the allegation Sammy was at a cab company with his friends eating lunch and stayed there for two hours afterward shooting the breeze. Sammy acknowledged that he often was out of route when he took his lunch hour at the cab Company with his friends. He knew it was wrong to be out of route and goofing off but he assured the arbitrator that he always completed his job assignments by the end of each day. He testified that he had not been near the location where the sexual incident allegedly occurred.

On cross-examination Attorney Thompson ask Sammy did he know where Jenny lived. Sammy said he did not recall being in that area on any job assignments. Thompson then produced a printout of previous assignments over the past year where Sammy had worked in that community. Thompson walked back to the table and slowly and deliberately took a peace of paper from the supervisor setting next to Christina. He paused as if he was reading from the document. After what seemed a minute of silence he said, Mr. Mason have you ever repaired a phone at the home of Jenny Withers and her mother? With a very strong voice Sammy acknowledged it was possible but he did not remember. Thompson then placed into evidence a work order where Sammy had repaired Jenny's phone six months previously.

Thompson then asked Sammy had he ever had sex with Jenny? Sammy glancing toward his wife said, "No". Sammy volunteered that he had heard other technicians talk about women wanting sex but the technicians said they always resisted the advances. He volunteered that it was very common for the technicians to go into homes where women had on thin nightgowns. He had heard of technicians working in a house where the woman would take off her clothes and when the technician's refused the advances the woman in anger would turn them into South Central Bells security, accusing them of making sexual advances. He had read where technicians had been fired because of these unfair accusations. Thompson then asked for a short Company recess.

Patrick grabbed Sammy, took him to the phone bank outside the hearing room and asked him why didn't he keep his mouth shut as he had been instructed to do rather than volunteering information. Sammy answered that the arbitrator needed to know that technicians get propositioned and are accused of things they do not do. Patrick responded, "Well, you did not help your case."

Christina had left the hearing room and now was returning with a lady by her side. Patrick, still angry with Sammy, was sipping coffee from a styrofoam cup when he saw the two women. He turned to the local president and asked who was the lady. The local president stared at her and said, "that's Jenny Withers, I wonder how they found her?"
Patrick's Irish face began to flush. He had been assured that a diligent search had been made to find Jenny. He turned to Sammy; "do you see who is here?" Sammy just shrugged his shoulders as his wife held on to his arm.

Patrick, taking the last sip of coffee and holding the cup, walked over to Christina and ask to speak to her in private. "Who is the lady"? Looking straight into Patrick's eyes she said very firmly. "It's Jenny Withers'.
"She was not living in Louisville, where did you find her?"
" We found her in Richmond, Virginia."
" How long has she been in Louisville?"
" Since yesterday morning when we met her and her mother at the airport."
"Where have you kept her?"
"Here in the hotel."

Crushing the coffee cup in his hand, Patrick said, "Christina Preston, you have sandbagged me. I don't arbitrate cases where the facts do not support our case. I take strong exception to your not telling me about Jenny being here. Marvin and I have arbitrated a number of cases together. He should have advised you that I demand to know the facts of the Company's case before we go to arbitration. We will probably lose this case that we would not have arbitrated had we known of Ms. Wither's testimony. You haven't heard the last of this." Christina responded more relaxed, reflecting on what she had done.

She said softly but directly, "If we had told you Jenny was here, we didn't know what your people would have done to intimidate her. She is not well and we are protecting her."

" Christina, you are really pissing me off. You will regret what you have done."

Patrick turned and headed for his room and called South Central Bell headquarters and asked to speak to Christina's boss, Richard Rainer. After holding for 5 minutes, a voice said, "Rainer".

"Richard this is Calvin Patrick. I am in Louisville arbitrating a case. Christina Preston and Marvin Thompson are handling the Company's case. Richard, I have been sandbagged and don't appreciate it. The Company has a witness here that they did not tell us about. Had we known she was here, we would not be arbitrating this case as we knew her testimony would contradict the grievant's. We could not locate her and had no choice but to go forward if she was not going to testify. Now we find out at this late hour that she is here and testifying. You know dam well when you have the evidence and give it to me I do not pursue a case that I did not want to pursue anyway. If Christina had advised me she had this witness and some other evidence I just found out you have, I would have withdrawn our case. I want this cleared up today and for Christina and Marvin to have a clear understanding of how we do business."

Rainer responded" Well Calvin, you know we don't always have the evidence ahead of time and often find out at the last minute."

" Richard I understand that, but they have had this woman locked up for two days and are telling me they were afraid of what the Union would do to her if they had known she was in town. I am not going to put up with this kind of nonsense. I will appreciate your getting Thompson, who should know better, and Christina on board."

Back in the hearing the Company said they had a rebuttal witness, Ms. Jenny Withers. She looked much older than her 23 years. She had on a new blue dress and new shoes. It was clear that she had mental problems and it was not comfortable to look at her. No rational person would have sex with a poor wretch like her.

She was sworn in and Company attorney Marvin Thompson asked her. "Ms. Withers do you know Sammy Mason?"

" Yes I do."

"Has he ever been to your house?"

"Yes sir."

"Why was he there?"

He was repairing my phone".

"Was this the only time he ever came to your house?"

"No, he has been there several times."

'Did you have sex when he visited your house? '

" Yes we did."

"Did you meet Sammy Mason on June 2nd at 12:30 p.m. in the park near your home?"

"Yes I did."

"What kind of vehicle was he in?"

"He was driving a telephone Company bucket truck".

"'Why did you meet him in the park?"

" He had called and wanted to come to the house but my mother was at home."

" Where did you meet him in the park?"

"He was parked close to some shrubbery."

"Did you have sex with him in the park?"

" Yes sir."

"Where did you have sex with him?"

"Standing by the driver's door."

"Can you tell the arbitrator how you had sex standing by the driver's door?"

"Well, I went down on him while he was standing by the door."
"Ok, so you went down on him, how did you and Sammy clean up?"
"He had some rags he pulled out of a box."
" What did you do with the rags?"
" We put them on the back of the truck."

Thompson turned to the arbitrator: "Mr. Arbitrator I want to place in evidence these rags that were found on the back of the bucket truck. They are covered with human semen."

Patrick was a tough union representative. In his earlier years with the Union he had been an organizer. His delight was to take on management and out smart them. He liked to find a manager of a Company that the employees did not like and then hand out handbills at the gate regurgitating what workers had said about that manager. The workers would vote for the Union because they saw in Patrick a person who would stand up for them against management. But now, on the inside Patrick was a real softy; he loved people and had given his life to helping the underprivileged.

He stood to cross-examine the witness.
"Now Ms. Withers: When Sammy Mason came to your house to fix your phone, this was the only time he ever came to your house wasn't it?"
'Yes sir this was the only time.'
Now "Ms. Withers, when Mr. Mason came to your house to fix your phone he never had sex with you did he?"
"No he did not."
"You never met Mr. Mason in the park did you?"
"No we only met at my house when he fixed my phone."

Patrick turned his back to the witness and the arbitrator and walked toward the back of the room telling himself that with her mental condition you can lead her anywhere. He thought of his own son who had mental problems, Jenny's demeanor reminded him of his son. His eyes were misty. He took a couple of deep breaths, turned around and told the arbitrator that the Union "rest" our case.

Walking by Christina, he leaned over and whispered, you aught to be ashamed of your self. He walked outside the hearing room and stood by the phone bank trying desperately to hold back the tears as he continued to think of his own son.
Christina followed him out to the telephone bank and stood behind him. He did not turn around. She said, Calvin, you called Richard. He called me an hour ago and asked me why I couldn't get along with the Union. I am so sorry. I am so sorry. She started choking up. Patrick responded "Christina you really screwed up".

He was regretting that he had called her boss in anger and wanted to apologize to her; he was having so many mixed emotions.

She dabbed the corner of her eye with a Kleenex, took a deep breath and said firmly, "I am not going to cry." With his back still to her he said, "Christina we need to have a good conversation." Christina said; "I would appreciate that." Patrick was now feeling as sorry for her as he did for Jenny. He wanted to turn around and give her some comfort but he said without turning around, "I will call you."

It was late afternoon. Christina and Marvin Thompson headed for the airport and Birmingham. Patrick was driving back to Johnson City and decided to stay over and get an early start the next morning. Several of the local officers and job stewards were talking in low tones and now were saying the case should not have been tried. Patrick headed for the dining room along with the local president and Sammy Mason and his wife. They ordered dinner and ate mostly in silence. After dinner he whispered to the local president to stay and got up and paid the bill. He got

Sammy's attention and motioned for him to come out in the hall by the phone bank.

"Sammy, I believed you last night but after what has happened today I don't know. You really had me fooled, and I haven't been fooled many times. You did not tell me you had been to Jenny's house to work on her phone. You did not tell me a lot of things. I did not ask Jenny any more questions because I could get her to say anything I wanted her to say. So could the Company. She is so helpless. The arbitrator will understand her problems and believe her because there is a thread of truth in everything she says. I feel sorry for your wife. Maybe I am wrong but I think you are a very good pathological liar. We will have to wait for the arbitrator's decision to really know. If I were you I would be looking for another job." Patrick stuck out his hand and said: "Sammy, I hope I am wrong. Good Luck and tell your wife goodbye for me." He turned and went to his room.

Case #9 Do Unions Support Bad Employees?

The Union constantly gets inquires as to why does the Union support employees who have screwed up. Some do not come to work every day, some are tardy, some do not do a days work for a days pay, etc. Another question is why do you have irresponsible people in the leadership of the Union? The facts are that ninety-eight percent of all employees are very loyal to the Company who has employed them.

For the other two percent the simple answer is: The Company hired them, not the Union. And the Union cannot discriminate against any employee. If the Union was responsible for the hiring process then we could be held accountable.

When a Union goes in to an organizing drive in a non-union company, usually the first employees they come into contact with are employees in trouble of one kind or another. One of the first tasks is, to work with these individuals in helping identify other union sympathizers. Leadership is then developed from employees that the workforce respects.

Sometimes, after the organizing victory and a contract has been negotiated, someone who has not been involved with the Union will come out of the woodwork and run for a elected leadership position in the new local and are elected. In those instances even though the Union would prefer to keep the leadership that has been developed through the organizing drive and the negotiation process, at this point the members make the decisions and the Union may lose its influence. The Landrum-Griffin Act, which controls how elections are to be conducted, takes over. As a result, the majority of the members elect whom they want. The Union can use its influence in the election, but if the members are unhappy with the outcome of bargaining or any other issue they elect new leadership of their choosing.

Management sometimes has a perception that the Union processes every grievance regardless of merit. However, decisions at the executive level are made after a thorough investigation, much consultation with attorneys, staff and local officers. Many times after the investigation, the local officers will agree the case should not be arbitrated and wonder why this decision could not have been made sooner.

Unions do not have a problem resolving disputes quickly and determining if a grievance has merit. The Union's problem is getting enough information to make an intelligent decision with the case. The Company is in the position to supply that information where the grievance occurs. However, supervisors who have their decisions questioned do not like to be cooperative, they feel that the Union is really challenging their right to manage. Therefore, they throw road-blocks in the way or withhold information. This may be because of a personality conflict or simply two strong willed individuals, a supervisor and an employee. The supervisor and local Union representative may forget that at some point in the grievance procedure, information to substantiate their case must be provided. This problem is not just at the local supervisory level. The Company Personnel and labor relations departments are sometimes just as bad. Often it is acknowledged that there is more politics in management than the Union. So these so-called decision makers who earn high salaries simply pass the buck.

The Union's statistics over several years prove that we withdraw 25% of all cases approved for arbitration.

A study of 1018 cases that came to the Executive level

of the Union in CWA District 10 with a request to arbitrate by the CWA staff, shows that over the four year period of 1981-1984 there was a need for more investigation of cases by the Union and the Company before they are escalated and a request to arbitrate is made. The facts are not developed until a case is set for arbitration and Company and Union attorneys get involved. In researching and approving cases for arbitration, the Union tries to encourage a company to give the Union all its facts early on, so that an educated decision can be made as to whether a case has merit. Until a case reaches the arbitration level, it seems both sides want to withhold information hoping to sandbag the other. Usually by the time a case is properly prepared, both sides know what the other side's evidence is. But by then, a lot of time and resources that could be put to use helping the member in other ways has been wasted. Of the 1018 cases coming to the arbitration level in the four-year study (1981-1984) the results show:

	1981	1982	1983	1984
Arbitration approved but withdrawn after investigation by Union	21%	32%	22%	26%
-Not approved and withdrawn	31%	31%	32%	22%
-Settlement agreed to by both parties	37%	27%	26%	34%
-Cases lost by Union at Arbitration	9%	6%	15%	6%
-Wins at arbrtration by the Union	3%	5%	5%	6%

Collectively this tells us for the four years in question, 54%

of the 1018 cases did not have enough merit to allow an arbitrator to decide the issue. Of the 143 cases arbitrated over the four years the Union won 49 decisions (34% of cases arbitrated) or 4.8% of total cases submitted for arbritration.. We would not win this often if the company has looked responsibly at all the cases.

Case #10   Company Sandbagged by Supervisor

Sometimes the Union and Company gets sandbagged by our own constituents. In 1980 we had a member who had allegedly taunted his supervisor and made threatening physical gestures toward the supervisor. In our preparations, the grievant was very humble. He had never been in trouble, and in this instance had been provoked by his supervisor. We put our witness on the stand and he presented a good believable story. On cross-examination the Company started asking about his background. Was he good in sports, etc.? He started bragging about his boxing experiences. The arbitrator believed the supervisor and the case was lost.

In another case a grievant was fired for an accident involving a highway patrol vehicle on a four-lane highway. The grievant kept telling the Union he had witnesses who were mechanics and they had inspected the Company vehicle and the brakes had failed, causing him to hit the patrol car from the rear. The Company did not provide all their evidence prior to the hearing, which hampered the Union from making a decision based on all the facts. Well, you guessed it. The employee's mechanic witness did not show up for the hearing. The highway patrolman testified the patrol car had its blue lights flashing, the weather was clear, the road was straight, and the grievant knocked the highway patrol car over the rail and 100 feet down the embankment. This case became an embarrassment to Union counsel early in the hearing. Of course we lost it. Had the Company provided the Union their evidence, the case would have never gone to arbitration.

In a case in Nashville, Tennessee in 1984 the Company felt they had a good case. The Union was alleging that a clerical employee was performing a higher rated work, and should receive a wage differential. The supervisor kept denying it saying she was simply performing her job. After the Union presented our case to the arbitrator, the Company asked for a recess, came to us and offered to settle. It became very clear the supervisor was misrepresenting his case.

Case #11 Finally

Most managers care for their employees and if there is a problem they will work with the local Union to resolve the issues. Usually in these cases there will be no grievance and the executive level of the Union is never involved. On the other hand, when local problems are not resolved they fester until the employee(s) get so frustrated they reluctantly go against their manager and file a grievance.

Of course there are issues where management must act such as insubordination, misconduct, etc. In these situations if the Company follows practices established such as progressive discipline, usually the Union at all levels will have the facts and can make the appropriate decision.

When a Company and its managers treat its employees with respect and dignity, responds to their legitimate complaints, shows that the Company cares about their working conditions and gives the employees an honest answer even when the answer might not be what the employees wants to hear, usually these actions will go a long way in keeping a happy workforce, keep unity and respect for managers, and usually if there is no Union then there will not be a need for one.

It's left up to the Company and their leadership. If a Company does not live up to the above principles then the employees call the Union for help. The Union is always ready to respond.

Biography

Calvin Patrick worked in the Telephone industry 31 years and was an unpaid Local Union officer for 21 of those years. In 1972 he went to work for the Communications Workers of America responsible for 15 companies handling grievances, arbitration & contract administration

In 1980 he was promoted to the CWA District 10 headquarters and served as co-chair of the CWA bargaining committee with South Central Bell/Bellsouth in 1980, 1983, 1986. In 1989 and 1992 he was responsible for negotiations for the benefit plans with Bellsouth.

Involved in politics he was on the Tennessee Carter for President steering committee and a Tennessee congressional district chairman. He served as Washington County Tennessee party Chairman.

In his community he served as a scoutmaster, President of the Lions Club, the local PTA among others. Active in his church he Co-founded a Food-bank and Furniture ministry which is still flourishing after 24 years.

www.ingramcontent.com/pod-product-compliance
Lightning Source LLC
Chambersburg PA
CBHW061503180526
45171CB00001B/18